OXFORD

take off in

# French

Marie-Thérèse Bougard

**OXFORD**
UNIVERSITY PRESS

# OXFORD

UNIVERSITY PRESS

Great Clarendon Street, Oxford OX2 6DP

Oxford University Press is a department of the University of Oxford.
It furthers the University's objective of excellence in research, scholarship,
and education by publishing worldwide in

Oxford New York

Athens Auckland Bangkok Bogotá Buenos Aires Calcutta
Cape Town Chennai Dar es Salaam Delhi Florence Hong Kong Istanbul
Karachi Kuala Lumpur Madrid Melbourne Mexico City Mumbai
Nairobi Paris São Paulo Singapore Taipei Tokyo Toronto Warsaw

with associated companies in Berlin Ibadan

Oxford is a registered trade mark of Oxford University Press
in the UK and in certain other countries

Published in the United States
by Oxford University Press Inc., New York

British Library Cataloguing in Publication Data

Data available

Library of Congress Cataloging in Publication Data

Data available

ISBN 0-19-860906-X (Book and cassettes)
ISBN 0-19-860907-8 (Book and CDs)
ISBN 0-19-860993-0 (Coursebook)
This coursebook is only available as a component of Take Off In French

1

Commissioning, development, and project management: Tracy Miller
Project management (2nd edition): Natalie Pomier
Audio production: Gerald Ramshaw; Daniel Pageon, Actors World Production Ltd
Music: David Stoll
Design: Keith Shaw
Editorial: Brigitte Lee
Teaching consultant: Jenny Ollerenshaw

The author and publisher would like to thank the following for
permission to use copyright material: SNCF, Libération, the
Ministère de la Culture et de la Communication, France

Printed in Great Britain by
Clays Ltd, Bungay, Suffolk

# Contents

|  | Introduction | iv |
|---|---|---|
| 1 | Starting out<br>**Ça va?** | 1 |
| 2 | Asking the way<br>**Pour aller … ?** | 15 |
| 3 | Numbers, times, and dates<br>**Quel jour et à quelle heure?** | 29 |
|  | *Review 1* | 43 |
| 4 | Accommodation<br>**L'hébergement** | 47 |
| 5 | Personal information<br>**Renseignements personnels** | 61 |
| 6 | Shopping<br>**Dans les magasins** | 75 |
| 7 | Eating out<br>**Au restaurant** | 89 |
|  | *Review 2* | 103 |
| 8 | Getting around<br>**En route** | 107 |
| 9 | Health and fitness<br>**En bonne santé** | 121 |
| 10 | Free time<br>**Les loisirs** | 135 |
|  | *Review 3* | 149 |
| 11 | At home<br>**Chez nous** | 153 |
| 12 | Making plans<br>**Faire des projets** | 167 |
| 13 | All in the past<br>**Le passé** | 181 |
| 14 | The world of work<br>**Au travail** | 195 |
|  | *Review 4* | 209 |
|  | Answers | 213 |
|  | Grammar Summary | 224 |
|  | Vocabulary | 237 |
|  | Glossary of Grammatical Terms | 245 |
|  | Grammar index | 248 |

# Introduction

*Oxford Take Off In French* is designed to help the beginner develop the basic language skills necessary to communicate in French in most everyday situations. It is intended for learners working by themselves, providing all the information and support necessary for successful language learning.

## How to use the course

The book and the recording are closely integrated, as the emphasis is on speaking and listening. The recording contains step-by-step instructions on how to work through the units. The presenter will tell you when to use the recording on its own, when to use the book, and when and how to use the two together. The book provides support in the form of transcriptions of the recording material, translations of new vocabulary, and grammar explanations. You'll find this icon ⓐ in the book when you need to listen to the recording.

1 (recording/book) Read the unit objectives on the first page telling you what you will learn in the unit, and then begin by listening to the **dialogue** on the recording. You may not understand everything the first time you hear it, but try to resist the temptation to look at the transcript in the book. The first activity on the recording will help you develop your listening skills by suggesting things to concentrate on and listen out for. You'll be given the opportunity to repeat some of the key sentences and phrases from the dialogue before you hear it a second time. You may need to refer to the vocabulary list (book) before completing the second activity (book). Listen to the dialogue as many times as you like, but as far as possible try not to refer to the dialogue transcript (book).

2 (book) Once you have listened to all the new language, take some time to work through the **transcript, Vocabulary, Language Building**, and **activities** in the book to help you understand how it works.

3 (recording) Then it's time to practise speaking: first **Pronunciation practice** and then the **Your turn** activity. You will be given all the instructions and cues you need by the presenter on the recording. The first few times you do this you may need to refer back to the vocabulary and language building sections in the book, but aim to do it without the book after that.

4 (book) The fourth learning section, **Dossier**, concentrates on reading practice. Try reading it first without referring to the vocabulary list to see how much you can already understand,

making guesses about any words or phrases you are not sure of. The activities which accompany the text will help you develop reading comprehension skills.

5 (recording/book) For the final learning section, return to the recording to listen to the **Story**. This section gives you the opportunity to have some fun with the language and hear the characters in the story use the language you have just learnt in different situations. The aim is to give you the confidence to cope with authentic French. There are activities in the book to help you.

6 (book) Return to the book, and work through the activities in the **Test** section to see how well you can remember and use the language you have covered in the unit. This is best done as a written exercise. Add up the final score and, if it is not as high as you had hoped, try going back and reviewing some of the sections.

7 (recording/book) As a final review, turn to the **Summary** on the last page of the unit. This will test your understanding of the new situations, vocabulary, and grammar introduced in the unit. Use the book to prepare your answers, either by writing them down or speaking aloud, then return to the recording to test yourself. You will be given prompts in English on the recording, so you can do this test without the book.

8 (book) At the very end of each unit you will find some suggestions for **revision** and ideas for further practice.

Each unit builds on the work of the preceding units, so it's very important to learn the vocabulary and structures from each unit before you move on. There are review sections after units 3, 7, 10, and 14 for you to test yourself on the material learnt so far.

*Other support features*
If you want a more detailed grammar explanation than those given in the Language Building sections, you will find a *Grammar Summary* at the end of the book. For a definition of the grammar terms used in the course, see the *Glossary of Grammatical Terms* on page 245.

The *Answers* section will give you the answers to all the book activities. Some activities require you to give information about yourself, so you may also need to check some vocabulary in a dictionary.

At the end of the book you'll find a comprehensive French–English Vocabulary.

For additional practice, your *Take Off In French* pack contains an extra CD or cassette you can listen to while on the go without having to refer to the coursebook. You will also find a travel dictionary and phrasebook that easily slips into your handbag or pocket when you travel around.

## The French Language

The aim of this course is to introduce French as it is spoken in France and French-speaking countries. Even if you are a complete beginner, you are probably already familiar with a good range of French words such as **bonjour**, **au revoir**, **baguette**, **croissant** and expressions such as **c'est la vie**, **carte blanche**, **déjà vu**, or **je ne sais quoi**. Moreover, as French and English share a common source in Latin, many words are similar in both languages.

Despite the efforts of the Académie Française, an association of scholars and writers founded by Richelieu in the seventeenth century with the aim of preserving the purity of the French language, French has borrowed many English words over the years. **Le sandwich**, **le tee-shirt**, **le week-end**, and, more recently, **le web** and **on-line** are but a few examples. Beware! The meanings of some of these words have evolved in mysterious ways. **Un parking** is a car park and **un smoking** is a tuxedo ...

As French (like Italian, Spanish, Portuguese, and Romanian) belongs to the Romance group of European languages that are derived from Latin, nouns are either masculine or feminine, and articles and adjectives have to agree with the nouns they accompany. French has a greater range of tenses and more variation in verbs parts than English. French also has two ways of addressing people (**tu** being the informal and **vous** the formal 'you' form), which affects pronouns, possessives, and verb forms.

Like English, French is not a phonetic language: a single sound can be represented by a variety of different spellings and a single letter can correspond to a variety of different pronunciations.

Learning to communicate in another language may be challenging, but it is also a very rewarding and enriching experience. Most French speakers you will come across will be impressed by your attempts and very encouraging. We have made this course as varied and entertaining as possible, and we hope you enjoy it.

## Pronunciation

To achieve good pronunciation, there is no substitute for listening carefully to the recording and, if possible, to French native speakers, and trying to reproduce the sounds you hear. Here are a few guidelines for you to keep in mind when doing so. You will find this section most useful if you listen to the Pronunciation section on the recording as you read it.

## Vowels

The vowel sounds are represented by a variety of written forms.

| Written as | Phonetic symbol | English approximation | Example |
|---|---|---|---|
| a, à, ha- | /a/ | cat | café, papa |
| â, as | /ɑ/ | arm | âge, gâteau |
| e | /ə/ | ago | le, demi |
| eu, œu-, heu-, œ | /œ/ | fun | coiffeur, acteur |
| eu, eux | /ø/ | her (*but shorter*) | deux, bleu |
| é, ée, hé, er, es, ez, et | /e/ | tray (*but shorter*) | été, allé |
| ê, è, e, ai, ais, ait, ei, aî, ë, et | /ɛ/ | pet | maison, frère |
| i, ie, is, î, hi, y, ï | /i/ | treat | fille, midi |
| o, au, eau, aux, eaux, os, ô, hô | /o/ | course | numéro, château |
| o, ho, hô | /ɔ/ | hot | comme, téléphone |
| u, û, hu | /y/ | ee *but with rounded lips* | tu, rue |
| ou, où, oû, oo, hou, oux | /u/ | flute | douze, rouge |

*Nasal vowels*

| an | /ɑ̃/ | | chambre, prendre |
|---|---|---|---|
| on | /ɔ̃/ | | mon, comprendre |
| in | /ɛ̃/ | | cinq, main |
| un | /œ̃/ | | brun, lundi |

*Semi-vowels*

| i, y, il, ill | /j/ | yes | bien, ciel, yaourt |
|---|---|---|---|
| oi, oî, ou | /w/ | was | bonsoir, oui |
| ui, hui | /ɥ/ | we *but with rounded lips* | nuit, huit |

## Consonants

Most consonants are pronounced as in English. The exceptions are:

| Written as | Phonetic symbol | English approximation | Example |
|---|---|---|---|
| h | | not pronounced, but either with 'liaison' (the n of un is pronounced) or without | un hotel, un haricot |
| r, rr, rh | /R/ | pronounced at the back of the throat | trois roses rouges |
| c, qu, q, cc, k, ck, ch | /k/ | cat | acteur, coiffeuse |
| c + e/i | /s/ | sing | cent, ici |
| ç | /s/ | sing | garçon, français |
| g, gu, gg | /g/ | ground | gare, grand |
| g + e/i | /ʒ/ | leisure | gentil, région |
| w, v | /v/ | van | WC |
| w | /w/ | in foreign words w | |

*Consonant combinations*

| ch, sh | /ʃ/ | shoe | chaussure |
|---|---|---|---|
| th | /t/ | tent | théâtre |
| gn | /ɲ/ | onion | agneau |

# Starting out
## Ça va?

---

**OBJECTIVES**

In this unit you'll learn how to:

- ✓ greet people in French
- ✓ use simple everyday phrases
- ✓ order snacks and drinks
- ✓ count up to 30

And cover the following grammar and language:

- ✓ intonation
- ✓ different forms of address
- ✓ the definite and indefinite articles
- ✓ masculine and feminine nouns

---

### LEARNING FRENCH 1

Make the most of the time you have available to study. You need to set time aside to go through the material in the book and the recording, but you can make use of other opportunities – perhaps when you are travelling to work or doing household chores – to do less demanding but nonetheless essential exercises. You could, for example, do some pronunciation practice, memorize vocabulary and structures, or listen again to some of the recorded material.

Practise speaking French as often as you can – even speaking to yourself is good practice. If you can, record yourself regularly – you can learn a lot from playing it back.

*Answers to the activities are in the Answer section on page 213.*

Now start the recording for Unit 1.

# Bonjour!

 **ACTIVITY 1** is on the recording.

**ACTIVITY 2**
In each case decide if the people are meeting or parting.

**DIALOGUE 1**
○ Bonjour!
■ Bonjour! Ça va?
○ Ça va.

○ Bonne nuit, Papa! Bonne nuit, Maman!
■ Bonne nuit, ma chérie.
▼ Bonne nuit.

○ Au revoir, tout le monde! À bientôt!
■ À bientôt!

○ Salut, Christine.
■ Salut, Alexandre. À demain.

○ Bonsoir, Monsieur Laffont. Bonsoir, Madame Laffont.
■ Bonsoir, Mademoiselle.
▼ Bonsoir, Mademoiselle.

| VOCABULARY | |
|---|---|
| bonjour | hello, good morning, good afternoon |
| ça va? | how are you? [*literally* that goes?] |
| ça va | fine |
| bonne nuit | goodnight |
| papa | dad(dy) |
| maman | mum(my), mom(my) |
| ma chérie (*f*) | my darling |
| au revoir | goodbye |
| tout le monde | everyone |
| à bientôt | see you soon |
| salut | goodbye [*also* hi, hello] |
| à demain | see you tomorrow |
| bonsoir | good evening, hello |
| monsieur | Mr, Sir |
| madame | Mrs, Madam, Ms |
| mademoiselle | Miss |

*If you are uncertain about any of the grammatical terms used in the*
***Language Building*** *sections, see the Glossary of Grammatical Terms on*
*page 245.*

### ✔ Intonation

Intonation is important in French as it affects the meaning of what you
say. For example, a phrase like **ça va** can be used both as a question and
as an answer. As you heard in Dialogue 1, when it's a question, the voice
goes up at the end; for a statement it goes down.

> **Ça va?** How are you?
> **Ça va.** Fine.

**Salut** means 'hi', 'hello', or 'goodbye'; again, its meaning is determined by
the intonation used.

There will be more about intonation in later units.

### ✔ *Monsieur, Madame, Mademoiselle*

Forms of address such as **Monsieur** (to a man), **Madame** (to a woman),
and **Mademoiselle** (to a young woman) are more widely used in French
than the English equivalents of 'Sir', 'Madam', and 'Miss'.

> Bonsoir, **Monsieur**. Good evening, (Sir).
> Au revoir, **Madame**. Goodbye, (Madam).

### ✔ *Messieurs Dames*

This colloquial form of address is widely used in cafés, shops, and
restaurants as a greeting to a mixed group.

---

### ACTIVITY 3

Match each situation 1–4 with the appropriate phrase a–d.

1 You're saying goodnight to a group of French friends.
2 You're greeting your French neighbour in the morning.
3 A French colleague in your office is going home at the end
  of the day.
4 You're arriving at your hotel and are greeting the man at
  reception.

a Bonjour. Ça va?
b Bonsoir, Monsieur.
c Au revoir. À demain.
d Bonne nuit, tout le monde.

🎧 Now do activities 4 and 5 on the recording.

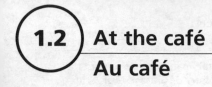

# 1.2 At the café
# Au café

**ACTIVITY 6** is on the recording.

**ACTIVITY 7**

A Which phrases do you hear in the dialogue?

1 Merci.          4 Au revoir.
2 Bonjour.        5 Bon appétit.
3 D'accord.       6 S'il vous plaît.

B Which of the phrases above would you use:

a when you leave?        c on starting a meal?
b to thank someone?

**DIALOGUE 2**

○ Messieurs Dames?
▼ Une salade et un Perrier, s'il vous plaît.
○ Une salade et un Perrier pour madame. Et pour monsieur?
■ Un sandwich et un café, s'il vous plaît.
○ Un sandwich et un café. D'accord.

○ Alors … la salade et le Perrier pour madame …
▼ Merci.
○ Le sandwich et le café pour monsieur.
■ Merci.
○ Bon appétit!
▼ Merci.

| VOCABULARY | |
|---|---|
| **une salade** | a salad |
| **et** | and |
| **un Perrier** | a Perrier [*mineral water*] |
| **s'il vous plaît** | please |
| **un/une** | one, a |
| **pour** | for |
| **un sandwich** | a sandwich |
| **un café** | café; a (cup of) black coffee |
| **d'accord** | OK |
| **alors** | so |
| **merci** | thank you |
| **bon appétit!** | enjoy your meal! |

## ✓ le/la/l' ('the'), un/une ('one', 'a')

All French nouns have a gender, that is, they are either masculine or feminine, and this affects the accompanying definite article ('the') and indefinite article ('a'):

|  | 'the' | 'a' |
|---|---|---|
| (m) | le | un |
| (f) | la | une |

When you learn a new French word, learn it with its article as it's important to know whether it's masculine or feminine.

| (m) | | (f) | |
|---|---|---|---|
| le papa | dad | la maman | mum |
| le monsieur | man | la dame | woman |
| le jour | day | la nuit | night |
| le sandwich | sandwich | la salade | salad |
| le Perrier | Perrier | la soupe | soup |
| le café | coffee | la table | table |

When a noun starts with a vowel or mute h, le and la change to l'.

| (m) | | (f) | |
|---|---|---|---|
| l'hôtel | hotel | l'eau minérale | mineral water |

### ACTIVITY 8

Guess the meaning of each of the items below, and copy them under two separate headings: food and drink. Don't forget to include un or une.

un gâteau / un hamburger / un jus d'orange / un thé / une bière / une limonade / une omelette / une pizza

| Food | Drink |
|---|---|
| _____ | _____ |
| _____ | _____ |
| _____ | _____ |
| _____ | _____ |

### ACTIVITY 9

Choose from the items mentioned in section 1.2, and practise ordering some food and drink for yourself.

Example: Un hamburger et un café, s'il vous plaît.

🔊 Now do activities 10 and 11 on the recording.

# How much is it?
# C'est combien?

ACTIVITY 12 is on the recording.

### ACTIVITY 13

Complete the price list, using the numbers on page 7 to help you.

tea _____ euros
coca cola _____
coffee _____
sandwich _____
They pay _____ in total.

### DIALOGUE 3

○ Le plat du jour, c'est combien?
■ Le plat du jour, 6€.
○ 6€! Et un sandwich, c'est combien?
■ Un sandwich? 5€.
○ 5€! Et une bière, c'est combien?
■ La bière, 3€.
○ 3€!! Et un coca?
■ Le coca? 3,25€.
○ 3,25€! Oh là, là! Et un thé?
■ Le thé? 3€.
○ 3€, le thé! Pff!
■ Mais le café, c'est 2,15€.
○ Alors, deux cafés, ça fait 4 euros et 30 centimes. On prend deux cafés? D'accord?
■ D'accord.

### VOCABULARY

| | |
|---|---|
| ça fait | that comes to, that costs [*literally* that makes] |
| le plat du jour | dish of the day, special |
| c'est combien? | how much is it? |
| l'euro (*m*) | euro |
| le coca | coke |
| mais | but |
| c'est | it is, it's |
| le centime (d'euro) | cent |
| on prend … ? | shall we have … ? |

## ✓ Numbers up to 30

| | | | | | |
|---|---|---|---|---|---|
| 1 | un/une | 11 | onze | 21 | vingt et un/une |
| 2 | deux | 12 | douze | 22 | vingt-deux |
| 3 | trois | 13 | treize | 23 | vingt-trois |
| 4 | quatre | 14 | quatorze | 24 | vingt-quatre |
| 5 | cinq | 15 | quinze | 25 | vingt-cinq |
| 6 | six | 16 | seize | 26 | vingt-six |
| 7 | sept | 17 | dix-sept | 27 | vingt-sept |
| 8 | huit | 18 | dix-huit | 28 | vingt-huit |
| 9 | neuf | 19 | dix-neuf | 29 | vingt-neuf |
| 10 | dix | 20 | vingt | 30 | trente |

### ACTIVITY 14

Match the following words and numbers.

| | |
|---|---|
| 2 | cinq |
| 12 | trois |
| 20 | deux |
| 3 | treize |
| 13 | douze |
| 30 | trente |
| 4 | quinze |
| 14 | quatorze |
| 5 | vingt |
| 15 | quatre |

### ⓐ ACTIVITY 15

Practise saying the following prices. Then use the recording to check that you've got them right, and to check your pronunciation.

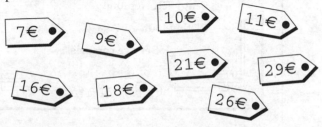

Now do activities 16 and 17 on the recording.

**DOSSIER**

# Café Neptune

| | |
|---|---|
| Bière | 1,50 € |
| Coca | 1,20 € |
| Limonade | 1,20 € |
| Jus de fruit | 1,25 € |
| Perrier | 1,25 € |
| Évian | 1 € |
| | |
| Café | 1 € |
| Thé | 1,20 € |
| Chocolat | 1,50 € |
| | |
| Soupe à la tomate | 1,90 € |
| Soupe Neptune | 2 € |
| | |
| Salade niçoise | 3,20 € |
| Salade Neptune | 3,70 € |
| | |
| Omelette nature | 2,75 € |
| Omelette Neptune | 3,35 € |
| | |
| Pizza Neptune | 3,95 € |
| | |
| Sandwich Neptune | 2,15 € |
| | |
| Plat du jour | 4,90 € |

**Service compris**

*Bon appétit!*

Note: In France, service is almost always included in a bill, so there's no need to tip.

| le jus de fruit | fruit juice |
| le chocolat | chocolate |
| la soupe | soup |
| la tomate | tomato |
| la salade niçoise | *salad with tomatoes, tuna, eggs, anchovies, and olives* |
| nature | plain |
| service compris | service included, tip included |

## ACTIVITY 18

You're at Café Neptune with a friend who's forgotten his reading glasses. Look at the menu and answer his questions in English.

1 Do they serve beer?
2 Do they only serve cold food?
3 Do they serve any egg dishes?
4 What's the most expensive item?

## ACTIVITY 19

You're at Café Neptune and want to order a drink and something to eat. Practise your side of the conversation with the waiter.

**La Bonne Étoile**

## UN PERRIER POUR ALEXANDRA
## A PERRIER FOR ALEXANDRA

The story takes place at La Bonne Étoile, a café in a small French town. One of the regular customers is Alexandra, a young journalist.

| | |
|---|---|
| **la bonne étoile** | lucky star [*literally* good star] |
| **excusez-moi** | excuse me |
| **allô?** | hello? [*on the phone*] |
| **bon** | good |
| **à tout à l'heure** | see you later |
| **oui** | yes |
| **non** | no |
| **ah bon?** | really? |

### ACTIVITY 20

Listen to the recording and decide whether the following statements are true (**vrai**) or false (**faux**).

1 Monsieur Delaine, the café owner, takes Alexandra's order. V / F
2 Monsieur Delaine's first name is Jean-Luc. V / F
3 Alexandra orders a sandwich and a coffee. V / F
4 Jérôme calls Alexandra on her mobile phone. V / F
5 The name of the second caller is Monsieur Weber. V / F
6 Alexandra is planning to see Monsieur Weber later on that day. V / F

### ACTIVITY 21

Who's speaking: Alexandra or Madame Delaine?

1 Allô?
2 Jean-Luc!
3 À demain.
4 Bon appétit!
5 Excusez-moi.
6 À tout à l'heure.

| | |
|---|---|
| Alexandra | Bonjour, Madame Delaine. |
| Mme Delaine | Bonjour, Alexandra. Ça va? |
| Alexandra | Ça … |
| | Ah, excusez-moi. Allô? Oui … Ah, Jérôme. Salut. Ça va? … Ça va, oui. Euh … oui, d'accord. Bon, Jérôme, salut, à tout à l'heure. |
| | Excusez-moi, Mme Delaine … Un sandwich et un Perrier, s'il vous plaît. |
| Mme Delaine | Un sandwich et un Perrier. D'accord. |
| | Jean-Luc! Un sandwich et un Perrier pour Alexandra! |
| | … |
| Mme Delaine | Alors … un sandwich et un Perrier. Bon appétit! |
| Alexandra | Merci … Ah, excusez-moi. Allô? Oui … Ah, bonjour, Monsieur Weber … D'accord … Oui … Merci … Au revoir, Monsieur Weber. À demain. |
| | Excusez-moi, Madame Delaine. Merci … Allô? Jérôme … Non!? … Ah bon? |

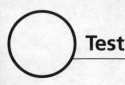

# Test

Now it's time to test your progress in Unit 1.

1 Match the following words and phrases with their English equivalents.

| 1 | merci | a | enjoy your meal |
|---|---|---|---|
| 2 | bonsoir | b | good evening |
| 3 | bonjour | c | goodnight |
| 4 | d'accord | d | thank you |
| 5 | au revoir | e | goodbye |
| 6 | bonne nuit | f | please |
| 7 | bon appétit | g | hello |
| 8 | s'il vous plaît | h | OK |

8

2 Pair up each of the sentences 1–6 with the correct sentence from a–f to make up six mini-dialogues.

| 1 | Ça va? | a | C'est vingt-cinq francs. |
|---|---|---|---|
| 2 | Au revoir! | b | Bonjour, Monsieur. |
| 3 | Bon appétit! | c | À demain. |
| 4 | Bonjour, Madame. | d | D'accord. |
| 5 | Le sandwich, c'est combien? | e | Merci. |
| 6 | Une bière et un jus d'orange, s'il vous plaît. | f | Ça va. |

6

3 Use **un** or **une** to complete the following dialogue.

● Madame?
■ _____ omelette et _____ bière, s'il vous plaît.
● Oui. Et pour monsieur?
▼ _____ sandwich et _____ jus d'orange, s'il vous plaît.
 Non. _____ pizza et _____ café, s'il vous plaît.
● D'accord.

6

*Answers to the Test sections are in the Answer section on page 213.*

4 Complete each number sequence.

1 neuf, sept, cinq, _____ , un
2 deux, quatre, six, _____ , dix
3 un, onze, _____ , trente et un
4 douze, vingt-quatre, _____
5 dix, quinze, vingt, vingt-cinq, _____
6 deux, treize, _____ , trente-cinq
7 vingt, douze, deux, trente, _____ , trois
8 seize, quinze, quatorze, treize, _____ , onze
9 six, douze, _____ , vingt-quatre, trente

**9**

5 How would you express the following things in French? (2 points for each correct answer, 1 point if you make only one error.)

1 Give the price of a pizza – 6,30€.
2 Order a salad and a coffee in a café.
3 Order a sandwich and a beer in a café.
4 Say 'goodbye' to someone.
5 Greet a group of French people in the evening.
6 Greet the female hotel receptionist in the morning.
7 Thank the male hotel receptionist who gives you your messages.
8 Wish some friends 'goodnight' and say you'll see them tomorrow.

**16**

 **TOTAL SCORE** **45**

If you scored less than 35, go through the dialogues and the Language Building sections again before completing the Summary on page 14.

# Summary 1

 Now try this final test summarizing the main points covered in this unit.

How would you:
1 greet someone during the day? in the evening?
2 say 'goodbye' and 'goodnight'?
3 address a man? a woman? a young woman?
4 say 'please' and 'thank you'?
5 order a sandwich and a coffee?
6 say 'enjoy your meal'?
7 count up to 10?

## REVISION

Before moving on to Unit 2, play Unit 1 through again and compare what you can say and understand now with what you knew when you started. Go over any vocabulary you still feel unsure of.

Once you have worked through the next few units, come back to Unit 1 and work through the dialogues and activities again. It will help you reinforce what you have learnt.

# Asking the way
# Pour aller ... ?

**OBJECTIVES**

In this unit you'll learn how to:

- ✓ find out about town-centre locations
- ✓ ask the way
- ✓ understand and give simple directions
- ✓ count up to 69

And cover the following grammar and language:

- ✓ the plural forms of nouns and articles
- ✓ the use of **il y a** ('there is', 'there are')
- ✓ the prepositions **à** ('to', 'at', 'in') and **de** ('of', 'from')
- ✓ the imperative
- ✓ the verb **être** ('to be')
- ✓ **c'est** ('it is')

## LEARNING FRENCH 2

Each unit has been divided into manageable sections (2.1, 2.2, 2.3, etc.), so it is a good idea to aim to do one complete section at a time, then stop to practise and learn the vocabulary. You will find that you can learn more effectively in that way.

It also helps if you can learn with someone else. If you can persuade a friend or family member to study with you, it will give you an extra impetus to keep working. Agree times to meet and goals for the week, and test each other regularly.

🔊 Now start the recording for Unit 2.

## En ville

**ACTIVITY 1** is on the recording.

**ACTIVITY 2**

Which plan matches the designers' discussion?

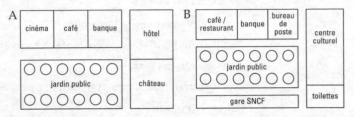

**DIALOGUE 1**

○ Là, il y a un café et un restaurant. En face, il y a un jardin public. Et à côté, il y a une banque et un bureau de poste.

■ Et là, qu'est-ce qu'il y a?

○ Le centre culturel.

■ Il y a des distributeurs de billets?

○ Oui, il y a deux distributeurs de billets. Un à la banque et un à la gare.

■ Où est la gare?

○ La gare SNCF est là.

■ Et les toilettes? Il y a des toilettes?

○ Oui, là. Il y a aussi des téléphones.

| VOCABULARY | |
|---|---|
| là | there |
| il y a | there is, there are |
| en face | opposite |
| le jardin public | park |
| à côté | next (to it) |
| la banque | bank |
| le bureau de poste | post office |
| qu'est-ce qu'il y a? | what is there? |
| le centre culturel | arts centre |
| le distributeur de billets | cash dispenser, ATM |
| où est? | where is? |
| la gare (SNCF) | (train) station |
| les toilettes | toilet(s) |

## LANGUAGE BUILDING

### ✓ Plurals of nouns and articles

Normally an **-s** is added to make a noun plural. Some words add -x instead of **-s**. For more detail, see the Grammar Summary on page 224.

Articles also change in the plural: **le, la,** and **l'** become **les**; **un** and **une** become **des**.

| (*sing.*) | (*pl.*) | |
|---|---|---|
| **la** salle de concert | **les** salles de concert | the concert halls |
| **le** musée | **les** musées | the museums |
| **un** feu | **des** feux | the traffic lights |
| **une** église | **des** églises | the churches |

Note that in French the word for 'toilet' is always in the plural – **les toilettes** – whether it refers to a toilet in a house or to public toilets.

### ✓ *il y a*

**il y a** can mean either 'there is' or 'there are':

**Il y a** un téléphone en face. There is a telephone opposite.
**Il y a** deux distributeurs de billets. There are two cash dispensers.

In informal speech, it can also be used to ask questions – meaning 'is there … ?' or 'are there … ?':

**Il y a** un hôtel / un cinéma? Is there a hotel / a cinema?
**Il y a** des toilettes? Are there any toilets?

---

### ACTIVITY 3

Use the following words to make up as many sentences as possible about the facilities in town.

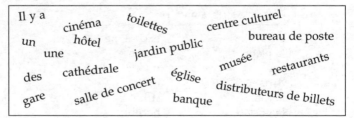

Il y a
cinéma   toilettes   centre culturel
un   hôtel   bureau de poste
une   jardin public
des   cathédrale   musée   restaurants
gare   salle de concert   église   distributeurs de billets
banque

### ACTIVITY 4

Imagine the set designers' discussion about plan A (page 16).

Example: Il y a un cinéma. En face, il y a …

 Now do activities 5 and 6 on the recording.

## 2.2 · Right or left?

## À droite ou à gauche?

**ACTIVITY 7** is on the recording.

### ACTIVITY 8

Which of these sketches corresponds to the directions given?

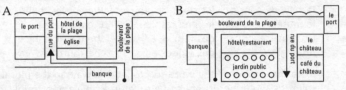

### DIALOGUE 2

- ○ Pardon, l'Hôtel de la plage, s'il vous plaît?
- ■ L'Hôtel de la plage. C'est sur le boulevard de la plage!
- ▲ Mais non! L'Hôtel de la plage, c'est dans la rue du port.
- ■ Ah, oui. Rue du port. Alors, pour aller à l'Hôtel de la plage, tournez à droite après la banque …
- ▲ Non, non! Pas à droite. À gauche! Tournez à gauche après la banque.
- ■ Ah, oui! À gauche. Tournez à gauche après la banque. Continuez tout droit jusqu'aux feux. Aux feux, tournez à gauche.
- ▲ Mais non! À droite! Aux feux, tournez à droite.
- ■ Ah, oui. Aux feux, tournez à droite. L'Hôtel de la plage est en face du port, à côté de l'église.

| VOCABULARY | |
| --- | --- |
| **pardon** | excuse me |
| **la plage** | beach |
| **sur** | on |
| **dans** | in |
| **la rue** | street |
| **le port** | harbour |
| **à côté de** | next to |
| **pour aller à** | to go to |
| **tournez** | turn |
| **après** | after |
| **pas** | not |
| **continuez tout droit** | continue straight ahead |
| **jusqu'à** | as far as |

## ✓ The prepositions à and *de*

A preposition is a word or phrase used before a noun or pronoun to relate it to another part of the sentence.

| | | |
|---|---|---|
| **sur** on | **à** to | **dans** in |
| **en face de** opposite | **à côté de** next to | **jusqu'à** as far as, until |

The prepositions **à** (meaning 'to', 'at', or 'in') and **de** (meaning 'of' or 'from') require special attention. When followed by **le** or **les**, their form changes. Note that they don't change when followed by **la** or **l'**:

à + le = au    de + le = du
à + les = aux    de + les = des

| | |
|---|---|
| **la** gare | Allez jusqu'**à la** gare. Go as far as the station. |
| **l'**église | Allez jusqu'**à l'**église. Go as far as the church. |
| **le** pont | Allez jusqu'**au** pont. Go as far as the bridge. |
| **les** feux | Allez jusqu'**aux** feux. Go as far as the traffic lights. |
| **la** banque | C'est à côté **de la** banque. It's next to the bank. |
| **l'**hôtel | C'est à côté **de l'**hôtel. It's next to the hotel. |
| **le** château | C'est à côté **du** château. It's next to the castle. |
| **les** toilettes | C'est à côté **des** toilettes. It's next to the toilets. |

## ✓ The Imperative

The imperative is the form of the verb used to give orders or instructions, or to suggest that someone does something. In French, there are three different forms of the verb depending on who you are speaking to.
To an adult or group of people:

**Tournez** à droite. Turn right.

To a child, a member of your family, or a close friend:

**Tourne** à droite. Turn right.

To a group in which the speaker is included:

**Allons** à la plage. Let's go to the beach.

How imperatives are formed is covered on page 230.

---

**ACTIVITY 9**

Find the right phrase to go with each symbol.

A → B ← C ↑ D ? E $£

Allez jusqu'à la banque.    Tournez à droite.
Continuez tout droit.    Je ne sais pas.
Tournez à gauche.

 Now do activities 10 and 11 on the recording.

## 2.3   Counting up to 69

## Compter jusqu'à 69

**ACTIVITY 12** is on the recording.

**ACTIVITY 13**

Using the numbers on page 21, complete the restaurant addresses.

1   Café des Amis, ___ rue de Bordeaux
2   Chez Abdel, ___ boulevard de la gare
3   Chez Nicole, ___ rue Victor-Hugo
4   Restaurant du Jardin, ___ avenue de la liberté

**DIALOGUE 3**

○   Le café des Amis, c'est où?
■   Le café des Amis, c'est dans la rue de Bordeaux. Au numéro 46.
○   Le café des Amis, 46 rue de Bordeaux. D'accord … Et le restaurant du Jardin?
■   Le restaurant du Jardin … C'est dans l'avenue de la liberté. Au numéro 37.
○   37 avenue de la liberté. Bien … Et le restaurant Chez Nicole?
■   Alors, là, c'est dans la rue Victor-Hugo. 69 rue Victor-Hugo.
○   Chez Nicole. 69 rue Victor-Hugo.
■   Mais moi, je recommande Chez Abdel.
○   Chez Abdel. C'est où?
■   C'est au 55 boulevard de la gare.
○   55 boulevard de la gare. Chez Abdel. D'accord, merci.

| VOCABULARY | |
| --- | --- |
| compter | to count |
| les amis | friends |
| c'est où? | where is it? |
| le numéro | number |
| le jardin | garden |
| la liberté | liberty |
| bien | fine |
| moi | personally [*literally* me] |
| je recommande | I recommend |

20

## LANGUAGE BUILDING

### ✓ Numbers up to 69

| | | | |
|---|---|---|---|
| 30 | trente | 40 | quarante |
| 31 | trente et un | 41 | quarante et un |
| 32 | trente-deux | 42 | quarante-deux |
| 33 | trente-trois | 43 | quarante-trois |
| 34 | trente-quatre | 44 | quarante-quatre |
| 35 | trente-cinq | 45, etc. | quarante-cinq, etc. |
| 36 | trente-six | 50 | cinquante |
| 37 | trente-sept | 51, etc. | cinquante et un, etc. |
| 38 | trente-huit | 60 | soixante |
| 39 | trente-neuf | 61, etc. | soixante et un, etc. |

### ✓ être ('to be') – irregular verb

| | | | |
|---|---|---|---|
| je **suis** | I am | nous **sommes** | we are |
| tu **es** | you are (*sing.*) | vous **êtes** | you are (*pl. or formal sing.*) |
| il/elle **est** | he/she/it is | ils/elles **sont** | they are (*m/f*) |

**c'est**, meaning 'it is', is used to describe location:

**C'est** dans la rue Victor-Hugo. It's in Victor Hugo Street.
**C'est** en face du port. It's opposite the harbour.
**C'est** où? Where is it?

---

#### ACTIVITY 14

Rewrite the following numbers in ascending order.

vingt et un
trente-trois
soixante-six
trente-deux
soixante-sept
cinquante-huit
quarante-neuf
cinquante-cinq
quarante-quatre

#### ACTIVITY 15

Practise saying the following numbers. You can also use the recording to check that you've got them right.

31, 34, 36, 42, 45, 47,
53, 56, 58, 64, 67, 69

Now do activities 16 and 17 on the recording.

# 2.4 Town map
## Le plan de la ville

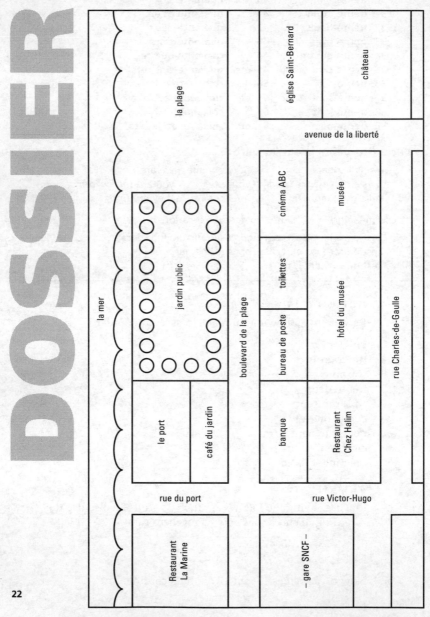

## ACTIVITY 18

Study the map for two or three minutes. Then cover it with a sheet of paper, and decide whether the following statements are true (vrai) or false (faux).

1  Il y a un café en face de l'église. V / F
2  Le château est en face du musée. V / F
3  Le musée est dans la rue du port. V / F
4  Le jardin public est à côté du port. V / F
5  Le cinéma ABC est en face de la gare. V / F
6  Les toilettes sont en face du jardin public. V / F
7  La gare SNCF est dans l'avenue de la liberté. V / F
8  Il y a une banque à côté du bureau de poste. V / F
9  Le château est dans la rue Charles-de-Gaulle. V / F
10  L'église Saint-Bernard est dans la rue Victor-Hugo. V / F
11  Le restaurant La Marine est sur le boulevard
de la plage. V / F
12  Le restaurant Chez Halim est en face du café
du Jardin. V / F

## ACTIVITY 19

Correct the false statements from Activity 18. For example:

1  Il y a un café en face de l'église. V̶ / F
Le café est en face de la banque.

## ACTIVITY 20

Imagine you're at the beach. Someone asks you the way to the station. Work out what you would reply.

# 2.5 ) La Bonne Étoile

## EN FACE DU CAFÉ
## OPPOSITE THE CAFÉ

Alexandra's still at La Bonne Étoile and still on the phone.

| | |
|---|---|
| **le bureau d'Alexandra** | Alexandra's office |
| **c'est ça** | that's right |
| **le pont** | bridge |
| **très bien** | very good, very well |
| **voilà** | there you are |

### ACTIVITY 21

Listen to the recording and choose the correct ending for the following statements.

1 Le bureau d'Alexandra est …
   a dans la rue de la liberté.
   b dans l'avenue de la gare.

2 Le bureau d'Alexandra est …
   a au numéro 14.
   b au numéro 44.

3 Le bureau d'Alexandra est …
   a à côté du café La Bonne Étoile.
   b en face du café La Bonne Étoile.

4 Le bureau d'Alexandra est …
   a à côté d'une banque.
   b en face d'une banque.

5 Pour aller au bureau d'Alexandra …
   a tournez à droite à la banque, continuez tout droit jusqu'aux feux, et tournez à droite dans la rue de la liberté …
   b tournez à gauche à la gare, continuez tout droit jusqu'au pont, et tournez à droite dans la rue de la liberté …

Look at the doodles produced by Madame Martinez during her conversation with Alexandra. Replace them with the correct information.

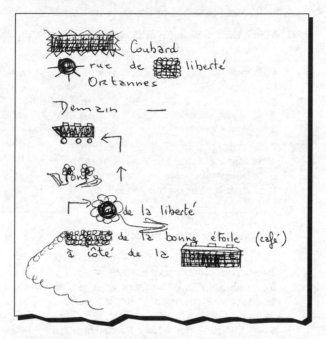

## STORY TRANSCRIPT

| | |
|---|---|
| Mme Delaine | Ça va, Alexandra? |
| Alexandra | Ça va. Merci. |
| Mme Delaine | Un café? |
| Alexandra | Oui, un café, s'il vous plaît. |
| Mme Delaine | D'accord. |
| | Jean-Luc! Un café pour Alexandra! |
| Alexandra | Allô? Oui, c'est moi, oui. … Monsieur Kolkowski? … Oui, bien sûr … Mon bureau? … C'est à Ortannes, dans la rue de la liberté, au numéro 44. 44 rue de la liberté … Oui c'est ça. À la gare, tournez à gauche. Continuez tout droit jusqu'au pont. Là, tournez à droite dans la rue de la liberté … Oui, c'est à côté de la banque, en face du café La Bonne Étoile … D'accord … À tout à l'heure, Monsieur Kolkowski. |
| Mme Delaine | Un café. Voilà. |
| Alexandra | Ah, merci. Alors, il y a … Ah, excusez-moi … Allô? Oui, c'est moi. Ah, non, je regrette. Demain? Oui? Très bien. Alors, c'est à Ortannes, dans la rue de la liberté, au numéro 44 … Oui … à la gare, tournez à gauche et continuez tout droit jusqu'au pont. Là, tournez à droite dans la rue de la liberté … C'est en face du café La Bonne Étoile, à côté de la banque … Très bien … Au revoir, Madame Martinez. À demain. |

# Test

Now it's time to test your progress in Unit 2.

1 Match the following words and phrases with their English
  equivalents.

| | | | |
|---|---|---|---|
| a | la gare | 1 | concert hall |
| b | l'église | 2 | station |
| c | le pont | 3 | traffic lights |
| d | la plage | 4 | post office |
| e | les feux | 5 | cash dispenser |
| f | le jardin public | 6 | beach |
| g | la salle de concert | 7 | bridge |
| h | le bureau de poste | 8 | park |
| i | le distributeur de billets | 9 | church |

9

2 Find the odd one out in each group of words.

1 à gauche / alors / à droite / tout droit
2 tournez / allez / continuez / jusqu'à
3 une église / une rue / une avenue / un boulevard
4 quarante / cinquante / treize / soixante
5 en face du port / à côté du café / dans la rue / d'accord
6 les toilettes / les feux / les distributeurs / les jardins

6

3 Complete the following signs with **du, de la**, or **des**.

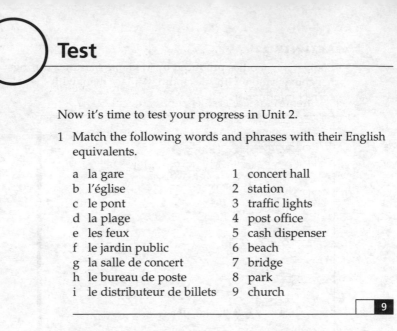

1 café _____ gare

4 rue _____ cathédrale

2 HÔTEL _____ PORT

3 avenue _____ plage

5 MUSÉE _____ CHÂTEAU

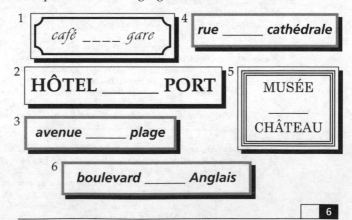

6 boulevard _____ Anglais

6

4 Complete each number sequence.

1 vingt, trente, _____ , cinquante, soixante
2 soixante-six, _____ , quarante-quatre, trente-trois
3 trente et un, quarante et un, cinquante et un, _____
4 _____ , quarante-quatre, cinquante et un, cinquante-huit
5 onze, vingt-deux, _____ , quarante-quatre,
   cinquante-cinq
6 trente-sept, quarante, _____ , quarante-six,
   quarante-neuf
7 cinquante-cinq, _____ , quarante-cinq, quarante,
   trente-cinq
8 vingt-trois, trente-quatre, quarante-cinq, cinquante-six,
   _____

|  | 8 |

5 Put the words in order to make sentences. (2 points for
  each correct answer, 1 point if you make only one error.)

1 à / aller / la / s'il / pour / gare / vous / plaît?
2 billets / y / il / distributeurs / a / des / de?
3 pont / allez / jusqu'au
4 tout / continuez / droit
5 à / aux / tournez / feux / droite
6 tournez / banque / gauche / à / après / la
7 il / y / a / du / à / un / café / côté / public / jardin
8 église / restaurant / face / en / du / a / y / il / une

|  | 16 |

**TOTAL SCORE** | 45 |

If you scored less than 35, go through the dialogues and the
Language Building sections again before completing the
Summary on page 28.

# Summary 2

 Now try this final test summarizing the main points covered in this unit.

How would you:
1 ask the way to the station?
2 say there is a post office next to the cinema?
3 say there is a telephone opposite the toilet?
4 tell someone to turn left?
5 tell someone to turn right?
6 tell someone to continue straight on?
7 tell someone to go as far as the traffic lights?
8 count in tens from 30 to 60?

## REVISION

Think of the area where you live or your nearest town centre. How would you describe it to a French-speaking friend, using the vocabulary and structures you have just learnt?

First, think of all the main buildings and facilities – such as cafés, restaurants, museums, banks, churches, cinemas, etc. – in your town, and list them in French starting with **il y a**. Look up any words you don't know.

Then try to describe their positions in relation to each other, using the structures you have learnt so far. For example:

**Il y a un jardin public en face de l'église.**
**Le château est dans l'avenue de la gare.**
**Pour aller au port, allez jusqu'au cinéma et tournez à gauche.**

# Numbers, times, and dates
# Quel jour et à quelle heure?

---

### OBJECTIVES

In this unit you'll learn how to:

- ✓ tell the time
- ✓ say the days of the week
- ✓ ask simple questions
- ✓ count up to 100

And cover the following grammar and language:

- ✓ the present tense of regular **-er** verbs
- ✓ interrogative adjectives **quel(s)/quelle(s)** ('which', 'what')
- ✓ the present tense of regular **-ir** verbs
- ✓ simple questions
- ✓ negatives using **ne ... pas**

---

### LEARNING FRENCH 3

When learning a language, it's important to use a variety of strategies (using the book, listening to the recording, rehearsing dialogues, learning vocabulary, writing things down, listing verb forms, etc., aloud, and so on), to practise the different skills of listening, speaking, reading, and writing. Work out your preferred learning style and use it to your advantage without neglecting any particular skill.

The first stage is for you to work out what kind of learner you are. The following questions will help you. Do I learn something better when I see it written down? Do I only need to hear something a few times before I know it? Do I like to learn grammar rules by heart? Are there other strategies that work well for me? If you recognize your strengths, you can use them to work more effectively.

Now start the recording for Unit 3.

# What time is it?

# Il est quelle heure?

**ACTIVITY 1** is on the recording.

**ACTIVITY 2**

At what time …

1  are they eating dinner?
2  does the football match start?
3  does the film start?
4  does the film finish?

**DIALOGUE 1**

○ Qu'est-ce que tu regardes à la télé?
■ Je regarde une interview avec Céline Dion.
○ Ah, je n'aime pas Céline Dion. Je prépare le dîner.
■ D'accord! On dîne à quelle heure?
○ On dîne à huit heures. Après le dîner, je regarde le match de foot. Nantes joue contre Marseille. Ça commence à huit heures et demie.
■ Il y a un film avec Jean Reno à dix heures et quart. Ça finit à minuit moins le quart.
○ On regarde le film ensemble après le match de foot?
■ D'accord!

| VOCABULARY | |
| --- | --- |
| qu'est-ce que tu regardes? | what are you watching? |
| à la télé | on TV |
| je regarde | I watch, I'm watching |
| l'interview (f) | interview |
| avec | with |
| je n'aime pas | I don't like |
| je prépare | I prepare, I'm preparing |
| le dîner | dinner |
| on dîne | we eat, we're eating dinner |
| à quelle heure? | at what time? |
| le match de foot | football match, soccer game |
| joue | plays, is playing |
| contre | against |
| ça commence | it starts, it's starting |
| le film | film, movie |
| ça finit | it finishes, it's finishing |
| on regarde | we watch, we're watching |
| ensemble | together |

## ✓ Telling the time

| Il est | **une heure.** It's one o'clock. (**une** because **heure** is feminine) |
| | **midi/minuit.** It's midday/midnight. |
| À | **deux heures.** At two o'clock. |
| Il est | **trois heures <u>cinq</u>.** It's five past three. |
| Il est | **cinq heures <u>moins vingt</u>.** It's twenty to five. |
| Il est | **neuf heures <u>et quart</u>.** It's quarter past nine. |
| À | **quatre heures <u>moins le quart</u>.** At quarter to four. |
| Il est | **deux heures <u>et demie</u>.** It's half past two. (**demie** after **heure(s)**) |
| À | **midi/minuit <u>et demi</u>.** At half past twelve (midday/midnight). |
| | (**demi** after **midi/minuit** – masculine) |

## ✓ Regular -er verbs

Regular French verbs are classified in three groups. You can work out which group a verb belongs to by the ending of the infinitive: **-er**, **-ir**, or **-re**. Most verb tenses are formed by adding specific endings to the infinitive minus its **-er**, **-ir**, or **-re** ending: this is known as the stem.

**-er** verbs, such as **travaill<u>er</u>** ('to work'), **jou<u>er</u>** ('to play'), **regard<u>er</u>** ('to watch'), **prépar<u>er</u>** ('to prepare'), or **aim<u>er</u>** ('to love'), take the following endings in the present tense:

| | |
|---|---|
| je **travaille** I work | nous **travaill<u>ons</u>** we work |
| tu **travaill<u>es</u>** you work | vous **travaill<u>ez</u>** you work |
| il/elle/on **travaille** he/she/it works, we work | ils/elles **travaill<u>ent</u>** they work |

1 French only has one form of the present tense, so **je travaille** can mean both 'I work' and 'I'm working'.
2 The **tu** form is only used to a child or someone you know well.
3 The **vous** form is used to a person you don't know well or to a group of people – including children. When in doubt, use the **vous** form.
5 In everyday conversation, **on** is very often used instead of **nous**, meaning 'we'. Note that it takes the **il/elle** form of the verb: **on regarde la télévision** ('we watch television').

---

### ACTIVITY 3

Add the correct ending and write the time in English.

1 Vous dîn__ à neuf heures?
2 Le match commenc__ à midi et quart.
3 Ils jou__ à une heure dix.
4 Tu travaill__ à deux heures moins le quart.

🔊 Now do activities 4 and 5 on the recording.

## Compter jusqu'à 100

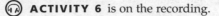 **ACTIVITY 6** is on the recording.

**ACTIVITY 7**

Correct the six mistakes in the following advert.

---

### CLUB MULTILINGUE

#### ANGLAIS, ESPAGNOL, ALLEMAND, JAPONAIS

Pour l'anglais, appelez le 01 64 75 92 98.     Pour l'allemand, appelez le 01 64 77 81 71.
Pour l'espagnol, appelez le 01 64 95 83 97.     Pour le japonais, appelez le 01 64 72 88 93.

de 8 heures à 20 heures du lundi au vendredi
de 10 heures à 16 heures le samedi et le dimanche

---

### DIALOGUE 2

Au Club Multilingue, nous proposons des cours d'anglais, d'espagnol, d'allemand et de japonais. Pour plus de renseignements, appelez le 01 64 75 82 98 pour les cours d'anglais, le 01 64 75 83 97 pour les cours d'espagnol, le 01 64 77 81 91 pour les cours d'allemand, et le 01 64 72 88 93 pour les cours de japonais. Je répète le 01 64 75 82 98 pour l'anglais, le 01 64 75 83 97 pour l'espagnol, le 01 64 77 81 91 pour l'allemand, et le 01 64 72 88 93 pour le japonais. Nous sommes ouverts de 8 heures à 22 heures du lundi au vendredi, et de 10 heures à 18 heures le samedi. Alors, à bientôt … au Club Multilingue!

### VOCABULARY

| | |
|---|---|
| **proposer** | to offer |
| **le cours** | class |
| **l'anglais** (*m*) | English |
| **l'espagnol** (*m*) | Spanish |
| **l'allemand** (*m*) | German |
| **le japonais** | Japanese |
| **plus de renseignements** | more information |
| **appeler** | to call |
| **je répète** | I repeat |
| **nous sommes ouverts** | we're open |
| **de … à, du … au** | from … until, from … to |

## ✓ Days of the week

| | | | | | |
|---|---|---|---|---|---|
| **lundi** | Monday | **jeudi** | Thursday | **samedi** | Saturday |
| **mardi** | Tuesday | **vendredi** | Friday | **dimanche** | Sunday |
| **mercredi** | Wednesday | | | | |

The days of the week are masculine: **le lundi**, etc. Unlike English, they don't begin with a capital. Note when the article is included:

Je travaille **lundi**. I'm working on Monday.
Je travaille **le lundi**. I work on Mondays.

## ✓ Numbers up to 100

| | | | |
|---|---|---|---|
| 70 **soixante-dix** | 77 **soixante-dix-sept** | 91 **quatre-vingt-onze** |
| 71 **soixante et onze** | 78 **soixante-dix-huit** | 92 **quatre-vingt-douze** |
| 72 **soixante-douze** | 79 **soixante-dix-neuf** | 93 **quatre-vingt-treize** |
| 73 **soixante-treize** | 80 **quatre-vingt(s)** | 100 **cent** |
| 74 **soixante-quatorze** | 81 **quatre-vingt-un** | 101 **cent un** |
| 75 **soixante-quinze** | 82 **quatre-vingt-deux** | 102 **cent deux** |
| 76 **soixante-seize** | 90 **quatre-vingt-dix** | |

Note the patterns:
From 70: **soixante-dix** [*literally* sixty-ten], **soixante et onze** [*literally* sixty and eleven], **soixante-douze** [*literally* sixty-twelve], etc.
From 80: **quatre-vingt(s)** [*literally* four-twenties], **quatre-vingt-un** [*literally* four-twenty-one], etc.

## ✓ Using *quel(s)/quelle(s)* ('which?', 'what?')

The interrogative adjective **quel** changes to **quelle** with a feminine noun. Both masculine and feminine forms add an **-s** in the plural.

| | (*sing.*) | (*pl.*) |
|---|---|---|
| (*m*) | **quel** | **quels** |
| (*f*) | **quelle** | **quelles** |

C'est **quel** numéro? What number is it?
Ça commence à **quelle** heure? What time does it start?
**Quels** jours? Which days?
Dans **quelles** rues? In which streets?

---

### ACTIVITY 8

What are the following numbers in French?

| | | | | |
|---|---|---|---|---|
| 96 | 82 | 74 | 105 | 91 |
| 70 | 84 | 99 | 80 | 71 |

 Now do activities 9 and 10 on the recording.

# 3.3 A busy schedule
## Un emploi du temps chargé

**ACTIVITY 11** is on the recording.

**ACTIVITY 12**

Pierre and Thierry can't have a game of tennis together this week, because Pierre (1) _____ on Monday and Tuesday. Thierry (2) _____ on Wednesday night. Pierre (3) _____ on Thursday night. Thierry (4) _____ on Friday night and he doesn't know whether he (5) _____ on Saturday or Sunday.

**DIALOGUE 3**

- ■ Pierre, on joue au tennis lundi soir?
- ○ Lundi? Non, Thierry, ce n'est pas possible. Je travaille jusqu'à 10 heures. Et mardi aussi. Mercredi?
- ■ Non, ce n'est pas possible. J'ai un cours d'anglais le mercredi soir. Jeudi alors?
- ○ Non, jeudi soir, ce n'est pas possible. Nathalie travaille le jeudi soir. Alors, je garde les enfants.
- ■ Après, c'est le week-end. Je pars vendredi soir avec Juliette et Halim. On rentre samedi soir ou dimanche matin.
- ○ On joue au tennis la semaine prochaine?

---

| VOCABULARY | |
|---|---|
| **on joue?** | shall we play? |
| **le tennis** | tennis |
| **le soir** | evening |
| **ce n'est pas possible** | it's not possible |
| **travailler** | to work |
| **aussi** | too, as well |
| **j'ai** | I have |
| **garder** | to look after |
| **l'enfant** (*m/f*) | child |
| **je pars** | I'm going away, I'm leaving |
| **en week-end** | for the weekend |
| **rentrer** | to come back |
| **le matin** | morning |
| **la semaine prochaine** | next week |

### ✓ Regular -ir verbs

Regular -ir verbs, such as **finir** ('to finish') and **choisir** ('to choose') follow this pattern in the present tense:

je **finis** I finish

tu **finis** you finish

il/elle/on **finit** he/she/it finishes, we finish

nous **finissons** we finish

vous **finissez** you finish

ils/elles **finissent** they finish

### ✓ Simple questions

There are three ways of asking simple questions.

1  The formal way is to put the verb before the subject:

**Travaillez-vous** le lundi? Do you work on Mondays?

2  Less formally, you use the sentence word order with a question intonation.

**Vous travaillez** le lundi? Do you work on Mondays?

3  You can also add **est-ce que** at the beginning of a sentence:

**Est-ce que** vous travaillez le lundi? Do you work on Mondays?

### ✓ Negative ne ... pas

The most common way of forming a negative is to use **ne ... pas**, with **ne** in front of the verb (**n'** before a vowel) and **pas** after the verb:

Je **ne** comprends **pas**. I don't understand.

Je **ne** sais **pas**. I don't know.

Ce **n'**est **pas** possible. It's not possible.

**ne/n'** is often dropped in informal contexts: **c'est pas possible**, etc.

---

**ACTIVITY 13**

Find the right sentence for these situations, and add the correct day.

1  You want to suggest a game of tennis on Sunday.
2  You want to say you're going away on Wednesday.
3  You want to say you aren't working on Tuesday nights.
4  You're asking a friend if she's working on Thursday night.
5  A friend has invited you out on Friday night. You can't go.

a  Ce n'est pas possible _____ soir.
b  Je ne travaille pas le _____ soir.
c  On joue au tennis _____ ?
d  Tu travailles _____ soir?
e  Je pars _____ .

🔊 Now do activities 14 and 15 on the recording.

DOSSIER

━━━━ **SÉLECTION TÉLÉ** ━━━━

## TF1:

**14.25–16.25**
FORMULE 1
Grand Prix de Monaco

## F2:

**22.55–0.30**
CANNES: LES 400 COUPS
Documentaire sur le
Festival de Cannes

## F3:

**22.25–23.35**
DIMANCHE SOIR
Spécial Éducation. Débat
animé par Christine
Ockrent

## C+:

**22.45–23.15**
L'ÉQUIPE DU
DIMANCHE
Spécial football. Émission
présentée par Thierry
Gilardi

## La Cinquième:

**6.45–7.15**
LANGUES
Cours d'anglais et
d'espagnol

## ARTE:

**20.40–1.45**
SOIRÉE THEMATIQUE
**20.45:** MASH, comédie
américaine de Robert
Altman
**22.40:** Documentaire sur
Robert Altman
**23.35:** Prêt-à-porter, film
américain de Robert
Altman

## M6:

**22.55–23.25**
CULTURE PUB
Magazine présenté par
Christian Blachas: la lutte
anti-tabac

| | |
|---|---|
| **le coup** | blow |
| **le documentaire** | documentary |
| **sur** | on, about |
| **l'éducation** (*f*) | education |
| **le débat** | debate |
| **animé(e) par** | led by |
| **l'équipe** (*f*) | team |
| **l'émission** (*f*) | programme |
| **présenté(e) par** | presented by |
| **la langue** | language |
| **la soirée thématique** | theme evening |
| **la comédie** | comedy |
| **américain(e)** | American |
| **la culture** | culture |
| **la pub** | publicity |
| **la lutte anti-tabac** | anti-smoking campaign |

## ACTIVITY 16

A Look at the TV selection and work out:
  • what the seven French TV channels are called
  • what day of the week the selection is for

B Recommend two programmes for:
  • a film buff
  • a sports fan
  • someone who follows current affairs

## ACTIVITY 17

**Vrai ou faux?** Correct the false statements.

1 Le documentaire sur Robert Altman finit à onze heures moins vingt.
2 Le Grand Prix de Formule 1 commence à quatre heures vingt-cinq.
3 L'émission de football commence à onze heures moins le quart.
4 Le débat sur l'éducation commence à dix heures vingt-cinq.
5 Il y a des cours d'anglais et d'espagnol le matin.
6 Il y a deux films de Robert Altman sur Arte.

## ACTIVITY 18

Look at the TV selection, decide what you would like to watch, and suggest it to a French-speaking friend, giving as much information as possible (channel, starting time, finishing time).

## ON DÎNE ENSEMBLE?
## SHALL WE HAVE DINNER TOGETHER?

Alexandra is at La Bonne Étoile with her friend Jérôme.

| | |
|---|---|
| **en Espagne** | to Spain [*also* in Spain] |
| **chez moi** | home, to my house |
| **le basket** | basketball |
| **j'arrive** | I'm coming |
| **je suis désolé(e)** | I'm sorry |
| **je te téléphone** | I'll call you |

### ACTIVITY 19

Listen to the recording and correct the following summary. There are six mistakes.

Alexandra is having a coffee with Jérôme, and suggests first of all they go out for dinner on Tuesday night. Unfortunately, Jérôme is leaving for Spain on Sunday morning and may not be back until nine or ten on Wednesday night. He has a Spanish class which finishes at ten o'clock on Thursday nights and Alexandra plays basketball on Saturday nights. Jérôme suggests they go out on Sunday instead, but Alexandra takes a call on her mobile and leaves immediately without giving Jérôme an answer.

### ACTIVITY 20

Listen to the dialogue again. Which of the following sentences do you hear?

1 Je pars en Espagne dimanche soir.
2 Je pars en Espagne lundi matin.
3 Tu commences à quelle heure?
4 Tu finis à quelle heure?
5 Tu rentres quel jour?
6 Tu pars quel jour?
7 C'est le 02 84 41 70 96.
8 C'est le 02 47 81 70 96.
9 J'ai un cours d'anglais.
10 J'ai un cours d'espagnol.

## ACTIVITY 21

Who's speaking: Madame Delaine, Alexandra, or Jérôme?

1  On dîne ensemble lundi soir?
2  On dîne ensemble samedi?
3  J'ai un cours d'espagnol.
4  C'est dans quelle rue?
5  Je joue au basket.
6  Ça va, Jérôme?

## STORY TRANSCRIPT

| | |
|---|---|
| Mme Delaine | Deux cafés? |
| Alexandra | Oui, deux cafés, s'il vous plaît. |
| Mme Delaine | Jean-Luc! Deux cafés pour Alexandra et Jérôme! |
| Alexandra | On dîne ensemble lundi soir? |
| Jérôme | Oui, d'accord! Ah, non! Ce n'est pas possible. Je travaille. |
| Alexandra | Mardi alors? |
| Jérôme | Ce n'est pas possible. Je travaille, je pars en Espagne lundi matin. |
| Alexandra | Tu pars en Espagne? Tu rentres quel jour? |
| Jérôme | Je rentre mercredi soir. |
| Alexandra | À quelle heure? |
| Jérôme | Oh, je ne sais pas. Onze heures et demie … minuit … |
| Alexandra | On dîne ensemble jeudi soir alors? |
| Jérôme | Jeudi soir, ce n'est pas possible, j'ai un cours d'espagnol. |
| Alexandra | Tu finis à quelle heure? |
| Jérôme | À dix heures. |
| Alexandra | On dîne après? |
| Jérôme | Après? Non, après, je rentre chez moi. Vendredi soir? On dîne ensemble vendredi soir? |
| Alexandra | Vendredi … Allô? … Oui. C'est le 02 47 81 70 96 … D'accord … Salut. |
| Jérôme | On dîne ensemble vendredi soir? D'accord? |
| Alexandra | Le vendredi soir, je joue au basket. Tu sais bien. |
| Jérôme | Et samedi soir? |
| Alexandra | Samedi … Euh … Allô? Oui. Oh, là, là! C'est dans quelle rue? … Quel numéro? … 91, d'accord, j'arrive. Bon, écoute, Jérôme, je suis désolée … Je te téléphone demain. OK? |
| Jérôme | Mais … on dîne ensemble samedi? |
| Alexandra | Euh … je ne sais pas. Je … Salut. |
| Mme Delaine | Alors, deux cafés. Mais où est Alexandra? Ça va, Jérôme? |
| Jérôme | Ça va … |

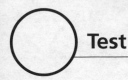

# Test

Now it's time to test your progress in Unit 3.

1 Complete the names of the days of the week.

- A - - I
- EU - I
- U - - I
- A - E - I
- E - C - E - I
- E - - - E - I
- I - A - - - E

Rewrite them in the right order, starting with Monday.
(3 points for the right order. Take off ½ point for each
mistake.)

10

2 Complete the clock faces.

a Il est minuit.

:

b Il est onze heures.

:

c Il est trois heures et quart.

:

d Il est dix heures vingt-cinq.

:

e Il est deux heures et demie.

:

f Il est quatre heures moins dix.

:

g Il est cinq heures moins le quart.

:

7

3 Complete these **-er** verbs.

1 Je gard- les enfants.
2 Tu prépar-- le dîner.
3 Elle jou- au tennis.
4 On dîn- au restaurant.
5 Nous travaill--- le samedi.
6 Vous rentr-- dimanche soir.
7 Ils regard--- la télévision.

7

4 Rewrite the following numbers in ascending order.

cent                      quatre-vingt-dix-neuf
soixante et onze          quatre-vingt-treize
quatre-vingt-un           soixante-quatorze
soixante-dix-sept         quatre-vingt-huit
quatre-vingt-onze         soixante et un

10

5 Find the right answer from a–i for the questions 1–9.

1 Qu'est-ce que tu regardes à la télévision?
2 Le film commence à quelle heure?
3 Vous travaillez le dimanche?
4 Thierry apprend l'anglais?
5 Nathalie joue au tennis?
6 Vous partez quel jour?
7 Quelle heure est-il?
8 C'est quel numéro?
9 C'est possible?

a  Minuit et demi.
b  Oui, je travaille.
c  Un match de foot.
d  Je pars lundi matin.
e  Quatre-vingt-douze.
f  À neuf heures et quart.
g  Non, ce n'est pas possible.
h  Non, elle n'aime pas le sport.
i  Oui, il a un cours le jeudi soir.

9

**TOTAL SCORE**  43

If you scored less than 33, go through the dialogues and the
Language Building sections again before completing the
Summary on page 42.

# Summary 3

 Now try this final test summarizing the main points covered in this unit.

How would you:
1 say the days of the week starting with Monday?
2 ask what the time is?
3 say it's ten o'clock?
4 say it's half past four?
5 say it's quarter to eight?
6 ask what time something starts?
7 say it finishes at a quarter past four?
8 say you don't work on Saturdays?
9 count in tens from 70 to 100?

## REVISION

First, how would you describe a typical week to a French-speaking friend, using the vocabulary and structures you have just learnt? Which days of the week do you work? At what time do you start and at what time do you finish work? When do you learn French? Do you have other regular commitments?

Then work out what questions you would ask your friend to find out about his/her typical week. Finally, how would you suggest doing something together next week? Revise the vocabulary and grammar in Unit 3 until you feel able to do this.

# Review 1

## VOCABULARY

1 Which is the odd one out in each group?

| | | | |
|---|---|---|---|
| 1 Madame | Mademoiselle | merci | Monsieur |
| 2 bonjour | bonsoir | s'il vous plaît | salut |
| 3 à bientôt | à demain | au revoir | d'accord |
| 4 un thé | un musée | un café | une bière |
| 5 une étoile | une omelette | une salade | un sandwich |

2 Which of the following words are names of buildings?

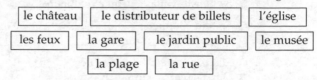

le château | le distributeur de billets | l'église

les feux | la gare | le jardin public | le musée

la plage | la rue

3 Rémy Deschamps works in a museum. Look at his diary and decide whether the following statements are true or false. Correct those which are false.

| **L** | | **J** | |
|---|---|---|---|
| 9.00 musée | 19.00 italien | 9.00 musée | 19.00 |
| | | **V** | |
| **M** | | 9.00 musée | 19.00 dîner Marie |
| 9.00 | 19.00 | **S** | |
| | | 9.00 musée | 19.00 |
| **M** | | **D** | |
| 9.00 musée | 19.00 foot | 9.00 tennis Philippe | 19.00 |

1 Dimanche matin, il joue au tennis avec Philippe.
2 Jeudi soir, il regarde un match de foot.
3 Vendredi matin, il part en week-end.
4 Lundi soir, il a un cours d'italien.
5 Samedi soir, il dîne avec Marie.
6 Mardi, il ne travaille pas.
7 Mercredi, il travaille.

*Answers to the Review sections are in the Answer section on page 213.*

4 Complete the following dialogue using the correct form of
à, de, or the definite article (le, la, les).

○ _____ musée, s'il vous plaît?

■ Alors, pour aller _____ musée, continuez tout droit …

○ Tout droit?

■ Oui, continuez tout droit jusqu'_____ feux et tournez à
gauche. Allez jusqu'_____ gare et tournez à droite dans
_____ rue de Bordeaux. _____ musée est à côté _____
café _____ jardins, en face _____ jardin public.

5 Write the correct ending for each verb.

○ Tu dîn__ avec Éric?

■ Non, je travaill__ jusqu'à dix heures.

○ Le film commenc__ à dix heures heures?

■ Oui, et il fini__ à minuit.

○ Elle par__ en Italie avec Jules?

■ Oui, ils rentr__ dimanche soir.

○ Vous part__ en week-end?

■ Non, nous travail__ samedi.

○ On jou__ au tennis avec Jules et Sarah?

■ Non, ils regard__ la télé.

6 Make the following calculations.

1 six x douze = _____
2 cinq x treize = _____
3 quarante + quinze = _____
4 trente-six – vingt = _____
5 quatre x vingt-cinq = _____
6 quatre-vingt-dix-huit – quatorze = _____
7 quarante-deux + cinquante et un = _____
8 trente-huit + quarante et un = _____

## 🎧 LISTENING

7 Two friends, Amina and Julie, haven't seen each other for a
long time. Listen to their conversation and correct Amina's
account. There are six mistakes.

Before coming to the class, I saw my friend Julie. She suggested we had a cup of tea, but I said it wasn't possible because I had an English class at half past seven. We agreed to meet at a quarter to six tomorrow. Julie asked me if I knew the Grand Café, and I said 'yes, of course'. It's next to a cinema in the rue de Paris, opposite the station.

8 Guillaume is talking about his new job. Listen to the conversation and complete the transcript.

G Je _____ dans un café.
X Quel café?
G Le café du terminus, en face de la _____
X Tu travailles quels jours?
G Je travaille le lundi et le _____ Le mercredi et le _____ j'ai des _____ de piano.
X Ah bon? Et le vendredi? Tu _____ des cours de clarinette?
G Non! Le _____ je travaille au café. Et le samedi aussi.
X Et le _____ ? Tu travailles?
G Non, je _____ travaille _____ le dimanche.
X Tu commences à _____ heure le matin?
G Le lundi et le mardi, je _____ à six heures _____ le quart et je _____ à trois heures et _____ .
X Et le vendredi et le samedi?
G Le vendredi et le _____ , je travaille le soir. Je commence à cinq _____ et quart, et je finis à _____ et demi.

 **SPEAKING**

9 Read the phrases aloud, and then listen to the recording to check your pronunciation.

1 Bonjour. Ça va?
2 Le mercredi et le vendredi.
3 Numéro quarante-quatre.
4 À quelle heure?
5 À trois heures et quart.
6 Au revoir et merci.

10 A friend rings one morning and suggests going out for a meal on Friday night. Use the cues below to help with your side of the conversation. Prepare what you're going to say first, then listen to the recording and talk in the pauses.

Nicolas: Allô. Ici Nicolas.
You: (Say hello and ask how he is.)
1 _____ .

Nicolas: Ça va. On dîne ensemble vendredi soir?
You: (Say you can't. You're working until midnight.)
2 _____ .

Nicolas: Samedi alors?
You: (Say OK. Where?)
3 _____ .

Nicolas: Tu connais le Restaurant du Jardin?
You (Ask if it's opposite the park.)
4 _____ .

Nicolas: Oui. C'est ça. À quelle heure?
You: (Suggest half past eight.)
5 _____ .

Nicolas: D'accord. À samedi soir.
You: (Say goodbye. See you on Saturday.)
6 _____ .

Now try the dialogue again without referring to the book.

11 Someone's asking you to recommend a restaurant. Use the information in the advert below to answer the questions on the recording.

*Restaurant Bienvenue*

**92 rue de la République**
**44600 Saint-Nazaire**
**Tél 02 40 61 73 94**

ouvert du mardi au dimanche
de 12 heures à 15 heures
et
de 19 heures à 23 heures

*À bientôt*
*et*
*bon appétit!*

**4**

# Accommodation
# L'hébergement

---

### OBJECTIVES

In this unit you'll learn how to:

- ✓ give your name and spell it out
- ✓ check into a hotel, a campsite, or a gîte
- ✓ say what kind of accommodation you require
- ✓ ask for accommodation details
- ✓ use higher numbers

And cover the following grammar and language:

- ✓ the present tense of **avoir** ('to have')
- ✓ the present tense of **s'appeler** ('to be called')
- ✓ the months of the year
- ✓ the present tense of **-re** verbs
- ✓ adjectives: position and agreements

---

### LEARNING FRENCH 4

When listening to the recorded material – especially the dialogues and the story – you aren't expected to understand everything first time round. If you play the same piece several times, you will most probably understand something new each time. Learn to make maximum use of all the clues you can pick up. For example, what do the speakers sound like? Happy? Angry? Calm? etc.

 Now start the recording for Unit 4.

# 4.1 Checking into a hotel
## À l'hôtel

**ACTIVITY 1** is on the recording.

**ACTIVITY 2**

Correct the statements which are false.

1  The man has booked a room for two nights.   V / F
2  It costs 89 euros a night.   V / F
3  It's a double room with toilet and shower.   V / F
4  His room number is 307.   V / F
5  It's on the second floor.   V / F

**DIALOGUE 1**

○ Bonsoir, Monsieur. Je regrette, mais l'hôtel est complet.
■ Oui, mais j'ai une réservation. Je m'appelle Christophe Waller. W-A-deux L-E-R.
○ Avec un W! Ah, oui. Nous avons une chambre pour une personne, avec douche et WC. Pour deux nuits.
■ Oui, c'est ça. Quel est le prix de la chambre?
○ 129 euros pour la nuit.
■ D'accord. Il y a la télévision dans la chambre?
○ Oui, bien sûr. Vous avez la chambre 307. Voici la clé. C'est au troisième étage. L'ascenseur est là-bas, à droite.
■ Oh, je n'aime pas les ascenseurs. Je prends l'escalier.

| VOCABULARY | |
| --- | --- |
| **complet (complète)** | full (up) |
| **la réservation** | reservation |
| **je m'appelle** | my name is ... |
| **la chambre** | room |
| **une personne** | one person |
| **la douche** | shower |
| **les WC** | toilet |
| **le prix** | price |
| **voici** | here is, here's |
| **la clé** | key |
| **au troisième étage** | on the third floor |
| **l'ascenseur (m)** | lift, elevator |
| **là-bas** | over there |
| **prendre** | to take |
| **l'escalier** | stairs |

## ✓ avoir ('to have') – irregular verb

| | |
|---|---|
| j'ai | nous **avons** |
| tu **as** | vous **avez** |
| il/elle/on **a** | ils/elles **ont** |

## ✓ s'appeler ('to be called')

The formal way to ask someone's name is to say **comment vous appelez-vous?** However, you will also hear **vous vous appelez comment?** When speaking to a child or someone you address as **tu**, the question becomes **comment t'appelles-tu?** or **tu t'appelles comment?** In both cases, the answer starts **je m'appelle** … ('my name is … ').

The verb **s'appeler** is a reflexive verb, which means there is an additional pronoun just before the verb. See Unit 5 for more details.

| | |
|---|---|
| je **m'appelle** | nous **nous appelons** |
| tu **t'appelles** | vous **vous appelez** |
| il/elle/on **s'appelle** | ils/elles **s'appellent** |

Note that when the final syllable is silent (i.e. not pronounced), l becomes ll: appe**ll**e and appe**ll**es. In other cases, when the final syllable is pronounced, only one l is needed: appe**l**er, appe**l**ons, appe**l**ez.

## ✓ More on numbers

| | | | | | |
|---|---|---|---|---|---|
| 100 | **cent** | 310 | **trois cent dix** | 2000 | **deux mille** |
| 200 | **deux cents** | 320 | **trois cent vingt** | 2500 | **deux mille cinq cent(s)** |
| 300 | **trois cents** | 1000 | **mille** | | |

### ACTIVITY 3

Rewrite the following prices in figures.

1 cent quarante-cinq euros
2 trois mille six cents dollars
3 quatre cent soixante-dix euros
4 vingt-deux mille cinq cents livres
5 mille deux cent trente-quatre euros
6 neuf cent quatre-vingt-dix neuf dollars

### ACTIVITY 4

Practise saying the following numbers. You can also use the recording to check that you've got them right.

109   654   345   4700   590   33,600   2345   9999

🎧 Now do activities 5 and 6 on the recording.

# Au camping

 **ACTIVITY 7** is on the recording.

**ACTIVITY 8**

1 Can you go in July?
2 Is there a supermarket?
3 Is there a swimming pool?
4 How much does it cost per day?
5 Do children pay as much as adults?

**DIALOGUE 2**

- Je voudrais réserver un emplacement pour une tente, s'il vous plaît.
- Et c'est pour quand?
- Pour une semaine, en juillet. Vous avez de la place?
- Oui, nous avons de la place en juillet.
- Quels sont vos tarifs?
- Alors, vous payez 4,25 euros par jour pour l'emplacement, 4,25 euros par jour pour la voiture et 5,90 euros par personne par jour. C'est gratuit pour les enfants de moins de huit ans.
- Vous avez une piscine?
- Oui, bien sûr. Nous avons une piscine et une épicerie.

| VOCABULARY | |
| --- | --- |
| je voudrais | I'd like |
| réserver | to book, to reserve |
| l'emplacement (m) | place, pitch [*for tent*] |
| la tente | tent |
| quand | when |
| la place | space, room |
| vos | your [*when followed by a plural noun*] |
| le tarif | rate |
| payer | to pay |
| par jour | per day |
| l'enfant (m) | child |
| la voiture | car |
| gratuit | free |
| de moins de huit ans | under eight (years) |
| la piscine | swimming pool |
| l'épicerie (f) | supermarket [*on campsite*] |

## ✓ Les mois ('months')

| | | | | | | | |
|---|---|---|---|---|---|---|---|
| **janvier** | January | **avril** | April | **juillet** | July | **octobre** | October |
| **février** | February | **mai** | May | **août** | August | **novembre** | November |
| **mars** | March | **juin** | June | **septembre** | September | **décembre** | December |

## ✓ Present tense of -re verbs

There are not many regular **-re** verbs, but the group does include such common verbs as **vendre** ('to sell'), **attendre** ('to wait'), **descendre** ('to go down'), **entendre** ('to hear'), and **répondre** ('to answer'). The forms in the present tense are as follows:

| | |
|---|---|
| je **vends** | nous **vendons** |
| tu **vends** | vous **vendez** |
| il/elle/on **vend** | ils/elles **vendent** |

**prendre** ('to take'), **apprendre** ('to learn'), and **comprendre** ('to understand') are slightly irregular: in the **nous** and **vous** forms, the **d** is dropped and in the **ils/elles** form, the **n** doubles:

| | |
|---|---|
| je **prends** | nous **prenons** |
| tu **prends** | vous **prenez** |
| il/elle/on **prend** | ils/elles **prennent** |

### ACTIVITY 9

Match the following dates in words with the correct form in numbers.

| | | |
|---|---|---|
| 1 | le quinze août deux mille seize | 14/07/1789 |
| 2 | le vingt février deux mille deux | 08/05/1945 |
| 3 | le trente juin deux mille vingt-cinq | 27/01/1995 |
| 4 | le huit mai mille neuf-cent quarante-cinq | 20/02/2002 |
| 5 | le quatorze juillet mille sept-cent quatre-vingt-neuf | 15/08/2016 |
| 6 | le vingt-sept janvier mille neuf-cent quatre-vingt-quinze | 30/06/2025 |

🎧 Now do activities 10 and 11 on the recording.

# Staying in a gîte
# Vacances en gîte

**ACTIVITY 12** is on the recording.

## ACTIVITY 13

1 Is the kitchen to the right or left of the living room?
2 How many bedrooms are there?
3 What other rooms are there in the gîte?

### DIALOGUE 3

○ Alors, voici le séjour.
■ Il est grand! C'est un beau séjour.
▼ Où est la cuisine?
○ Là, à gauche. Alors, il y a tout, cuisinière, four,
    réfrigérateur, lave-linge.
■ C'est une belle cuisine!
○ Là, vous avez une grande chambre avec un grand lit à
    droite, et une autre chambre avec deux petits lits à gauche.
    La salle de bains est là, et les WC sont à côté.
▼ C'est une belle maison: très agréable et très confortable!
○ Alors, bonnes vacances.

---

### VOCABULARY

| | |
|---|---|
| **le séjour** | living room |
| **grand(e)** | big |
| **beau/belle** | beautiful |
| **la cuisine** | kitchen |
| **tout** | everything |
| **la cuisinière** | cooker, stove |
| **le four** | oven |
| **le réfrigérateur** | refrigerator |
| **le lave-linge** | washing machine |
| **le lit** | bed |
| **autre** | other |
| **petit(e)** | small |
| **la salle de bains** | bathroom |
| **agréable** | pleasant |
| **confortable** | comfortable |
| **la maison** | house |
| **les vacances (f)** | holidays, vacation |

## ✅ Adjectives

Adjective endings change depending on whether the noun or pronoun they describe is masculine or feminine, singular or plural.

|  | (sing.) |  | (pl.) |  |
|--------|--------|--------|--------|--------|
|  | (m) | (f) | (m) | (f) |
| small | **petit** | petite | petits | petites |
| young | **jeune** | jeune | jeunes | jeunes |
| pretty | **joli** | jolie | jolis | jolies |
| modern | **moderne** | moderne | modernes | modernes |

Some adjectives are irregular. For example:

|  | (sing.) |  | (pl.) |  |
|--------|--------|--------|--------|--------|
|  | (m) | (f) | (m) | (f) |
| beautiful | **beau** | belle | beaux | belles |
| old | **vieux** | vieille | vieux | vieilles |
| good | **bon** | bonne | bons | bonnes |
| new | **nouveau** | nouvelle | nouveaux | nouvelles |

The Grammar Summary, page 225, has more on irregular adjectives.

Adjectives usually come after the noun they describe:

Vous avez une maison **confortable**. You have a comfortable house.
J'ai une cuisine **moderne**. I have a modern kitchen.
C'est un hôtel **agréable**. It's a pleasant hotel.

However, a few common adjectives – such as **grand**, **petit**, **bon**, **beau**, **jeune**, and **vieux** – are placed before the noun. (Note that **des** usually becomes **de** before a plural adjective.)

Vous avez un **joli** jardin. You have a pretty garden.
Ils ont une **belle** cuisine. They have a beautiful kitchen.
Nous avons une **vieille** maison. We have an old house.
Nous passons de **bonnes** vacances. We're having a good holiday.

---

### ACTIVITY 14

Find the right sentence to describe the following places, and insert the correct form of the adjective.

1  a hotel
2  a campsite
3  your garden
4  the lifts in a hotel
5  a friend's kitchen

a  Les ascenseurs sont ___ . (**moderne**)
b  C'est un camping ___. (**confortable**)
c  Nous avons un ___ jardin. (**petit**)
d  C'est un hôtel ___ . (**agréable**)
e  Tu as une ___ cuisine. (**beau**)

🎧 Now do activities 15 and 16 on the recording.

# Small ads
# Petites annonces

**DOSSIER**

| MAISONS & APPARTEMENTS | |
|---|---|
| **1**<br>**À louer**, Paris, 1<sup>er</sup> étage, 30 m², séjour, chambre, salle de bains<br>**tél 01 43 62 55 58** | **4**<br>**À vendre**, Paris, appartement, 2<sup>ème</sup> étage, ascenseur, chambre, séjour, cuisine, douche, 35 m²<br>**tél 01 45 04 61 78** |
| **2**<br>**À louer**, Paris, appartement, séjour, cuisine, 2 chambres, salle de bains<br>**tél 01 34 40 19 32** | **5**<br>**À vendre**, Nantes, maison, 3 étages, 3 chambres, bureau, séjour, grande cuisine, petit jardin<br>**tél 02 40 63 79 18** |
| **3**<br>**À louer**, Méditerranée, grande villa, juillet/août, 5/6 chambres, piscine<br>**tél 04 42 05 84 13** | |

| | |
|---|---|
| l'annonce (*f*) | advertisement |
| l'appartement (*m*) | apartment |
| à louer | for rent |
| 1er = premier | first |
| à vendre | for sale |
| 2ème = deuxième | second |
| le bureau | study |

## ACTIVITY 17

Look through the adverts on page 54.

Which properties are ...
1  in Paris?
2  for sale?
3  for rent?
4  houses?
5  flats?

Which properties have ...
6  two bedrooms or more?
7  only one bedroom?

Which property is ...
8  for holiday rent?
9  the smallest?

Which property has ...
10  a swimming pool?
11  a study?
12  a lift?

## ACTIVITY 18

Find the most suitable ad for the following people.

1  Parisian couple with 2 children wanting to buy house in smaller city.
2  Friends (4 couples + 3 children) looking for house to rent in summer.
3  Writer looking for flat to buy in Paris. Needs wheelchair access.
4  Couple with baby looking for flat to rent in Paris.
5  Retired person looking for flat to rent in Paris.

## ACTIVITY 19

Choose one of the properties and imagine you are the owner. Practise what you would say when showing people round it.

## J'AI UNE RÉSERVATION
## I HAVE A RESERVATION

As well as being a café, La Bonne Étoile is also a small but busy hotel. Alexandra listens to Madame Delaine's conversations with her clients.

| | |
|---|---|
| **seulement** | only |
| **le petit déjeuner** | breakfast |
| **voici la clé** | here's the key |
| **au premier étage** | on the first floor |
| **bienvenue (à)** | welcome (to) |
| **remercier** | to thank |
| **intéressant(e)** | interesting |

### ACTIVITY 20

Listen to the recording and fill in the missing numbers in the summary.

L'hôtel la Bonne Étoile est un petit hôtel avec seulement _____ chambres. Une chambre avec salle de bains coûte _____ euros par nuit plus _____ euros pour le petit déjeuner. Le café est ouvert de _____ heures du matin à _____ heures du soir. Monsieur Massoud a la chambre numéro _____ .

L'hôtel du Château est un grand hôtel moderne. Il y a _____ chambres. Le numéro de téléphone est le _____ .

### ACTIVITY 21

C'est quel hôtel? La Bonne Étoile ou Le Château?

1 Il y a une piscine.
2 C'est un petit hôtel.
3 C'est un grand hôtel.
4 Ce soir, il est complet.
5 Ce soir, il y a de la place.
6 Il y a une chambre pour Karim Massoud.

### ACTIVITY 22

Imagine you're checking into La Bonne Étoile. Practise the conversation you would have with Madame Delaine. To help you, follow the conversation between Madame Delaine and Monsieur Massoud and substitute your own details.

| | |
|---|---|
| Mme Delaine: | Ça va, Alexandra? |
| Alex | Ça va. |
| Mme Delaine | Et ça … Ah, excuse-moi … Allô? La Bonne Étoile. Bonsoir … Ah, je regrette, Madame, l'hôtel est complet … C'est un petit hôtel, nous avons seulement huit chambres … Il y a de la place à l'hôtel du Château … C'est un grand hôtel, il y a soixante chambres. Il y a une piscine. C'est moderne et confortable. J'ai le numéro de téléphone. C'est le 02 47 81 92 75 … Bonsoir, Madame. |

| | |
|---|---|
| Mme Delaine | Bonsoir, Monsieur. |
| M. Massoud | Bonsoir, Madame. J'ai une réservation. |
| Mme Delaine | Oui. Vous vous appelez comment? |
| M. Massoud | Massoud. Je m'appelle Karim Massoud. Ça s'écrit M-A- deux S-O-U-D. |
| Mme Delaine | Oui, Monsieur Massoud. Vous êtes là pour trois nuits. C'est ça? |
| M. Massoud | Oui, c'est ça. Quel est le prix de la chambre? |
| Mme Delaine | C'est 50 euros pour la nuit, plus 6,40 euros pour le petit déjeuner. Vous avez le téléphone et la télévision dans la chambre, vous avez une belle salle de bains, et le café est ouvert de sept heures du matin à onze heures du soir. |
| M. Massoud | Très bien. |
| Mme Delaine | Alors, vous avez la chambre 7. C'est au premier étage. Voici la clé. Bienvenue à La Bonne Étoile, Monsieur Massoud. |
| M. Massoud | Je vous remercie. |
| Alexandra | Karim Massoud … Intéressant … |

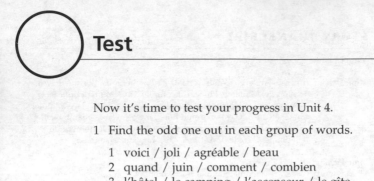

# Test

Now it's time to test your progress in Unit 4.

1 Find the odd one out in each group of words.

1 voici / joli / agréable / beau
2 quand / juin / comment / combien
3 l'hôtel / le camping / l'ascenseur / le gîte
4 la nuit / la chambre / le lit / le lave-linge
5 la tente / la caravane / le camping / la clé
6 le séjour / la chambre / la cuisine / l'escalier
7 le four / la cuisinière / la piscine / le réfrigérateur
8 vieille / jolie / mars / bonne

8

2 Write the following numbers in figures.

1 cent vingt-trois
2 deux mille deux
3 quatre cent cinquante-six
4 sept cent quatre-vingt-neuf
5 neuf mille huit cent soixante-seize
6 quatre mille cinq cent soixante-sept
7 neuf mille neuf cent quatre-vingt-dix-neuf

7

3 Complete the names of the months.

1 - ui - - e -        7 - o - e - - - e
2 - é - e - - - e     8 - ai
3 - é - - ie -        9 a - û -
4 a - - i -          10 - e - - e - - - e
5 - ui -             11 - a - -
6 - a - - ie -        12 o - - o - - e

12

4  Choose the appropriate form of the adjectives in brackets to complete the following description.

Nous passons de (**bon/bonnes**) vacances. L'hôtel est dans une (**vieux/vieille**) maison, mais il est (**confortable/confortables**). Nous avons une (**beau/belle**) chambre avec un (**grand/grande**) lit. Il y a la télévision, le téléphone et un (**petit/petite**) réfrigérateur. La salle de bains est (**joli/jolie**) et (**moderne/modernes**). Les jardins de l'hôtel sont très (**beau/beaux**), et il y a une (**grand/grande**) piscine.

10

5  Pair up the right parts to make up eight sentences.

| 1 | J' | as une tente ou une caravane? |
| 2 | Tu | m'appelle Jacqueline Simon. |
| 3 | Je | avons une belle chambre. |
| 4 | Ils | a une grande maison. |
| 5 | Elle | ont un beau jardin. |
| 6 | Vous | ai une réservation. |
| 7 | Nous | avez une piscine? |

7

6  Find the right answer from a–f for the questions 1–6.
(***s'écrire** – to spell)

1  C'est pour combien de personnes?
2  Comment vous appelez-vous?
3  Vous avez une chambre?
4  Comment ça s'écrit*?
5  Où est l'ascenseur?
6  C'est pour quand?

a  J-A-M-I-N.
b  Pierre Jamin.
c  À côté de l'escalier.
d  Pour le mois de juin.
e  Je regrette. L'hôtel est complet.
f  Pour deux adultes et un enfant.

6

**TOTAL SCORE** 50

If you scored less than 40, go through the dialogues and the Language Building sections again before completing the Summary on page 60.

# Summary 4

 Now try this final test summarizing the main points covered in this unit.

How would you:
1  say your name is Chris Martin and spell it?
2  say the months of the year?
3  say you would like to book a room?
4  ask where the bathroom is?
5  say the living room is small?
6  say the kitchen is big?
7  tell some friends they have a beautiful garden?

## REVISION

First, how would you describe your home to a French speaker using the vocabulary and structures you have learnt so far? Is your home big or small? Old or modern? How many rooms do you have? What equipment do you have in the kitchen? Do you have a garden?

Then imagine a French speaker is showing you round his/her house. Think of all the complimentary comments you could make, such as: **Vous avez une belle cuisine, Le jardin est agréable**, etc.

# Personal information
# Renseignements personnels

**OBJECTIVES**

In this unit you will learn how to:

- ✓ say where you come from and where you live
- ✓ talk about your family
- ✓ talk about your job
- ✓ talk about your daily routine

And cover the following grammar and language:

- ✓ adjectives of nationality
- ✓ the use of **de** ('of') to show possession
- ✓ possessive adjectives: **mon**, **ton**, **son**, **notre**, **votre**, **leur**
- ✓ reflexive verbs

## LEARNING FRENCH 5

It is important to practise speaking aloud as often as possible, because it will help you memorize vocabulary and structures. Going through the same dialogue several times is a good idea, too. A fun way of doing it is to vary the tones – happy, sad, shy, angry, etc. – as if you were auditioning for a part. And don't be afraid to exaggerate! It is also helpful to record yourself as often as possible, so that you can replay it, improve your performance, and keep track of your progress.

Now start the recording for Unit 5.

## Je ne suis pas marié

ACTIVITY 1 is on the recording.

**ACTIVITY 2**

Which of these 3 women has most in common with Éric?
Choose one and write a letter to Éric on her behalf.

**Sylvie**, 35 ans, séparée, 1 enfant, originaire de Nice, infirmière, Lille

**Linda**, 40 ans, portugaise, interprète de conférence, Paris

**Karima**, 38 ans, divorcée, 2 enfants, professeur d'espagnol, Marseille

**DIALOGUE 1**

○ Bonjour. Je m'appelle Éric et j'ai trente-huit ans. Je suis suisse et j'habite Genève. J'ai un petit appartement près du lac. Je parle français et allemand, et je comprends l'italien. En ce moment, j'apprends l'anglais. J'ai un magasin d'antiquités et je vends des objets anciens. C'est un métier passionnant. Je ne suis pas marié, je n'ai pas d'enfants. Je suis seul, et je cherche l'âme sœur. J'attends vos messages. À bientôt!

| VOCABULARY | |
| --- | --- |
| **avoir … ans** | to be … years old |
| **suisse** | Swiss |
| **habiter** | to live |
| **près de** | near |
| **le lac** | lake |
| **parler** | to speak |
| **l'italien** (*m*) | Italian |
| **en ce moment** | at the moment |
| **le magasin d'antiquités** | antique shop |
| **vendre** | to sell |
| **les objets anciens** | old objects, antique objects |
| **le métier** | job |
| **passionnant** | fascinating |
| **seul(e)** | alone, single |
| **chercher** | to look for |
| **l'âme sœur** (*f*) | soulmate |
| **attendre** | to wait for |

## ⊘ Talking about age

Remember to use **avoir** rather than **être**: elle a **18 ans** ('she is 18 years old'). When asking someone's age, the formal way is **quel âge avez-vous?** In everyday conversation, however, you'll hear **vous avez quel âge?**

## ⊘ Adjectives of nationality

Many adjectives of nationality end in **-ais**. Like other regular adjectives they add an **e** in the feminine.

| French | français | française |
| English | anglais | anglaise |
| Scottish | écossais | écossaise |
| Irish | irlandais | irlandaise |
| Japanese | japonais | japonaise |
| Portuguese | portugais | portugaise |

Others end in **-ain(e)**, **-ien(ne)**, **-ois(e)**, and **-and(e)**.

| American | américain | américaine |
| Moroccan | marocain | marocaine |
| Italian | italien | italienne |
| Canadian | canadien | canadienne |
| Tunisian | tunisien | tunisienne |
| Welsh | gallois | galloise |
| Chinese | chinois | chinoise |
| German | allemand | allemande |

And finally there are a few which don't fit these patterns:

| Belgian | belge | belge |
| British | britannique | britannique |
| Spanish | espagnol | espagnole |
| Swiss | suisse | suisse |

Like most other adjectives, they add an **-s** in the plural unless they already end in **-s**. They are placed after the noun:

| un restaurant **marocain** | a Moroccan restaurant |
| une chanteuse **canadienne** | a Canadian singer |
| les hôtels **britanniques** | British hotels |
| trois enfants **portugais** | three Portuguese children |

---

### ACTIVITY 3

Introduce yourself in French, giving your name, your age, nationality, where you live, and what languages you speak and are learning.

 Now do activities 4 and 5 on the recording.

63

## 5.2 The family
## La famille

 **ACTIVITY 6** is on the recording.

**ACTIVITY 7**

Choose the right ending for each sentence.

1 Madame Leblanc's daughter is called: **a** Anne. **b** Émilie.
2 She works in a hospital: **a** as a doctor. **b** as a nurse.
3 Madame Leblanc's grandson is: **a** 7. **b** 2½.
4 Madame Leblanc's granddaughter is: **a** 3½. **b** 2½.
5 Madame Lenoir's son: **a** works a lot. **b** is looking for work.

**DIALOGUE 2**

○ Madame Leblanc, vos petits-enfants, ça va?
■ Eh bien, Léo a sept ans et il est très mignon.
○ Et sa petite sœur Émilie. Elle a quel âge?
■ Elle a deux ans et demi. Elle est très drôle!
○ Et votre fille, Anne, est infirmière. C'est ça?
■ Oui, c'est ça. Et Laurent, son mari, est informaticien. Il s'occupe d'ordinateurs. Il est adorable … très gentil. Et vous, Madame Lenoir? Comment va votre fils Philippe?
○ Oh, là, là! Il est divorcé, il ne voit pas ses enfants et il est au chômage.

---

| VOCABULARY | |
| --- | --- |
| **les petits-enfants** | grandchildren |
| **mignon(ne)** | sweet |
| **la sœur** | sister |
| **drôle** | funny |
| **la fille** | daughter |
| **l'infirmière** (*f*) | nurse |
| **le mari** | husband |
| **l'informaticien** (*m*) | computer engineer |
| **s'occuper de** | to take care of, to be in charge of |
| **l'ordinateur** (*m*) | computer |
| **adorable** | adorable |
| **gentil(le)** | kind |
| **le fils** | son |
| **divorcé(e)** | divorced |
| **voir** | to see |
| **au chômage** | unemployed |

## ✓ The use of *de*

The preposition **de** is used to show possession. Note that the word order is different from English:

> le mari **d'**Anne      Anne's husband [*literally* the husband of Anne]
> le métier **de** ma mère   my mother's job

Remember to use **du** instead of **de** + **le** and **des** instead of **de** + **les**:

> la maison **du** professeur   the teacher's house
> la chambre **des** enfants   the children's room

## ✓ Possessive adjectives

There is no distinction in French between 'his' and 'her'. The form of the possessive adjective is determined by the gender of the person or thing possessed:

| | | | |
|---|---|---|---|
| **mon** fils | my son | **notre** frère | our brother |
| **ma** fille | my daughter | **notre** sœur | our sister |
| **mes** enfants | my children | **nos** frères et sœurs | our brothers and sisters |
| **ton** mari | your husband | **votre** beau-père | your father-in-law/stepfather |
| **ta** femme | your wife | **votre** belle-mère | your mother-in-law/stepmother |
| **tes** amis | your friends | **vos** beaux-parents | your parents-in-law |
| **son** père | her/his father | **leur** grand-père | their grandfather |
| **sa** mère | her/his mother | **leur** grand-mère | their grandmother |
| **ses** parents | her/his parents | **leurs** grands-parents | their grandparents |

**ACTIVITY 8**

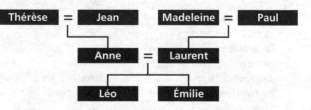

**La famille d'Anne:** \_\_\_\_\_ père s'appelle \_\_\_\_\_ et \_\_\_\_\_
mère s'appelle \_\_\_\_\_ . \_\_\_\_\_ mari s'appelle \_\_\_\_\_ , et
\_\_\_\_\_ beaux-parents s'appellent \_\_\_\_\_ et \_\_\_\_\_ . Anne et
Laurent ont deux enfants: \_\_\_\_\_ fils s'appelle Léo et \_\_\_\_\_
fille s'appelle Émilie.

 Now do activities 9 and 10 on the recording.

65

**What job do you do?**

**Que faites-vous comme métier?**

ACTIVITY 11 is on the recording.

**ACTIVITY 12**

Correct the statements which are false.

| | |
|---|---|
| 1  Mona works as a DJ. | V/F |
| 2  She loves her job. | V/F |
| 3  She usually works until 8 o'clock in the morning. | V/F |
| 4  When she gets home, she goes straight to bed. | V/F |
| 5  She gets up around 5 o'clock. | V/F |
| 6  She takes her dog out for a walk in the afternoon. | V/F |

**DIALOGUE 3**

○ Mona, vous aimez votre métier?

■ Oui, j'aime beaucoup mon métier! Je suis DJ. Je travaille dans des boîtes de nuit, et je m'occupe de la musique.

○ Vous travaillez la nuit alors?

■ Généralement, je travaille jusqu'à six heures du matin, et je rentre chez moi à sept heures du matin. Je promène mon chien, je dîne et je me couche à huit heures et demie.

○ Vous vous levez à quelle heure?

■ Je me lève à quinze heures et je prends mon petit déjeuner. L'après-midi, je travaille: j'écoute de la musique, j'achète des disques, et je choisis la musique pour la nuit.

---

| VOCABULARY | |
|---|---|
| aimer | to like |
| beaucoup | very much |
| la boîte de nuit | nightclub |
| la musique | music |
| généralement | generally |
| promener le chien | to take the dog for a walk |
| se coucher | to go to bed |
| se lever | to get up |
| l'après-midi (m/f) | afternoon |
| écouter | to listen to |
| acheter | to buy |
| le disque | record |
| choisir | to choose |

## ✓ Talking about work

The indefinite article is omitted when you say what your job is.

| **Je suis ...** ('I'm a/an ...') | **Il/Elle est ...** ('He/She's a ...') |
|---|---|
| **vendeur/vendeuse** sales assistant | **secrétaire** secretary |
| **serveur/serveuse** waiter/waitress | **réceptionniste** receptionist |
| **pharmacien/pharmacienne** pharmacist | **gardien/gardienne** caretaker |
| **comédien/comédienne** actor/actress | **instituteur/institutrice** primary |
| **technicien/technicienne** technician | school teacher |
| **directeur/directrice** director | |

**Je travaille dans ...** ('I work in')

**un magasin** a shop    **une école** a school    **un bureau** an office
**une usine** a factory    **un hôpital** a hospital

## ✓ Reflexive verbs

Reflexive verbs require an extra pronoun between the subject and the verb. Many verbs describing daily activities are reflexive, for example: **se réveiller** ('to wake up'), **se lever** ('to get up'), **se laver** ('to get washed'), **s'habiller** ('to get dressed'), **se coucher** ('to go to bed').

| je **me** réveille | nous **nous** réveillons |
|---|---|
| tu **te** réveilles | vous **vous** réveillez |
| il/elle/on **se** réveille | ils/elles **se** réveillent |

Note that **me**, **te**, and **se** change to **m'**, **t'**, and **s'** in front of a vowel or mute h: **je m'habille, elle s'amuse**.

Note that the spelling of **se lever** varies slightly. When the final syllable is silent, the **e** of the stem becomes **è**: **je me lève, tu te lèves, il/elle/on se lève, ils/elles se lèvent**. The same applies to **promener** and **acheter**.

Other reflexive verbs: **se promener** ('to go for a walk'), **s'inquiéter** ('to worry'), **s'amuser** ('to enjoy oneself'), **s'ennuyer** ('to be bored').

---

### ACTIVITY 13

Complete this summary about a typical day in Mona's life.

Mona aime _____ son métier. Elle _____ DJ, elle s' _____ de la musique dans les boîtes de nuit. Elle _____ réveille vers trois heures de l'après-midi, elle se _____ et elle prend son petit déjeuner. Elle travaille l'après-midi et la nuit jusqu'à six heures du matin. Elle rentre chez elle, elle _____occupe de son chien, elle mange, et elle se _____ vers huit heures et demie.

 Now do activities 14 and 15 on the recording.

# 5.4 The French-speaking world
## Le monde francophone

There are more than 104 million French speakers in the world. More than 67 million have French as their mother tongue, and a further 38.5 million speak French as their second language.

### ACTIVITY 16

French is spoken in different countries in the world, but there are variations. Here are a few examples. Try to match them with their English equivalents.

\* **avant** before

| | | | |
|---|---|---|---|
| 1 | hier nuit (Mali) | a | to have had enough |
| 2 | un quartier (Belgique) | b | to feel depressed |
| 3 | camembérer (Sénégal) | c | small apartment |
| 4 | avoir les bleus (Canada) | d | last night |
| 5 | la fin de semaine (Canada) | e | weekend |
| 6 | avoir son voyage (Canada) | f | morning |
| 7 | l'avant\*-midi (Belgique, Canada, et Suisse) | g | to stink |

### ACTIVITY 17

In Switzerland, numbers over 69 are different from the French equivalents. Try to match the following Swiss and French numbers.

| Swiss | French |
|---|---|
| septante-un | soixante et onze |
| septante-sept | quatre-vingt-cinq |
| huitante-cinq | quatre-vingt-dix |
| huitante-huit | quatre-vingt-huit |
| nonante | quatre-vingt-dix-neuf |
| nonante-neuf | soixante-dix-sept |

Note that **septante** and **nonante** are also used in Belgium.

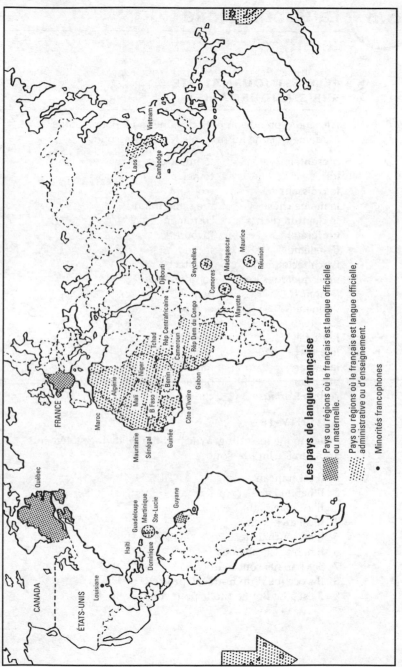

**Les pays de langue française**

▨ Pays ou régions où le français est langue officielle ou maternelle.

⬚ Pays ou régions où le français est langue officielle, administrative ou d'enseignement.

● Minorités francophones

CANADA

ÉTATS-UNIS

Québec

Louisiane

Haïti
Dominique
Guadeloupe
Martinique
Ste-Lucie

Guyane

FRANCE

Maroc

Mauritanie
Sénégal
Guinée

Algérie

Mali
B Faso

Niger

Tchad

Rép Centrafricaine

Bénin
Cameroun

Côte d'Ivoire

Gabon

Rép Dém du Congo

Djibouti

Seychelles
Comores

Madagascar
Mayotte
Maurice
Réunion

Vietnam

Laos

Cambodge

69

#### ELLE EST JOURNALISTE
#### SHE'S A JOURNALIST

Alexandra prend son petit déjeuner à La Bonne Étoile.
Madame Delaine lui présente Karim Massoud.

| | |
|---|---|
| présenter | to introduce |
| lui | to her |
| le croissant | croissant |
| la même chose | the same thing |
| le client/la cliente | customer |
| préféré(e) | favourite |
| deuxième | second |
| l'architecte (m/f) | architect |
| pour quelques jours | for a few days |
| le nom | name |
| l'origine (f) | origin |
| ici | here |
| le travail | work |
| le projet | project |
| la région | region |
| attention | be careful, watch out |
| curieux/curieuse | curious |

#### ACTIVITY 18

Listen to the recording. Which of the following statements
apply to Karim Massoud?

1  Il est français.
2  Il habite Paris.
3  Il est marocain.
4  Il est architecte.
5  Il est journaliste.
6  Il habite Casablanca.
7  Ses parents sont marocains.
8  Il s'occupe d'un nouveau projet.
9  Il est à La Bonne Étoile pour son travail.

**ACTIVITY 19**

Complete this transcript of a conversation between Alexandra and one of her colleagues.

○ Il y a un client intéressant à La Bonne Étoile.

■ Il s'appelle _____ ?

○ Il s'_____ Monsieur Massoud.

■ Il _____ marocain?

○ Non, il est _____ , mais ses parents _____ marocains.

■ Il habite _____ ?

○ Il _____ Paris.

■ Il a _____ âge?

○ Je ne sais pas! Vingt-huit, trente _____ .

■ Qu'est-ce qu'il fait à La Bonne Étoile?

○ Il _____ architecte. Il _____occupe d'un nouveau projet dans la région.

■ Très intéressant!

**ACTIVITY 20**

Imagine you are Karim Massoud. Introduce yourself, giving your name, where you come from, what you do, etc.

**STORY TRANSCRIPT**

| | |
|---|---|
| M. Massoud | Bonjour, Madame. |
| Mme Delaine | Bonjour, Monsieur Massoud. Ça va? Votre chambre est confortable? |
| M. Massoud | Très confortable. Merci. |
| Mme Delaine | Qu'est-ce que vous prenez? |
| M. Massoud | Un café et un croissant, s'il vous plaît. |
| Mme Delaine | D'accord. Ah, bonjour, Alexandra. Tu prends un café? |
| Alexandra | Oui, et un croissant aussi, s'il vous plaît. |
| Mme Delaine | Jean-Luc, un café et un croissant pour Monsieur Massoud. Et la même chose pour Alexandra. Alexandra est notre cliente préférée. La Bonne Étoile, c'est son deuxième bureau. Monsieur Massoud est architecte et il est à La Bonne Étoile pour quelques jours. |
| Alexandra | Massoud, c'est un nom marocain? |
| M. Massoud | Oui, je suis d'origine marocaine, mes parents sont marocains. Mais je suis français. |
| Alexandra | Vous habitez où? |
| M. Massoud | J'habite Paris. |
| Alexandra | Vous êtes ici pour votre travail? |
| M. Massoud | Oui, je m'occupe d'un nouveau projet dans la région. |
| Alexandra | Un nouveau projet? C'est très intéressant! |
| M. Massoud | Oui, c'est un projet très intéressant, mais … |
| Alexandra | Ah, excusez-moi … Allô? … |
| Mme Delaine | Attention, Monsieur Massoud. Nous aimons beaucoup Alexandra, elle est adorable. Mais elle est journaliste, et elle est très curieuse! |
| M. Massoud | D'accord. Je comprends. |

# Test

Now it's time to test your progress in Unit 5.

1 Match the following words and phrases with their English equivalents.

| | | | |
|---|---|---|---|
| 1 | un informaticien | a | shop |
| 2 | une infirmière | b | nurse |
| 3 | une serveuse | c | school |
| 4 | un vendeur | d | factory |
| 5 | un magasin | e | waitress |
| 6 | une école | f | sales assistant |
| 7 | une usine | g | computer engineer |

`7`

2 Find the right answer from a–f for the questions 1–6.

1 Où habite ta sœur?
2 Quel âge a votre fils?
3 Comment s'appelle ta fille?
4 Que faites-vous comme métier?
5 À quelle heure vous levez-vous?
6 Combien de langues parlez-vous?

a Trois: le français et l'anglais et j'apprends l'espagnol.
b Je suis au chômage en ce moment.
c À sept heures et demie.
d Dix-sept ans.
e À Marseille.
f Annabelle.

`6`

3 Take one item from each column to make up six correct sentences. (2 points for each correct answer, 1 point if you make only one error.)

| Je | t' | lève | dans la salle de bains. |
| Tu | s' | lavez | dans le jardin. |
| Elle | m' | occupe | à trois heures. |
| Nous | se | amusent | d'ordinateurs. |
| Vous | ne nous | inquiètes | beaucoup. |
| Ils | vous | ennuyons | pas. |

`12`

4 Choose the right possessive adjective to complete the following dialogue.

- Comment vont (**votre/vos**) enfants?
- Ça va, merci. (**Mon/Ma**) fils travaille en Écosse, et (**mon/ma**) fille est mariée. (**Son/sa**) mari est italien. Alors (**mes/notre**) petits-enfants parlent français et italien.
- Ils parlent italien avec (**leur/son**) père?
- Oui, et aussi avec (**ses/leurs**) grands-parents italiens.
- Et comment va (**votre/son**) mari?
- Ça va, merci.
- Et (**sa/son**) mère?
- Ça va. Elle a quatre-vingt-quinze ans maintenant!

| | 9 |

5 How would you express the following things in French? (2 points for each correct answer, 1 point if you make only one error.)

1 Say that your sister is a journalist.
2 Say that she likes her job very much.
3 Say that your brother-in law is American.
4 Say that your parents-in-law are Irish.
5 Say that your children's dog is called Tintin.
6 Ask friends if their children are learning German.
7 Ask a close friend at what time she gets up.
8 Ask someone if they sell computers.

| | 16 |

**TOTAL SCORE** | 50 |

If you scored less than 40, go through the dialogues and the Language Building sections again before completing the Summary on page 74.

# Summary 5

 Now try this final test summarizing the main points covered in this unit.

How would you:
1 say that your parents are divorced?
2 say that your father is 88 and lives in New York?
3 say that your sister speaks English, French, and German?
4 say that your brother is learning Japanese?
5 say that your sister's husband is unemployed?
6 say that you like your grandchildren a lot, they are very funny?
7 say that they get up at 6.30?

## REVISION

Can you describe your daily routine, and that of other members or your family/household, making the most of the language you have learnt so far?

- Say a few words about your job, and about theirs:

  **Je suis .../Il est .../Elle est ...**
  **Je travaille .../Il travaille .../Elle travaille ...**
  **dans un/une ...**
  **Je m'occupe de .../Il s'occupe de .../Elle s'occupe de ...**

- Say at what time you and they wake up/get up/have breakfast, etc., using reflexive verbs:

  **Je me lève/réveille/couche ...**
  **Il/Elle se lève/réveille/couche ...**

- Make the most of the possessive adjectives and family vocabulary you have learnt:

  **Mon/Son/Leur père/fils/frère/mari ...**
  **Ma/Sa/Leur mère/fille/sœur/femme ...**
  **Mes/Ses/Leurs/Nos enfants/parents/grands-parents ...**

- Also use the expressions of time you know:

  **... à sept heures et quart/et demie/moins le quart**

# Shopping
# Dans les magasins

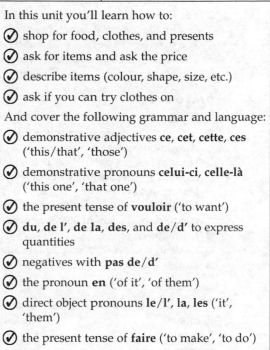

**OBJECTIVES**

In this unit you'll learn how to:

- ✓ shop for food, clothes, and presents
- ✓ ask for items and ask the price
- ✓ describe items (colour, shape, size, etc.)
- ✓ ask if you can try clothes on

And cover the following grammar and language:

- ✓ demonstrative adjectives **ce**, **cet**, **cette**, **ces** ('this/that', 'those')
- ✓ demonstrative pronouns **celui-ci**, **celle-là** ('this one', 'that one')
- ✓ the present tense of **vouloir** ('to want')
- ✓ **du**, **de l'**, **de la**, **des**, and **de/d'** to express quantities
- ✓ negatives with **pas de/d'**
- ✓ the pronoun **en** ('of it', 'of them')
- ✓ direct object pronouns **le/l'**, **la**, **les** ('it', 'them')
- ✓ the present tense of **faire** ('to make', 'to do')

## LEARNING FRENCH 6

Apart from listening to the course recordings, you could watch French films with subtitles, listen to a French radio station (try France Inter on 162 m long wave), or watch French-speaking TV stations if you have satellite or cable TV. Even if you don't understand much of what is being said, it is a good way of getting used to French sounds and intonations.

🎧 Now start the recording for Unit 6.

# Je peux vous aider?

$\textcircled{\scriptsize 1A}$ **ACTIVITY 1** is on the recording.

**ACTIVITY 2**

Correct those statements which are false.

1  A customer is looking for a present for her sister.     V / F
2  The assistant shows her some hand-painted pottery.  V / F
3  Finally the assistant shows her some pretty silk hats. V / F
4  The scarves cost between 30 and 85 euros.           V / F
5  The customer chooses a pretty blue and green scarf.  V / F
6  The assistant offers to gift wrap it.                V / F

**DIALOGUE 1**

○ Je peux vous aider?
■ Je cherche un cadeau pour une amie.
○ Alors, nous avons ce vase rond, ou cette assiette carrée.
  Nous avons ces plats et ces bols peints à la main … Ah! J'ai
  aussi de très jolis foulards en soie: des bleus, des verts, des
  jaunes, des orange, des rouges et des violets.
■ Ils sont très beaux. Ils coûtent combien?
○ Alors, ceux-ci coûtent 48€ et ceux-là 41,90€.
■ Je prends celui-ci.
○ Le bleu. Vous voulez un paquet-cadeau?
■ Oui, je veux bien.

| VOCABULARY | |
|---|---|
| **le cadeau** | present |
| **l'ami(e)** | friend |
| **le vase** | vase |
| **rond(e)** | round |
| **l'assiette (f)** | plate |
| **carré(e)** | square |
| **le plat** | dish |
| **le bol** | bowl |
| **peint(e) à la main** | hand-painted |
| **le foulard** | scarf |
| **en soie** | made of silk |
| **coûter** | to cost |
| **vous voulez un paquet-cadeau?** | do you want it gift-wrapped? |
| **oui, je veux bien** | yes please |

### ✓ Demonstrative adjectives

In French, the demonstrative adjectives (the words for 'this', 'that', 'these', or 'those' used before a noun) are:

| (*m*) | (*f*) | (*pl.*) |
|---|---|---|
| **ce/cet** | **cette** | **ces** |

**cet** is used before a masculine noun starting with a vowel or mute **h**.

> **ce** bracelet est cher. This/that bracelet is expensive.
> Je choisis **cet** objet. I'll choose this/that item.
> Je n'aime pas **cette** bague. I don't like this/that ring.
> Je déteste **ces** boucles d'oreilles. I hate these/those earrings.

If you need to be more specific, add **-ci** or **-là** after the noun:

> Je n'aime pas **cette** couleur-**ci**, je prends **ces** roses-**là**.
> I don't like this colour, I'll take those roses.

### ✓ Demonstrative pronouns

Demonstrative pronouns are the words for 'this (one)'/'that (one)' used in place of nouns. In French, the demonstrative pronouns are:

| (*sing.*) | | (*pl.*) | | |
|---|---|---|---|---|
| (*m*) | (*f*) | (*m*) | (*f*) | |
| **celui-ci** | **celle-ci** | **ceux-ci** | **celles-ci** | this one, these |
| **celui-là** | **celle-là** | **ceux-là** | **celles-là** | that one, those |

### ✓ *Les couleurs*

| **bleu(e)** blue | **jaune** yellow | **violet(te)** purple | **marron** brown |
|---|---|---|---|
| **noir(e)** black | **rouge** red | **vert(e)** green | **orange** orange |
| **gris(e)** grey | **blanc(he)** white | | |

**orange** and **marron** do not change in the feminine or plural.

### ✓ *vouloir* ('to want') – irregular verb

| je **veux** | nous **voulons** |
|---|---|
| tu **veux** | vous **voulez** |
| il/elle/on **veut** | ils/elles **veulent** |

---

#### ACTIVITY 3

Match each pronoun with the correct item.

| 1 | celui-ci | a | des boucles d'oreilles |
|---|---|---|---|
| 2 | celle-là | b | des foulards |
| 3 | ceux-ci | c | un bracelet |
| 4 | celles-là | d | une bague |

 Now do activities 4 and 5 on the recording.

# At the market
## Au marché

ACTIVITY 6 is on the recording.

### ACTIVITY 7

Which dish is the customer planning to prepare?

| Ratatouille | Navarin | Soupe au pistou |
|---|---|---|
| 750 g d'aubergines | 1 kg d'agneau | ³/₄ l d'eau |
| 750 g de poivrons | 1 kg de navets | 150 g de carottes |
| 600 g de tomates | 150 g de carottes | 150 g de navets |
| 1 kg de courgettes | 40 g de farine | 60 g d'oignons |
| 120 g d'oignons | huile d'olive | 100 g de tomates |
| huile d'olive | ¹/₂ l de bouillon | huile d'olive |
| ail, sel, poivre | 100 g d'oignons | ail, basilic, sel |

### DIALOGUE 2

○ Je voudrais des oignons et des tomates, s'il vous plaît.
■ Vous en voulez combien?
○ Une livre de tomates et une livre d'oignons.
■ Voilà. Et avec ça?
○ Je voudrais un kilo de carottes … et des navets.
■ Un kilo de carottes. Voilà. Je n'ai pas de navets aujourd'hui.
○ Vous n'en avez pas. Vous avez de l'ail et du basilic?
■ Oui, voilà. Vous voulez autre chose?
○ Non, c'est tout. Ça fait combien?

### VOCABULARY

| | |
|---|---|
| **l'huile d'olive** (f) | olive oil |
| **l'eau** (f) | water |
| **le sel et le poivre** | salt and pepper |
| **l'agneau** (m) | lamb |
| **la farine** | flour |
| **le bouillon** | stock |
| **l'oignon** (m) | onion |
| **vous en voulez combien?** | how many/much do you want? |
| **la livre** | pound [*equivalent to 500 grams*] |
| **et avec ça?** | anything else? |
| **la carotte** | carrot |
| **le navet** | turnip |
| **l'ail et le basilic** | garlic and basil |
| **autre chose** | anything else |

## ✓ Expressing quantities

**du, de l', de la**, and **des** are used to express unspecified quantities:

Je voudrais **du** fromage, **de l'**eau, **de la** bière et **des** olives.
I'd like (some) cheese, water, beer, and olives.

**de** (or **d'** before a vowel) is used to express more specific quantities:

| | | |
|---|---|---|
| un litre **d'**eau a litre of water | beaucoup **d'**argent a lot of money | |
| un peu **de** sel a little salt | une douzaine **d'**œufs a dozen eggs | |
| deux cents grammes **de** fromage 200 grammes of cheese | | |

## ✓ *de/d'* after a negative

After a negative **de/d'** replaces **un/une, du/de l'/de la/des**:

Il y a **un** marché ici? Is there a market here?
Non, il n'y a pas **de** marché. No, there is no market.
Vous avez **de l'**eau? Do you have any water?
Non, je n'ai pas **d'**eau. No, I have no water.
Je voudrais **des** tomates. I'd like some tomatoes.
Je n'ai pas **de** tomates. I don't have any tomatoes.

## ✓ *en* ('of it', 'of them')

The pronoun **en** is used to replace **de/du/de la/de l'/des** + noun:

Je voudrais **des pommes**. I would like some apples.
Vous **en** voulez combien? How much/many do you want?
Vous avez **des** abricots? Do you have any apricots?
Non, je n'**en** ai pas. No, I don't have any.
J'**en** voudrais trois. I'd like three (of them).

## ✓ *Les fruits et les légumes*

| | |
|---|---|
| **le fruit** fruit | **le légume** vegetable |
| **l'orange** (*f*) orange | **la pomme de terre** potato |
| **la pomme** apple | **le poireau** leek |
| **la poire** pear | **le poivron** pepper, capsicum |
| **la pêche** peach | **le haricot vert** French bean, green bean |
| **la banane** banana | **le petit pois** pea |
| **la fraise** strawberry | **l'aubergine** (*f*) aubergine, eggplant |
| **la framboise** raspberry | **la courgette** courgette, zucchini |

---

### ACTIVITY 8

Imagine you are shopping in the market before preparing a ratatouille. Look at the list of ingredients on page 78, and complete the following sentence. **Je voudrais ...**

 Now do activities 9 and 10 on the recording.

# Les vêtements

🎧 **ACTIVITY 11** is on the recording.

**ACTIVITY 12**

Correct the statements which are false.

| | | |
|---|---|---|
| 1 | The customer is looking for a skirt. | V / F |
| 2 | She normally takes a size 38. | V / F |
| 3 | She doesn't like the grey trousers. | V / F |
| 4 | The black trousers are made of wool and polyester and cost 140 euros. | V / F |
| 5 | They are too big. | V / F |
| 6 | She finally buys a pair of blue trousers in size 38. | V / F |

**DIALOGUE 3**

○ Je cherche un pantalon.

■ Vous faites quelle taille?

○ Je fais du 40.

■ Nous avons celui-ci en noir ou celui-là en gris.

○ Je n'aime pas le gris, mais le noir est très joli. Il est en coton?

■ Non. C'est un mélange laine-polyester.

○ Il coûte combien?

■ 114 euros.

○ Je peux l'essayer?

■ Bien sûr. … Ça va?

○ Non, il est trop grand. Vous l'avez en 38?

■ En 38, je l'ai en bleu, mais pas en noir. … Ça va? Il est assez long?

○ Oui, c'est parfait. Je le prends.

---

**VOCABULARY**

| | |
|---|---|
| **le pantalon** | (pair of) trousers, pants |
| **vous faites quelle taille?** | what size do you take? |
| **la taille** | size |
| **le coton** | cotton |
| **le mélange** | mixture |
| **essayer** | to try (on) |
| **trop** | too |
| **assez** | enough |
| **parfait(e)** | perfect |

### ✓ Direct object pronouns *le*, *la*, *l'* ('it'), and *les* ('them')

The direct object of a verb is the noun, pronoun, or phrase which is directly affected by the action of the verb. **le** refers to a masculine singular noun, **la** to a feminine singular noun, and **les** to a plural noun. Unlike English, French direct object pronouns come before the verb:

Ce pull est très joli. Je **le** prends. This sweater is very pretty. I'll take it.
Il y a **une** vendeuse là-bas. Tu **la** vois? There's a sales assistant over there. Can you see her?
J'aime **ces** chaussures. Je peux **les** essayer? I like these shoes. Can I try them on?

Note that **le** and **la** change to **l'** before a vowel or mute **h**:

J'aime ce pull. Je **l'**achète. I like this sweater. I'll buy it.
Il y a une vendeuse là-bas. Je **l'**appelle? There's a sales assistant over there. Shall I call her?

### ✓ *Les vêtements*

| | | | | | |
|---|---|---|---|---|---|
| **la robe** | dress | **la chaussure** | shoe | **le chapeau** | hat |
| **la jupe** | skirt | **la chaussette** | sock | **la chemise** | shirt |
| **l'imperméable** (*m*) | raincoat | **le pyjama** | pyjamas | **le jean** | jeans |
| **le manteau** | winter coat | **le collant** | tights | **le gant** | glove |

Note that the French for trousers, jeans, tights, and pyjamas is singular. The plural is only used when talking about more than one pair.

### ✓ *faire* ('to do, to make') – irregular verb

| | |
|---|---|
| je **fais** | nous **faisons** |
| tu **fais** | vous **faites** |
| il/elle/on **fait** | ils/elles **font** |

**faire** is an important verb to learn as it is used in a variety of phrases, such as **ça fait combien?** ('how much is that?'), **vous faites quelle taille?** ('what size [in clothes] do you take?'), or **vous faites quelle pointure?** ('what shoe size do you take?'). Find out more in later units.

---

### ACTIVITY 13

Rewrite Dialogue 3, replacing the trousers with a skirt and changing all the pronouns and the endings on the colours accordingly. Then read it aloud.

 Now do activities 14 and 15 on the recording.

## Les tailles et les pointures

**ACTIVITY 16**

Look at the charts and answer the following questions.

1 Vous faites quelle taille? Et votre mari/femme/père/mère/sœur/frère?
2 Vous faites quelle pointure? Et votre mari/femme/père/mère/sœur/frère?

**Les tailles**

**Femmes**

| | | | | | | |
|-----|-----|-----|-----|-----|-----|-----|
| GB | 8 | 10 | 12 | 14 | 16 | 18 |
| USA | 6 | 8 | 10 | 12 | 14 | 16 |
| France | 36 | 38 | 40 | 42 | 44 | 46 |

**Hommes**

| | | | | | | |
|-----|-----|-----|-----|-----|-----|-----|
| GB | 36 | 38 | 40 | 42 | 44 | 46 |
| USA | 36 | 38 | 40 | 42 | 44 | 46 |
| France | 46 | 48 | 50 | 52 | 54 | 56 |

**Les pointures**

**Femmes**

| | | | | | | |
|-----|-----|-----|-----|-----|-----|-----|
| GB | 4 | 5 | 6 | 7 | 7.5 | 8 |
| USA | 6.5 | 7.5 | 8.5 | 9.5 | 10.5 | 11.5 |
| France | 37 | 38 | 39 | 40 | 41 | 42 |

**Hommes**

| | | | | | | |
|-----|-----|-----|-----|-----|-----|-----|
| GB | 6 | 7 | 8 | 9 | 10 | 11 |
| USA | 9.5 | 10.5 | 11.5 | 12.5 | 13.5 | 14.5 |
| France | 40 | 41 | 42 | 43 | 44 | 45 |

**ACTIVITY 17**

Look at this extract from a French mail order catalogue, and work out what you would say to a French friend asking:

1 Qu'est-ce que tu voudrais/cherches?
2 Pour qui?
3 Tu choisis quelle couleur?
4 Ça coûte combien?

Here are some phrases to help you:
**Je cherche un/une …**
**Pour moi/mon frère/ma sœur, etc.**
**Je choisis le noir/le bleu/le rouge, etc.**
**Ça coûte XXX euros.**

**A.** Tee-shirt
en jersey 100%
coton
Rose: 660603
Beige: 660601
Rouge: 660600
1, 2, 3, 4

**40 euros**

**B.** Boots
dessus cuir
Marron: 660942
Noir: 660943
36, 36$^1/_2$, 37, 37$^1/_2$,
38, 38$^1/_2$, 39, 39$^1/_2$,
40, 40$^1/_2$, 41

**116 euros**

**C.** Collant
70% polyamide,
30% élasthanne
Marron: 660762
Noir: 660763
1, 2, 3, 4

**15 euros**

**D.** Ceinture
en cuir
Marron: 660884
65, 70, 75, 80, 85

**39 euros**

**E.** Jupe droite
100% laine
Marron: 660109
36, 38, 40, 42, 44, 46

**62 euros**

**F.** Chemisier
100% coton
Blanc: 660400
36, 38, 40, 42, 44,
46, 48

**76 euros**

**G.** Jean 5 poches
97% coton, 3%
élasthanne Lycra
Noir: 660219 (36 au
44)
Marine: 660218 (36
au 44)
Marron: 660216 (36
au 46)
36, 38, 40, 42, 44, 46

**62 euros**

**H.** Veste
100% coton
Marron: 662005
1, 2, 3, 4, 5

**210 euros**

**I.** Pull jacquard
50% acrylique,
25% laine, 15%
alpaga, 10%
mohair
Bleu/marron/beige
: 662502
2, 3, 4, 5

**90 euros**

**J.** Chemise 100%
coton
Blanc: 662419
du 37 au 44

**55 euros**

**K.** Chemise 100%
coton
Indigo: 632408
du 37 au 44

**56 euros**

**L.** Chaussettes
75% laine, 22%
coton,
3% polyamide
Marron: 662761
Rouge: 662762
Marine: 662763
40/41, 42/43, 44/45

**19 euros**

83

**VOUS VOULEZ UN PAQUET-CADEAU?**
**DO YOU WANT IT GIFT-WRAPPED?**

Alexandra fait les magasins en ville. Elle rencontre Karim
Massoud dans la rue.

| | |
|---|---|
| **faire les magasins** | to shop |
| **en ville** | in town |
| **rencontrer** | to bump into, to meet |
| **on se tutoie?** | shall we say 'tu' to each other? |
| **l'anniversaire** (*m*) | birthday |
| **le copain/la copine** | (boy)friend/(girl)friend |
| **toi** | you, yourself |
| **peut-être** | maybe |
| **connaître** | to know |
| **artisanal(e)** | craft |
| **le collier** | necklace |
| **on entre?** | shall we go in? |
| **regarder** | to look |
| **hésiter** | to hesitate |
| **moi** | me, myself |
| **les boucles d'oreilles** | earrings |
| **assorti(e)** | matching |

**ACTIVITY 18**

Listen to the recording and put the summary back in the right
order.

1 Alexandra is in town, looking for a present for her friend
   Jérôme.
2 Karim decides to buy a necklace with matching earrings.
3 The shopkeeper mentions there are matching earrings.
4 He tells her he's looking for a present for his mother.
5 Inside, Alexandra notices some beautiful necklaces.
6 They see beautiful silk scarves in the window.
7 The shopkeeper offers to gift wrap the items.
8 Karim asks how much the necklaces are.
9 Alexandra suggests a gift shop nearby.

10 She bumps into Karim.

## ACTIVITY 19

Who says each of the following sentences: Karim, Alexandra, or the shop assistant?

1 Je prends ce collier-ci.
2 Vous voulez l'essayer?
3 Il y a un beau magasin à droite.
4 Vous voulez un paquet-cadeau?
5 Je cherche un cadeau pour ma mère.
6 Vous avez les boucles d'oreilles assorties.

## ACTIVITY 20

Alexandra goes to a shop to buy Jérôme a sweater. Imagine the conversation with the shop assistant. Follow Dialogue 3 on page 80 to help you.

## STORY TRANSCRIPT

| | |
|---|---|
| Karim | Alexandra. Bonjour. Ça va? |
| Alexandra | Oui. Et vous … Et toi? On se tutoie? |
| Karim | Oui, je préfère! Je m'appelle Karim. Qu'est-ce que tu fais ici? |
| Alexandra | Je cherche un cadeau d'anniversaire pour mon copain Jérôme. |
| Karim | Qu'est-ce que tu achètes? |
| Alexandra | Je ne sais pas. Peut-être, un pull ou un CD. Et toi? Qu'est-ce que tu fais? |
| Karim | Je cherche un cadeau pour ma mère, mais je ne connais pas les magasins ici. Alors, c'est difficile. |
| Alexandra | Il y a un beau magasin à droite. |
| Karim | Qu'est-ce qu'ils vendent? |
| Alexandra | Des objets artisanaux, des foulards en soie peints à la main, ou des colliers. Regarde. |
| Karim | Ah, oui. Ces foulards sont très beaux. C'est vrai. On entre? |
| | |
| Alexandra | J'adore ces colliers! Regarde! |
| Karim | Oui, c'est vrai. Ils sont très beaux. Ces colliers coûtent combien? |
| La vendeuse | Ceux-ci coûtent 39€ et ceux-là 47,50€. |
| Karim | J'hésite entre celui-ci et celui-là. Qu'est-ce que tu préfères, Alexandra? |
| Alexandra | Celui-ci … peut-être. |
| La vendeuse | Vous voulez l'essayer? |
| Alexandra | Non, non, ce n'est pas pour moi! |
| La vendeuse | Ah bon! Avec celui-ci, vous avez les boucles d'oreilles assorties. Regardez. C'est très joli! |
| Karim | Oui, c'est vrai. C'est très joli. Alors, je prends ce collier-ci, avec les boucles d'oreilles. |
| La vendeuse | Très bien. Vous voulez un paquet-cadeau? |
| Karim | Oui, je veux bien. Merci. |

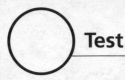

# Test

Now it's time to test your progress in Unit 6.

1 Match the following words with their English equivalents.

| | | | |
|---|---|---|---|
| 1 | un imperméable | a | shoe |
| 2 | une chaussure | b | skirt |
| 3 | une chemise | c | shirt |
| 4 | un pantalon | d | scarf |
| 5 | un foulard | e | dress |
| 6 | une veste | f | jacket |
| 7 | une robe | g | raincoat |
| 8 | une jupe | h | trousers |

**8**

2 Find the odd one out in each group of words.

1  un poireau / un cadeau / un oignon / un haricot / une pomme de terre
2  une poire / une pêche / une fleur / une framboise / une fraise
3  un kilo / un litre / une livre / une pomme / un gramme
4  vert / carré / bleu / blanc / rouge / jaune
5  une assiette / un plat / un bol / une fraise / un vase

**5**

3 Use **d'**, **de**, **de l'**, **de la**, **des**, **du**, or **en** to complete the following dialogue.

○ Je voudrais ____ poires.
■ Vous ____ voulez combien?
○ Un kilo, s'il vous plaît.
■ Un kilo ____ poires. Et avec ça?
○ Vous avez ____ framboises?
■ Je regrette, je n'____ ai pas. Vous voulez autre chose?
○ Oui, je voudrais une douzaine ____ œufs et un litre ____ lait.
■ Voilà. C'est tout?
○ Vous avez ____ coca?
■ J'ai ____ eau et ____ limonade, mais je n'ai pas ____ coca.

**11**

4  Choose the right word to complete the following dialogue.

○ (**Ce/Cet**) objet est très joli. Et j'aime beaucoup (**ce/ces**) vases. J'hésite entre (**celui-ci/celle-ci**) et (**celui-là/celle-là**).

■ Je ne sais pas.

○ Regarde (**ces/cette**) assiettes.

■ Elles coûtent combien?

○ (**Celles-ci/Ceux-ci**) coûtent 225 francs et (**celles-là/ceux-là**) 199 francs.

■ C'est cher!

○ (**Ces/Cette**) bols sont très beaux.

■ Je n'aime pas (**ceux-ci/celles-ci**), je préfère (**ceux-là/celles-là**).

○ D'accord. Alors, je choisis (**ce/cet**) bol et (**cet/cette**) assiette.

`12`

5  What are they talking about? Choose the correct item.

| | | | | |
|---|---|---|---|---|
| 1 | Je le prends. | a le pantalon | b la chemise |
| 2 | Tu l'achètes? | a les gants | b le foulard |
| 3 | Vous la prenez? | a la chemise | b le pull |
| 4 | Je peux les essayer? | a le chapeau | b les chaussures |
| 5 | Vous voulez l'essayer? | a les chaussures | b la veste |
| | | a les chaussettes | b l'imperméable |
| 6 | Vous les avez en rouge? | | |

`6`

6  Who's saying each sentence? The sales assistant or the customer?

1  C'est tout?             5  Vous faites quelle taille?
2  Ça fait combien?        6  Vous en voulez combien?
3  Je peux l'essayer?      7  Vous avez des gants blancs?
4  Je peux vous aider?     8  Vous voulez un paquet-cadeau?

`8`

**TOTAL SCORE** `50`

If you scored less than 40, go through the dialogues and the Language Building sections again before completing the Summary on page 88.

# Summary 6

 Now try this final test summarizing the main points covered in this unit.

How would you:
1 say you're looking for a present for your sister?
2 ask the price of the plate you're pointing at?
3 say it's too expensive?
4 say you'd like a kilo of potatoes?
5 ask the assistant if they have any milk?
6 and say you'd like a litre?
7 ask for the price of the shoes you're pointing at?
8 and ask if you can try them on?
9 say you take a size 42?
10 say they're too big?

## REVISION

Think of a recent conversation you have had with a very helpful shop assistant, and practise the same thing in French. Try to make the most of the language you have learnt so far, and be as precise as possible. Whenever applicable,

- describe the colour (**rouge**, **bleu**, **noir**, **vert**, etc.)
- describe the size and shape (**grand**, **petit**, **rond**, **carré**, **long**)
- describe the material (**en soie**, **en coton**)
- be precise about the quantity (**un kilo**, **une livre**, **100 grammes**, **un litre**, **une douzaine**)
- say why something is not suitable (**trop grand/petit/long**)

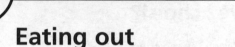

# Eating out
# Au restaurant

### OBJECTIVES

In this unit you'll learn how to:

- ✓ order food and drink
- ✓ ask for information about a menu item
- ✓ express appreciation
- ✓ ask for the bill

And cover the following grammar and language:

- ✓ disjunctive pronouns **moi, toi, lui, elle**, etc.
- ✓ the present tense of **aller** ('to go')
- ✓ **aller** ('to go') + infinitive
- ✓ indirect object pronouns **me/m', te/t', lui, nous, vous, leur**
- ✓ negatives using **ne ... plus** ('not ... any more', 'no ... left')
- ✓ the present tense of **pouvoir** ('to be able')
- ✓ **au, à l', à la, aux** to describe food
- ✓ **qu'est-ce que ... comme ... ?** to ask questions

## LEARNING FRENCH 7

Try recording yourself speaking French whenever you can – especially when doing the pronunciation practice activities. When you listen to it afterwards, don't worry if you sound hesitant or have made mistakes. It's important to evaluate your performance. Compare your pronunciation with the master version, see how you can do better, and have another go. If you do this several times, you will find that each version is better than the last.

Now start the recording for Unit 7.

# 7.1 | Are you ready to order?

## Vous avez choisi?

 **ACTIVITY 1** is on the recording.

**ACTIVITY 2**

Which order matches the conversation?

| Table 1 |
| --- |
| 1 moules |
| 1 tarte tomates |
| 1 lapin |
| 1 steak |

| Table 2 |
| --- |
| soupe pistou |
| 1 tarte tomates |
| 1 sole |
| 1 plat du jour |

| Table 3 |
| --- |
| 1 soupe poissons |
| 1 tarte tomates |
| 1 sole |
| 1 steak (BC) |

**DIALOGUE 1**

▼ Messieurs Dames, vous avez choisi?

○ Oui, alors, pour moi, le menu à 15 euros avec les moules marinières. Euh … non, la soupe de poissons. Ensuite … Le lapin à l'antillaise, qu'est-ce que c'est?

▼ Alors c'est du lapin avec des épices et de l'ananas. C'est très bon.

○ Euh … non. Je vais prendre le filet de sole aux courgettes.

▼ Le filet de sole aux courgettes. D'accord. Et pour monsieur?

■ Le plat du jour, qu'est-ce que c'est?

▼ Le plat du jour, c'est un navarin d'agneau.

■ Alors, je vais prendre la tarte aux tomates et le steak.

▼ Oui, vous voulez quelle cuisson pour le steak? À point?

■ Non, non. Bien cuit, s'il vous plaît.

---

| VOCABULARY | |
| --- | --- |
| la moule | mussel |
| le poisson | fish |
| ensuite | then |
| le lapin à l'antillaise | West Indian style rabbit |
| l'épice (f) | spice |
| l'ananas (m) | pineapple |
| le filet | fillet |
| le plat du jour | dish of the day |
| vous voulez quelle cuisson? | how would you like it done? |
| à point | medium rare |
| bien cuit(e) | well done [*literally* well cooked] |

## ✓ Disjunctive pronouns

|  | (sing.) |  | (pl.) |
|---|---|---|---|
| je | **moi** | nous | **nous** |
| tu | **toi** | vous | **vous** |
| il | **lui** | ils | **eux** |
| elle | **elle** | elles | **elles** |

Disjunctive pronouns can be used in different ways.

1 For emphasis, when used before the subject pronoun (in French the subject pronoun can't carry stress in the way it can in English):

**Lui**, il est végétarien. <u>He</u>'s a vegetarian.
**Elle**, elle n'est pas végétarienne. <u>She</u> isn't a vegetarian.

2 After prepositions, such as **pour**, **avec**, or **sans**:

Elle mange avec **toi**. She's eating with you.
Je travaille pour **lui**. I work for him.
Il part sans **moi**. He's leaving without me.

3 With **et** for the equivalent of 'and you?', etc.

Moi, je n'aime pas la viande. Et **toi**? I don't like meat. And you?

## ✓ *aller* ('to go') – irregular verb

| je **vais** | nous **allons** |
|---|---|
| tu **vas** | vous **allez** |
| il/elle/on **va** | ils/elles **vont** |

**aller** + an infinitive is often used to say what you're going to do:

Je **vais prendre** du vin rouge. I'm going to have some red wine.

---

### ACTIVITY 3

Use the words below to make as many correct sentences as possible.

Exemple: Moi, je vais prendre la soupe.

> moi   le poisson   eux   je   allons
> toi   prendre   nous   tu   vous   choisir
> vais   le steak   la soupe   allez
> lui   elle   vont   va
> la salade   ils   elles   vas   il   la tarte

 Now do activities 4 and 5 on the recording.

91

**ACTIVITY 6** is on the recording.

**ACTIVITY 7**

Here are some of the things the waiter said to the chef in the course of his shift: which ones refer to the diners you hear?

1  Il aime son steak.
2  Ils n'ont plus d'eau.
3  Ils n'ont plus de pain.
4  Elle n'aime pas la sole.
5  Elle n'a pas de couteau.
6  Il n'a pas de fourchette.

**DIALOGUE 2**

▼ Alors, la sole pour Madame.
○ Merci. Hmm! Ça sent bon!
▼ Et le steak pour Monsieur.
■ Merci.
▼ Attention! Les assiettes sont très, très chaudes.
○ D'accord.
▼ Bon appétit, Messieurs Dames.
■ Merci.
○ Je n'ai pas de couteau. Vous pouvez m'apporter un couteau, s'il vous plaît?
▼ Bien sûr. Je vous apporte ça tout de suite.

▼ Tout va bien?
■ Oui, le steak est très bon.
○ Et le poisson est délicieux.
■ Nous n'avons plus de pain. Vous pouvez m'apporter du pain, s'il vous plaît?
▼ Bien sûr. Je vous apporte ça tout de suite.

| VOCABULARY | |
| --- | --- |
| le couteau | knife |
| la fourchette | fork |
| ça sent bon | it smells good |
| chaud(e) | hot |
| apporter | to bring |
| tout de suite | right away |
| tout va bien? | is everything all right? |
| délicieux/délicieuse | delicious |
| le pain | bread |

## ✓ Indirect object pronouns

|        | (sing.)     |            | (pl.) |
|--------|-------------|------------|-------|
| je     | **me / m'** | nous       | **nous** |
| tu     | **te / t'** | vous       | **vous** |
| il, elle | **lui**   | ils, elles | **leur** |

Indirect object pronouns are used to replace nouns which would normally be preceded by **à**, in such phrases as **apporter à** ('to bring'), **donner à** ('to give'), **envoyer à** ('to send'), **téléphoner à** ('to telephone'). They come before the relevant verb.

> Elle téléphone à sa copine. Elle **lui** téléphone.
> She rings her friend. She rings her.
> Il apporte le menu **aux clients**. Il **leur** apporte le menu.
> He brings the customers the menu. He brings them the menu.
> Vous pouvez **m'**apporter un café, s'il vous plaît?
> Could you bring me a coffee, please?

## ✓ *ne ... plus* ('not ... any more', 'no ... left')

**ne ... plus** is used in exactly the same way as the negative **ne ... pas**, so it is followed with **de/d'** rather than **un/une** or **des**:

> Je **ne** mange **plus**. I'm not eating any more.
> Nous **n'**avons **plus de** moules. We have no mussels left.

## ✓ *pouvoir* ('to be able') – irregular verb

| je **peux** | nous **pouvons** |
|-------------|------------------|
| tu **peux** | vous **pouvez** |
| il/elle/on **peut** | ils/elles **peuvent** |

**pouvoir** is followed by a verb in the infinitive:

> Je **peux avoir** du pain, s'il vous plaît? Could I have some bread, please?

---

### ACTIVITY 8

The waitress is so overworked, she cannot make sense of the diners' requests. Put the words in order.

1 l' / on / de / eau / avoir / peut / ?
2 n' / de / nous / avons / plus / pain
3 d' / elle / ne / pas / peut / œufs / manger
4 je / de / une / vin / peux / avoir / bouteille / ?
5 le / me / une / peut / faire / chef / omelette / ?
6 le / leur / vous / menu / pouvez / apporter / ?
7 lui / une / vous / donner / pouvez / fourchette / ?

🔊 Now do activities 9 and 10 on the recording.

# What will you have?
## Qu'est-ce que vous prenez?

**ACTIVITY 11** is on the recording.

**ACTIVITY 12**

Correct the statements which are false.

| | |
|---|---|
| 1 There's apple cake on the menu. | V / F |
| 2 The man orders a crème brûlée. | V / F |
| 3 The woman orders pear with caramel. | V / F |
| 4 Nobody orders a sorbet. | V / F |
| 5 They don't have time for a coffee afterwards. | V / F |
| 6 They are in a bit of a hurry. | V / F |

**DIALOGUE 3**

▼ Qu'est-ce que vous prenez comme dessert?

■ Qu'est-ce qu'il y a?

▼ Alors, il y des fraises à la crème, du gâteau aux pommes, des poires au caramel, de la crème brûlée au chocolat ou des sorbets.

○ Alors, pour moi, une poire au caramel, s'il vous plaît.

■ Et pour moi, des fraises à la crème.

▼ Très bien. Et vous prendrez un petit café?

■ Oui, deux express, s'il vous plaît.

○ Et l'addition aussi, s'il vous plaît.

■ Vous pouvez nous apporter tout ça en même temps? Nous sommes un peu pressés.

▼ D'accord. Je vous apporte tout ça en même temps.

---

| VOCABULARY | |
|---|---|

| | |
|---|---|
| **le dessert** | dessert |
| **la crème** | cream |
| **le gâteau** | cake |
| **le sorbet** | sorbet, sherbet |
| **vous prendrez ...?** | will you have ... ? |
| **l'express (m)** | espresso |
| **l'addition (f)** | bill |
| **tout ça** | everything [*literally* all that] |
| **en même temps** | at the same time |
| **un peu** | a little, a bit |
| **pressé(e)** | in a hurry |

## ✓ Describing food

**au, à l', à la,** and **aux** are used with flavours or fillings in food:

| **le** jambon | un sandwich **au** jambon | a ham sandwich |
| **l'**oignon | une soupe **à l'**oignon | onion soup |
| **la** vanille | une glace **à la** vanille | vanilla ice cream |
| **les** pommes | une tarte **aux** pommes | apple tart |

## ✓ Asking questions using *qu'est-ce que ... comme ... ?*

This construction is very common in French. It often translates as 'what sort/kind of ... ?':

**Qu'est-ce que** vous avez **comme** sandwiches?
What sort of sandwiches do you have?
**Qu'est-ce que** vous aimez **comme** parfum?
What (kind of) flavour do you like?
**Qu'est-ce que** vous écoutez **comme** musique?
What kind of music do you listen to?

---

**ACTIVITY 13**

1 How would you ask the following questions?

What sort of    sandwiches    do you have?
                soups
                fish
                meat
                ice cream/sorbets
                tarts/cakes
                desserts

2 Choose from the list of ingredients below to order a sandwich and an ice cream.

| **le jambon** | ham | **la vanille** | vanilla |
| **le fromage** | cheese | **la framboise** | raspberry |
| **le poulet** | chicken | **la fraise** | strawberry |
| **l'avocat** | avocado | **le chocolat** | chocolate |
| **les œufs** | eggs | **le café** | coffee |
| **les crevettes** | prawns, shrimps | **l'ananas** | pineapple |

 Now do activities 14 and 15 on the recording.

# 7.4 Eating out

## Au restaurant

French eating habits are changing and becoming more and more similar to those of other countries. For example, French people are eating less bread and drinking less wine, while consuming more ketchup and breakfast cereals! More and more people are also willing to try 'exotic' cuisines. The changes especially affect young people: 21% of young people drink coke with their lunch and amongst the 15–19 age group the third most popular dish – after steak and chips and couscous – is a hamburger.

---

## NOTRE MENU MAISON

tarte à l'oignon

soupe de poisson

terrine de saumon

salade d'avocat aux crevettes

❖

côte d'agneau aux herbes de Provence

risotto aux champignons

filet de porc aux pommes

poulet basquaise

steak au poivre

filet de sole

❖

crème caramel

glace à l'ananas

tarte aux fraises

gâteau à l'orange

sorbet à la framboise

| la terrine | pâté |
| le saumon | salmon |
| la côte d'agneau | lamb chop |
| le champignon | mushroom |
| le porc | pork |

## ACTIVITY 16

You're looking at this menu with friends who do not understand French. Answer their questions in English.

What can I have as a starter?
1 I love seafood.
2 I fancy something with prawns.
3 I am allergic to all fish and shellfish.

What can I have as a main course?
4 I only eat chicken.
5 I fancy some lamb.
6 I don't eat fish or meat.

What can I have for dessert?
7 I love pineapple.
8 I am allergic to strawberries and raspberries.
9 I fancy something with fruit – but not sorbet or ice cream.

## ACTIVITY 17

Decide what you would like to order for yourself and imagine your conversation with the waiter.

## ACTIVITY 18

If you were in charge of a French restaurant, what would be your ideal menu? Write it down, including starters, main courses, and desserts. Remember to use **au**, **à l'**, **à la**, and **aux** to describe flavours and fillings, e.g. **soupe à l'oignon**, **omelette aux champignons**, **gâteau à la vanille**.

**L'ADDITION, S'IL VOUS PLAÎT**
**THE BILL, PLEASE**

Alexandra et Jérôme dînent à La Bonne Étoile.

| | |
|---|---|
| **sûr(e)** | sure |
| **tout(e) seul(e)** | on his/her own |
| **venir** | to come |
| **tu veux bien?** | you don't mind, do you? |

### ACTIVITY 19

Listen to the recording and read Alexandra's letter to an English friend. There are three factual mistakes. Can you correct them?

Tonight I had dinner with Jérôme at La Bonne Étoile. He had a salad and some fish, and I had a vegetable pâté and a chicken dish. It was delicious, but the evening didn't go too well. There was this guy called Karim who was eating on his own. He's very friendly, so I asked him to join us. Jérôme didn't like it and left the restaurant at half past eight without eating a dessert. I'll call him tomorrow morning ...

### ACTIVITY 20

Vrai ou faux? Correct the statements which are false.

1 Alexandra adore les tomates et les poivrons.
2 Jérôme ne prend pas de dessert.
3 Alexandra prend du poisson.
4 Alexandra déteste le poulet.
5 Jérôme déteste les oignons.
6 Jérôme prend du poulet.

### ACTIVITY 21

That evening Karim had onion soup and salmon. Imagine his conversation with Madame Delaine when ordering his meal.

| | |
|---|---|
| Mme Delaine | Vous avez choisi? Alexandra? |
| Alexandra | Je ne sais pas, je vais prendre … . la terrine de légumes … ou … la salade de crevettes. Non, la terrine de légumes. |
| Mme Delaine | La terrine de légumes. Tu es sûre? |
| Alexandra | Oui, oui, oui. La terrine de légumes. |
| Mme Delaine | D'accord. Et ensuite? |
| Alexandra | Ensuite … le saumon. |
| Mme Delaine | Le saumon. Oui. Et pour vous, Jérôme? |
| Jérôme | Pour moi, la soupe à l'oignon. |
| Mme Delaine | La soupe à l'oignon. Oui. |
| Jérôme | Et ensuite … Le plat du jour, qu'est-ce que c'est? |
| Mme Delaine | Alors, c'est du poulet basquaise. |
| Alexandra | Ah, du poulet basquaise! Du poulet avec des tomates et des poivrons! Super! J'adore ça! |
| Mme Delaine | Oui, c'est ça. |
| Alexandra | Ben, je ne vais pas prendre de saumon, je vais prendre ça. |
| Mme Delaine | Alors, le poulet basquaise pour Alexandra. Et Jérôme? Vous prenez aussi le poulet basquaise? |
| Jérôme | Non, je vais prendre le filet de porc. |
| Mme Delaine | Le filet de porc. D'accord. |
| | … |
| Alexandra | Ah, c'est Karim là-bas. |
| Jérôme | Qui? |
| Alexandra | Karim. Il est tout seul. Il va venir manger avec nous! Tu veux bien? |
| Jérôme | Euh … |
| | … |
| Mme Delaine | Vous voulez un dessert? |
| Jérôme | Pas pour moi. Je suis pressé. Je voudrais l'addition, s'il vous plaît. |
| Alexandra | Jérôme! Il est seulement neuf heures et quart! |
| Jérôme | Oui, je sais, mais je … Au revoir. |
| Alexandra | Jérôme, je te téléphone demain matin. D'accord? |
| Jérôme | Si tu veux … |

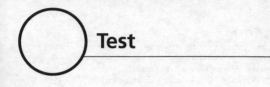

## Test

Now it's time to test your progress in Unit 7.

1 Work out the following anagrams to find eight different types of food.

| | | | | | |
|---|---|---|---|---|---|
| 1 | la ----- | pouse | 5 | les ------- | farisse |
| 2 | la ----- | ratte | 6 | la ------- | vlaneil |
| 3 | le ------ | touple | 7 | le ------- | gramofe |
| 4 | le ------ | jonmab | 8 | le ------- | snopois |

`8`

2 Rewrite the following pronouns in pairs (one subject and one object referring to the same person per pair).

je   me   il   lui   tu   te   elle   leur   ils   lui

`5`

3 Find the right response from a–f for each question 1–6.

1 Tout va bien?
2 L'addition, s'il vous plaît.
3 Vous voulez quelle cuisson?
4 Vous prendrez un petit café?
5 Le plat du jour, qu'est-ce que c'est?
6 Qu'est-ce que vous prenez comme dessert?

a Pour moi, une tarte aux fraises, s'il vous plaît.
b Non, nous sommes un peu pressés.
c C'est du poulet aux olives.
d Oui, le lapin est délicieux.
e Tout de suite, Madame.
f À point, s'il vous plaît.

`6`

4 Use **au**, **à l'**, **à la**, or **aux** to complete the following dialogue.

● Qu'est-ce que vous avez comme gâteaux?
■ Nous avons des gâteaux _____ crème, des gâteaux _____ café et des gâteaux _____ chocolat. Nous avons aussi des tartes _____ ananas et des tartes _____ pommes.
● Et vous avez des glaces?

- Oui, nous avons des glaces _____ vanille, des glaces
  _____ café et des sorbets _____ framboise.

8

5  Who is Pierre helping?

  1  Pierre te donne à manger.
     **a**  only you     **b**  all of you
  2  Pierre leur prépare un café.
     **a**  the men      **b**  the woman
  3  Pierre leur apporte du pain.
     **a**  the man      **b**  the women
  4  Pierre lui apporte l'addition.
     **a**  yourself     **b**  the woman
  5  Pierre vous prépare à manger.
     **a**  me           **b**  you
  6  Pierre nous apporte de la soupe.
     **a**  you          **b**  us
  7  Pierre m'apporte une fourchette.
     **a**  me           **b**  you
  8  Pierre va lui apporter un couteau.
     **a**  the man      **b**  you

8

6  Who is saying each sentence, the waiter or the diner?

  1  Vous prendrez un dessert?
  2  Nous sommes un peu pressés.
  3  Les assiettes sont très chaudes.
  4  Je vous apporte une fourchette.
  5  Vous pouvez me donner un couteau?
  6  Je vais prendre la tarte à l'ananas.
  7  Le lapin Marengo, qu'est-ce que c'est?
  8  Nous n'avons plus de tarte aux pommes.
  9  Qu'est-ce que vous avez comme dessert?
  10  C'est de l'agneau cuit avec des raisins et des épices.

10

**TOTAL SCORE**   45

If you score less than 35, go through the dialogues and the
Language Building sections again before completing the
Summary on page 102.

# Summary 7

 Now you've worked through Unit 7, test your progress by giving the French for the sentences and questions which follow. You can check your answers on the recording.

How would you:
1 say you don't have a knife?
2 say the chicken is delicious?
3 say you've run out of bread?
4 ask what the dish of the day is?
5 ask what sort of ice cream they have?
6 say you're going to have the vanilla ice cream?
7 ask the waitress if she can bring you a coffee?
8 ask for the bill?

## REVISION

Before moving on to Review 2, think of your last meal out and work out what you could have said to the waiter/waitress to order the meal, ask for things, or show your appreciation. See how much you can use of the language you have learnt so far. Make the most of structures such as:

> Je vais prendre ...
> Pour moi ...
> Je voudrais ...
> Qu'est-ce que c'est?
> Qu'est-ce que vous avez comme ... ?
> Vous pouvez m'apporter/me donner ... ?
> Je peux avoir ... ?
> Ça sent bon.
> C'est très bon/délicieux.

# Review 2

## VOCABULARY

1 Which is the odd one out in each group?

   1 bleu / blanc / rouge / poisson / jaune
   2 fraise / framboise / ananas / août / pomme
   3 lapin / laine / agneau / poulet / porc
   4 haricot / crevette / courgette / poireau / oignon
   5 veste / jupe / juin / manteau / chaussure
   6 couteau / cuiller / poire / fourchette / assiette

2 Use the following parts of words to make up 22 names of jobs. You can use the same piece more than once.

| | | |
|---|---|---|
| vend | eur | ière |
| serv | euse | direct |
| gard | ien | ienne |
| ferm | ier | informatic |
| réceptionn | iste | secrét |
| profess | rice | technic |
| journal | aire | infirm |
| un | une | coméd |

3 Match the following definitions with the right person.

| | |
|---|---|
| 1 Le fils de mon père est | a mes grands-parents |
| 2 La fille de ma mère est | b mes beaux-parents |
| 3 Le père de mes enfants est | c ma belle-sœur |
| 4 La femme de mon frère est | d mon beau-père |
| 5 Les parents de ma mère sont | e mon mari |
| 6 Les parents de mon mari sont | f mon frère |
| 7 La grand-mère de ma fille est | g ma mère |
| 8 Le nouveau mari de ma mère est | h ma sœur |

4 Match the words and figures.

| | |
|---|---|
| 1 cinq cent vingt-huit | 8396 |
| 2 six cent quarante et un | 7777 |
| 3 deux cent trente-quatre | 1252 |
| 4 mille deux cent cinquante-deux | 999 |
| 5 neuf cent quatre-vingt-dix-neuf | 641 |
| 6 sept mille sept cent soixante dix-sept | 528 |
| 7 huit mille trois cent quatre-vingt-seize | 234 |

5 Choose from the verbs in the box to complete the following dialogue.

> **voudrais voulez faites avons veux peux fais avez vais fait va**

- Je _____ une veste en laine. Qu'est-ce que vous_____ comme vestes?
- ○ Vous _____ quelle taille?
- Je _____ du 44.
- ○ Nous _____ celle-ci en marron et celle-là en noir.
- J'aime bien celle-ci.
- ○ Vous _____ l'essayer?
- Oui, je _____ bien. Je _____ aussi essayer celle-là?
- ○ Oui, bien sûr.

*Plus tard*

- ○ Ça _____ ?
- Oui, je _____ prendre cette veste et ce foulard.
- ○ Alors, en tout, ça _____ 99€.

6 Choose **du/de la/des** or **au/à la/aux** to complete the following speech.

«Mon menu préféré, c'est _____ moules marinières, ensuite _____ poulet cuit avec _____ poivrons et _____ tomates, et comme dessert _____ tarte _____ poires avec _____ glace _____ vanille.»

7 Complete the verbs in the following dialogues.

- Vous av___ des haricots verts?
- ○ Je regrette, nous n'en av___ plus.

- Tes beaux-parents compren___ le français?
- ○ Oui, ma belle-mère compre___ le français. Et moi, j'appren___ le portugais.

- Qu'est-ce que vous ven___ dans votre magasin?
- ○ On ven___ des objets en porcelaine.

- Tu appren___ l'anglais?
- ○ Oui, je pren___ des cours. Et mon mari appren___ l'allemand.

- Vous ___ réveill___ à quelle heure le matin?
- ○ Nous ___ réveill___ à six heures et demie. Mon mari ___ lèv___ à six heures et demie, il ___ lave et il ___ habille.

- Et toi, tu ne ___ lèv___ pas tout de suite?
- Moi, je ___ lèv___ à sept heures moins le quart, et je ___ occupe du bébé.
- Tes autres enfants ___ lèv___ à quelle heure?
- Ils ___ lèv___ à huit heures moins le quart, et on pren___ notre petit déjeuner tous ensemble.

## 🎧 LISTENING

You're going to hear an interview with a restaurant owner called Richard Lapierre.

8 Before listening, look at the following list of words and phrases and guess which ones you will hear. Then listen to the interview and check your answers.

| | |
|---|---|
| 1 métier | 6 un restaurant |
| 2 la cuisine | 7 un ordinateur |
| 3 américain | 8 nous travaillons |
| 4 le poisson | 9 les fruits de mer |
| 5 le pantalon | 10 la soupe de poissons |

9 Listen to the interview again, then read the following articles. Which one is the more accurate?

Richard Lapierre owns a restaurant called Les Fruits de mer, where he works with his wife and daughter. They specialize in seafood. When I went there, I had some delicious mussels and a fillet of salmon cooked with courgettes, while my companion had fish soup and tuna baked with tomatoes. It was very tasty. Richard Lapierre is very enthusiastic about his job despite the hard work: he generally doesn't go to bed until one or two o'clock in the morning and gets up at six. I hope he has an afternoon nap!

Les Fruits de mer is a friendly restaurant where you can enjoy all kinds of seafood dishes such as delicious fish soups, excellent fish pâtés served with courgettes, or sole cooked with tasty mushrooms. It is a family business run by Richard Lapierre and his wife, and their son works in the kitchen. Their passion for good food obviously makes up for the long hours they have to put in.

10 Read the sentences aloud and then listen to the recording to check your pronunciation.

1 Je peux l'essayer?
2 Ma belle sœur est britannique.
3 Je voudrais un kilo de poireaux.
4 Ce pantalon marron est trop long.
5 Ça coûte six cent soixante-seize francs.
6 Vous avez une chambre pour deux personnes?

11 You want to book a hotel room for the night. Use the cues to help with your side of the conversation.

Hôtel    Bonsoir.
You    (Say 'good evening', and ask if they have a room.)
Hôtel    Pour combien de personnes?
You    (Say it's for two people.)
Hôtel    Et pour combien de nuits?
You    (Say it's for one night.)
Hôtel    Nous avons une chambre avec salle de bains.
You    (Ask if there's a television in the room.)
Hôtel    Oui, bien sûr, toutes les chambres ont la télévision et le téléphone.
You    (Ask how much the room is.)
Hôtel    75 euros pour la nuit.
You    (Say very good, you'll take it.)

Now try the dialogue again without referring to the prompts in the book.

12 You're in a restaurant with a French-speaking friend. Using the menu, answer your friend's questions.

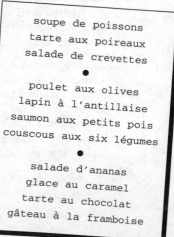

soupe de poissons
tarte aux poireaux
salade de crevettes

•

poulet aux olives
lapin à l'antillaise
saumon aux petits pois
couscous aux six légumes

•

salade d'ananas
glace au caramel
tarte au chocolat
gâteau à la framboise

# 8

# Getting around
# En route

## OBJECTIVES

In this unit you'll learn how to:

- ✓ talk about travel arrangements
- ✓ ask about train timetables
- ✓ book and buy travel tickets
- ✓ call a garage and explain what's wrong with your car

And cover the following grammar and language:

- ✓ the prepositions **à**/**en** + means of transport
- ✓ the pronoun **y** ('there') to show location
- ✓ the present tense of **devoir** ('to have to')
- ✓ the relative subject pronoun **qui** ('who', 'which', 'that')
- ✓ adverbs ending in **-ment**

## LEARNING FRENCH 8

When you are speaking a foreign language, it is impossible to translate everything word for word from one language to another. This unit contains many examples illustrating this point. For instance, although the French for 'to fly' is **voler**, 'I'm flying to Paris' is **je vais à Paris en avion**. To help you progress more easily and start sounding French more quickly, it is a good idea to learn short phrases by heart and use them whenever possible. With experience, you will be able to adapt them and reuse them in slightly different contexts.

🎧 Now start the recording for Unit 8.

## Transport

## Les moyens de transport

**ACTIVITY 1** is on the recording.

**ACTIVITY 2**

Choose the most accurate summary of the dialogue.

**A** Mathilde is going to Paris this weekend, but she has not decided how to get there. She could go on the motorway, but she's worried about her car breaking down. Flying would be very convenient, because she lives close to the airport, but she's afraid of flying. So she'll probably decide to travel by train.

**B** Mathilde normally drives when she goes to Paris, but her car has broken down. She's considering travelling by train or flying. Flying is expensive, but there are two flights a day and the airport is nearby, so she'll probably do that.

**DIALOGUE 1**

- Je vais à Paris ce week-end.
- Tu y vas comment?
- En train ou en avion. Je ne sais pas exactement.
- En train ou en avion! Tu n'y vas pas en voiture?
- Non, ma voiture est en panne.
- En avion, c'est cher, non?
- Oui, mais c'est rapide.
- Il y a combien de vols par jour?
- Normalement, il y a deux vols par jour, alors c'est pratique.
- Et l'aéroport n'est pas loin de chez toi!

| VOCABULARY | |
|---|---|
| le train | train |
| l'avion (*m*) | aeroplane |
| exactement | exactly |
| être en panne | to have broken down |
| rapide | quick |
| le vol | flight |
| normalement | normally |
| pratique | convenient |
| l'aéroport (*m*) | airport |
| loin | far |
| chez toi | your home |

## ✓ *en/à* + means of transport

The preposition **en** is used for means of transport such as trains, planes, cars, etc.

| | |
|---|---|
| **en voiture** | by car |
| **en train** | by train |
| **en métro** | by underground, by subway |
| **en bus** | by bus |
| **en car** | by coach, by bus |
| **en bateau** | by boat |
| **en avion** | by plane |

However, **à** is used for the following:

| | |
|---|---|
| **à pied** | on foot |
| **à vélo/à bicyclette** | by bike |
| **à moto** | by motorbike |
| **à cheval** | on horseback |

Although it is not strictly correct, you may hear **en vélo/en bicyclette/ en moto**, as more and more people are starting to say this.

## ✓ *y* to show location

The pronoun **y**, which usually means 'there', is used to avoid repeating a phrase that describes a location. It comes before the verb:

Je pars **en Écosse**. I'm off to Scotland.
Vous **y** allez comment? How are you going there?
Je mange **à la cantine**. I eat in the canteen.
Tu **y** manges toujours? Do you always eat there?

### ACTIVITY 3

Complete the summary about Mathilde, using **y** to describe location and **en** or **à** for the method of transport.

Mathilde va à Paris ce week-end. Normalement, elle ___ va ___ voiture, mais sa voiture est en panne. Elle ne peut pas ___ aller ___ pied ou ___ vélo, c'est trop loin! Elle va peut-être ___ aller ___ train ou ___ avion.

 Now do activities 4 and 5 on the recording.

# Voyage en train

(1A) **ACTIVITY 6** is on the recording.

**ACTIVITY 7**

Which of the tickets is the one that the customer bought?

**1**

| BILLET | | *SNCF* |
|---|---|---|
| aller simple 1ère classe | | |
| Toulouse – Bordeaux 41€ | | |
| Dép à | 12h 15 | de Toulouse |
| Arr à | 14h 36 | à Bordeaux |
| Dép à | | de |
| Arr à | | à |

**2**

| BILLET | | *SNCF* |
|---|---|---|
| seconde classe | | |
| Bordeaux – Toulouse 55,80€ | | |
| Dép à | 09h 52 | de Bordeaux |
| Arr à | 12h 09 | à Toulouse |
| Dép à | 13h 51 | de Toulouse |
| Arr à | 16h o6 | à Bordeaux |

**3**

| BILLET | | *SNCF* |
|---|---|---|
| aller retour seconde classe | | |
| Paris – Toulouse 140€ | | |
| Dép à | 10h 32 | de Paris |
| Arr à | 17h 05 | à Toulouse |
| Dép à | 14h 04 | de Toulouse |
| Arr à | 19h 10 | à Paris |

**DIALOGUE 2**

○ Je dois aller à Toulouse, et je voudrais des renseignements sur les horaires de trains, s'il vous plaît.

■ Vous voulez voyager quand?

○ Le mardi 30 mars. Je dois être à Toulouse avant 13 heures.

■ Il y a un train qui part de Bordeaux à 9 heures 52. Il arrive à Toulouse à 12 heures 09.

○ Et pour le retour? Je rentre à Bordeaux le vendredi 2 avril.

■ Il y a un train qui arrive à Bordeaux à 16 heures 06.

○ Il part de Toulouse à quelle heure?

■ Il part de Toulouse à 13 heures 51.

○ Très bien. Quel est le prix du billet?

■ Un aller retour … Première classe ou seconde?

○ Seconde.

■ L'aller retour coûte 55,80€.

---

## VOCABULARY

| | |
|---|---|
| **le renseignement** | information |
| **sur** | about |
| **l'horaire** (*m*) | timetable |
| **voyager** | to travel |
| **avant** | before |
| **partir (de)** | to leave (from) |
| **le retour** | return journey, round trip |
| **rentrer** | to return, come back |
| **le billet** | ticket |
| **l'aller retour** (*m*) | return ticket, round trip ticket |
| **la première classe/la seconde** | first/second class |
| **l'aller simple** (*m*) | single ticket, one-way ticket |

### ✓ *devoir* ('to have to') – irregular verb

| | |
|---|---|
| je **dois** | nous **devons** |
| tu **dois** | vous **devez** |
| il/elle/on **doit** | ils/elles **doivent** |

### ✓ *qui*

The relative subject pronoun **qui**, meaning 'who', 'which', or 'that', is used to refer to either people or objects mentioned earlier in the sentence:

Il y a un avion **qui** part à 10 heures. There's a plane that leaves at ten.
Téléphone à ton ami **qui** travaille à la gare. Ring your friend who works at the station.

See also the section on **que** on page 173.

### ✓ Using the 24-hour clock

The 24-hour clock is used in official contexts when talking about timetables, etc. However, more and more people use this way of telling the time in everyday conversations. Note that you don't use phrases such as **et quart**, **et demie**, or **moins le quart**. Instead you say:

| | |
|---|---|
| seize heures **quinze** | 16.15 |
| douze heures **trente** | 12.30 |
| treize heures **quarante-cinq** | 13.45 |

---

#### ACTIVITY 8

Look at the notes below and imagine the conversation between the traveller and the travel agent. To help you, follow Dialogue 2 and substitute the details below.

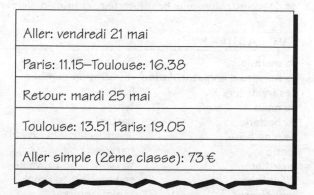

Aller: vendredi 21 mai

Paris: 11.15–Toulouse: 16.38

Retour: mardi 25 mai

Toulouse: 13.51 Paris: 19.05

Aller simple (2ème classe): 73 €

 Now do activities 9 and 10 on the recording.

## 8.3 Car breakdown
## La panne de voiture

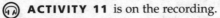

**ACTIVITY 11** is on the recording.

**ACTIVITY 12**
Complete the form.

Nom: _____

Voiture (marque, couleur): _____

Numéro d'immatriculation: _____

Problème: _____

essence ☐    pneu ☐    batterie ☐

freins ☐    huile ☐    pare-brise ☐

autre _____

Lieu: N138 entre Écommoy et Mulsanne

### DIALOGUE 3

○ Allô. Ma voiture est en panne. Les freins ne marchent plus. Vous pouvez me dépanner rapidement?

■ Bien sûr. Vous êtes où exactement?

○ Je suis sur la Nationale 138, entre Écommoy et Mulsanne.

■ Qu'est-ce que vous avez comme voiture?

○ C'est une Renault blanche.

■ Et le numéro d'immatriculation?

○ 3454 CP 93.

■ Vous vous appelez comment?

○ Je m'appelle Antoine Beaufort. B.E.A.U.F.O.R.T.

■ D'accord, Monsieur Beaufort. Je pars immédiatement.

### VOCABULARY

| | |
|---|---|
| la marque | make [car] |
| le numéro d'immatriculation | registration number |
| les freins (m) | brakes |
| le pneu | tyre |
| la batterie | battery |
| le pare-brise | windscreen, windshield |
| entre | between |
| marcher | to work [also to walk] |
| dépanner | to help out, to repair |
| rapidement | rapidly, quickly |
| immédiatement | immediately |

## ✓ Adverbs ending in *-ment*

Most French adverbs are constructed by adding **-ment** to the feminine form of the corresponding adjective.

| (m) | (f) | | | |
|-----|-----|------|------|------|
| facile | **facile** | easy | **facilement** | easily |
| heureux | **heureuse** | happy | **heureusement** | fortunately |
| lent | **lente** | slow | **lentement** | slowly |
| normal | **normale** | normal | **normalement** | normally |
| triste | **triste** | sad | **tristement** | sadly |

There are a few exceptions. For example:

| | | | | |
|-----|-----|------|------|------|
| gentil | **gentille** | kind | **gentiment** | kindly |
| poli | **polie** | polite | **poliment** | politely |
| vrai | **vraie** | true | **vraiment** | really |

## ✓ *Ma voiture est en panne*

**Je n'ai plus d'eau.** I have run out of water.
**Je suis en panne d'essence.** I have run out of petrol.
**Je n'ai plus d'huile.** I have run out of oil.
**J'ai un pneu crevé.** I have a flat tyre.
**La batterie est à plat.** The battery is flat.
**Le pare-brise est cassé.** The windscreen is broken.
**Les feux ne marchent plus.** The lights don't work any more.

---

### ACTIVITY 13

Look at the completed form below and imagine the conversation between the garage and the car driver.

| | |
|---|---|
| **Nom:** Rouillard | |
| **Voiture (marque, couleur):** Ford bleue | |
| **Numéro d'immatriculation:** 567 CP 11 | |
| **Problème:** | |

| essence ☐ | huile ☐ |
|-----------|---------|
| freins ☐ | batterie ☐ |
| pneu ☐ | pare-brise ☑ |

**autre**

**Lieu:** N116 entre Prades et Vernet

Now do activities 14 and 15 on the recording.

DOSSIER

| Billet |

## Réservation, achat

Tous les billets sont vendus dans les **gares**, les **boutiques SNCF** et les **agences de voyage** agréées. Vous pouvez les acheter à l'avance, **ils sont valables 2 mois.**

### Les guichets

Tous les guichets délivrent, en principe, l'**ensemble des prestations**. Certaines grandes gares disposent de guichets vous permettant de préparer votre voyage à l'écart des flux de départs immédiats.

### Les billetteries automatiques

Les billetteries automatiques délivrent les **titres de transport** (billets, réservations, suppléments) à destination de la France et pour les principales relations internationales. Vous pouvez également y réserver vos **titres repas** ou y **retirer vos commandes passées par Minitel**, téléphone ou sur Internet. **Vous pouvez payer par carte bancaire** (Visa française ou étrangère, Eurocard/ Mastercard, American Express et Diner's Club International). Les billetteries automatiques acceptent les pièces jusqu'à un montant de 100F.

### Par téléphone

LIGNE DIRECTE vous permet d'obtenir toute l'information utile à votre voyage et d'acheter votre billet. Ce service est disponible de **7 h à 22 h, 7 jours sur 7**, au **08 92 35 35 35** (0,45€/min).

### Par Minitel

**24 h sur 24**, composez le **3615 SNCF** (0,21€/min) ou, si vous disposez d'un Minitel à vitesse rapide (Magis-Club), le 3625 SNCF (0,21€/min). Ces serveurs vous fourniront les horaires de tous les trains sur les relations nationales et internationales. Vous pourrez réserver et même payer directement votre billet par carte bancaire.

### Sur Internet

A l'adresse **http://www. sncf.com**, vous pouvez obtenir toutes les informations utiles à la préparation de votre voyage et réserver votre billet. **Le paiement et le retrait des billets réservés s'effectuent dans les gares, aux guichets ou sur les billetteries automatiques.**

The text on page 114 is taken from a train user's guide published by the SNCF, the French Railway company. At this stage, you can extract a lot of information from it without understanding every word. The following activities will help you.

## ACTIVITY 16

Look through the text and circle at least six words you know.

## ACTIVITY 17

Find in the text the French equivalents of:

1 railshop
2 travel agent's
3 ticket office
4 automatic ticket machine

## ACTIVITY 18

Find the sentences/phrases which say that:

1 all tickets are sold in stations, railshops, and travel agents.
2 tickets are valid for two months.
3 you can pay by credit card.

## ACTIVITY 19

1 What phone number do you call to get information or buy a ticket?
2 Is that service available 24 hours a day? If not, when is it available?
3 Is it possible to book a ticket via the Internet? What is the address?

## ACTIVITY 20

Another way of getting information, booking and paying for rail tickets is via an interactive database system run by France Télécom.

1 What is this service called?
2 Is it available everyday?
3 During what hours?

### PANNE D'ESSENCE
### RUNNING OUT OF PETROL

Alexandra va à Châteauroux en voiture pour une réunion importante.

| | |
|---|---|
| **zut!** | bother!, damn! |
| **aider** | to help |
| **la réunion** | meeting |
| **sympa** | nice, friendly [*colloquial*] |
| **une demi-heure** | half an hour |
| **entendre** | to hear |
| **s'inquiéter** | to worry |
| **emmener** | to take |

### ACTIVITY 21

Listen to the recording and put the following information in the right order.

1  Alexandra doit aller à Châteauroux pour une réunion importante.
2  À trois heures et quart, elle appelle son copain Jérôme.
3  Malheureusement, elle n'a plus d'essence.
4  Heureusement, Karim Massoud arrive.
5  Il va l'emmener à Châteauroux.
6  Son téléphone ne marche plus.
7  Il ne veut pas l'aider.
8  Elle appelle son père.
9  Elle y va en voiture.

### ACTIVITY 22

Listen again, as many times as necessary, and fill in the gaps without looking at the transcript on page 117.

Allô, Papa? Tu _____ m'aider! J'ai une réunion importante.
Je _____ être à Châteauroux à _____ heures _____,
et ma _____ est en _____. Tu peux me dépanner? Je suis
… Allô? Papa, tu m'entends? Allô? … Zut! Ça ne _____
plus. Super! Je n'ai _____ d'_____, et mon
_____ est en panne.

## ACTIVITY 23

What do you think Jérôme said to Alexandra when she rang him? Imagine and practise their telephone conversation. You already have Alexandra's side of the conversation. To help you further, have another look at Dialogue 3, and adapt the garage owner's words. You need to decide on Jérôme's mood (sympathetic but too busy? unsympathetic?). Remember that Alexandra and Jérôme say **tu** to each other.

## STORY TRANSCRIPT

| | |
|---|---|
| Alexandra | Ah, zut! Je n'ai plus d'essence. Oh, là, là! |
| | Jérôme. Allô, c'est moi … Ça va? … Moi, ça ne va pas. Je suis en panne d'essence … Tu peux m'aider? … Il est quinze heures. J'ai une réunion à Châteauroux. Je dois y être à quinze heures trente. S'il te plaît, Jérôme! … Oh, tu n'es pas sympa. |
| | Allô, Papa? Tu dois m'aider! J'ai une réunion importante. Je dois être à Châteauroux à quinze heures trente, et ma voiture est en panne. Tu peux me dépanner? Je suis … Allô? Papa, tu m'entends? Allô? … Zut! Ça ne marche plus. Super! Je n'ai plus d'essence, et mon téléphone est en panne. Qu'est-ce que … Karim! |
| Karim | Qu'est-ce qui ne va pas? |
| Alexandra | Tout!!! J'ai une réunion importante dans une demi-heure. Je suis en panne d'essence et mon téléphone ne marche plus. |
| Karim | Ne t'inquiète pas. Je t'emmène. |

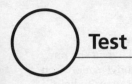

# Test

Now it's time to test your progress in Unit 8.

1 Match the following words with their English equivalents.

|   |   |   |   |
|---|---|---|---|
| 1 | le pare-brise | a | car |
| 2 | la batterie | b | oil |
| 3 | la voiture | c | flat |
| 4 | les freins | d | petrol |
| 5 | la panne | e | lights |
| 6 | l'essence | f | brakes |
| 7 | les feux | g | broken |
| 8 | l'huile | h | battery |
| 9 | à plat | i | punctured |
| 10 | cassé | j | breakdown |
| 11 | crevé | k | windscreen |

**11**

2 Choose **à** or **en** to complete the text below.

**Comment allez-vous travailler?**

1 _____ car
2 _____ bus
3 _____ vélo
4 _____ pied
5 _____ moto
6 _____ métro
7 _____ bateau
8 _____ voiture

**8**

3 Find the pairs.

|   |   |   |   |
|---|---|---|---|
| 1 | heureusement | a | partir |
| 2 | rapidement | b | retour |
| 3 | facilement | c | seconde |
| 4 | première | d | lentement |
| 5 | arriver | e | difficilement |
| 6 | aller | f | malheureusement |

**6**

4 Match the questions and answers.

1 Qu'est-ce qui ne va pas?  a  2755 ER 72.

2 Vous êtes où exactement?  b  Claude Molière.

3 Vous vous appelez comment?  c  J'ai un pneu crevé.

4 Qu'est-ce que vous avez comme voiture?  d  Une Peugeot rouge.

5 Quel est le numéro d'immatriculation?  e  Je suis sur la D456.

|  | 5 |

5 Unscramble each line in the following dialogue between a customer and a travel agent. (2 points for each correct sentence, 1 point if you make only one error.)

○ Je / à / dois / Lille / aller
■ Vous / quand / voyager / voulez / ?
○ Aujourd'hui / Je / à / y / 18 / être / dois / heures
■ Il / un / qui / de / y / a / à / Lyon / train / 14 heures 38 / part
○ Il / à / à / quelle / Lille / heure / arrive / ?
■ Il / Lille / arrive / 17 heures 45 / à / à
○ Quel / le / du / est / billet / prix / ?
■ Première / classe / seconde / ou / ?
○ Seconde
■ Un / 63 / simple / euros / aller / coûte

|  | 20 |

**TOTAL SCORE** | 50 |

If you scored less than 40, go through the dialogues and the Language Building sections again before completing the Summary on page 120.

# Summary 8

 Now try this final test summarizing the main points covered in this unit.

How would you:
1  ask a friend whether she goes to work by car or by bus?
2  ask a couple of friends if they're walking or cycling there?
3  say you have to go to Marseille?
4  say you're going there by boat or by plane?
5  ask what time the train leaves?
6  ask what time the train arrives?
7  ask for a return ticket?
8  say your car has broken down?
9  say you have a flat tyre?

## REVISION

Before moving on to Unit 9, think of the last time you had to arrange a train, coach, or plane journey and see if you could have held a similar kind of conversation in French. Try to make the most of what you have learnt so far and include as many details as possible about where you have to travel from and to, the dates and times, the means of transport, and fares. Even if it's not normally in your character, try to assume the personality of a very talkative traveller. Could you, for example, explain to the travel agent that you normally drive, but your car has broken down, you live very near the station, but you prefer to fly because it's convenient, quick, etc.?

# Health and fitness
# En bonne santé

## LEARNING FRENCH 9

When learning a language, it is important to practise the language so that you use what you have learnt in as many different contexts as possible. Opportunities for doing this have been provided throughout the course, but you can do more yourself to suit your own needs and interests. At the end of each unit, combine the structures you have just learnt with what you already know. For example, once you have learnt the perfect tense in this unit, you can combine it with the language of Unit 7 and say what you've eaten in a restaurant, or with the language of Unit 6 and say what you've bought at the market.

Now start the recording for Unit 9.

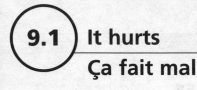

## 9.1 It hurts
## Ça fait mal

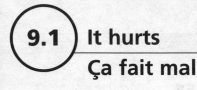 **ACTIVITY 1** is on the recording.

**ACTIVITY 2**

A  Which of the following ailments are mentioned?

| | | | |
|---|---|---|---|
| 1 | pain in foot/feet | 6 | sore throat |
| 2 | pain in hand(s) | 7 | toothache |
| 3 | pain in arm(s) | 8 | tiredness |
| 4 | pain in leg(s) | 9 | backache |
| 5 | rheumatism | 10 | headache |

B  Which ailment is only mentioned by one person?

**DIALOGUE 1**

■ Bonjour, Madame Legris. Vous allez chez le médecin?

○ Oui, j'ai mal à la gorge. Je suis fatiguée.

■ Moi aussi, j'ai mal à la gorge et je suis fatiguée. En plus, j'ai mal au pied droit. J'ai des rhumatismes.

○ Moi aussi, j'ai des rhumatismes, j'ai mal au pied et à la main. Alors, vous avez de la chance!

■ Moi, j'ai mal au pied droit, à la main droite et au bras gauche. Ça fait mal. Oh, là, là!

○ Mon mari aussi a des rhumatismes, mais il a mal au bras droit et au bras gauche. Alors, vous avez de la chance!

■ Mon mari aussi a des rhumatismes, il a mal aux bras et aux mains. Et en plus, il a mal au dos. Ce n'est pas drôle!

---

| VOCABULARY | |
|---|---|
| **en bonne santé** | in good health |
| **chez** | at, to [*someone's house*] |
| **le médecin** | doctor |
| **la gorge** | throat |
| **fatigué(e)** | tired |
| **en plus** | on top of that, also |
| **les rhumatismes** (*m*) | rheumatism |
| **avoir de la chance** | to be lucky |
| **la main** | hand |
| **le bras** | arm |
| **le dos** | back |
| **drôle** | funny |

### ✓ Parts of the body

| | | | |
|---|---|---|---|
| la tête | head | le nez | nose |
| les cheveux (m) | hair | la bouche | mouth |
| l'œil (m) | eye | la dent | tooth |
| les yeux (m) | eyes | le doigt | finger |
| l'oreille (f) | ear | la jambe | leg |

### ✓ Describing ailments

Using **avoir mal + à la/à l'/au/aux** is the most common way of saying where it hurts, what aches, or what is sore. Remember to use the appropriate form of **à**:

J'ai mal **à la** gorge. I have a sore throat.
Il a mal **à l'**oreille. He has earache.
Elle a mal **au** pied. Her foot hurts.
Ils ont mal **aux** dents. They have toothache.

Note that when referring to parts of the body, French uses the definite article whereas English uses a possessive adjective:

J'ai mal à **la** main. My hand hurts.

### ✓ Expressions with *avoir*

Here is a list of common expressions with **avoir**. Note that many of their English equivalents use 'to be' rather 'to have'.

| | |
|---|---|
| avoir de la chance | to be lucky |
| avoir besoin de | to need |
| avoir envie de | to feel like, to want |
| avoir peur (de) | to be afraid (of) |
| avoir froid | to be cold |
| avoir chaud | to be hot |
| avoir faim | to be hungry |
| avoir soif | to be thirsty |

### ACTIVITY 3

Here is what Madame Lenoir said to the doctor.
Fill in the gaps.

Oh, là, là! Ça ne va pas! Je suis fatiguée et j'ai mal _____ gorge. J'ai mal _____ pied. En plus, j'ai mal _____ main droite et _____ bras gauche. Et mon mari aussi a des rhumatismes. Il a mal _____ pieds et _____ mains. Et en plus, il a mal _____ dos!

 Now do activities 4 and 5 on the recording.

# Chez le médecin

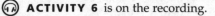

ACTIVITY 6 is on the recording.

## ACTIVITY 7

The doctor noted down the patient's symptoms as she talked.
Which of these is her set of notes?

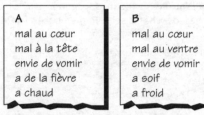

| A | B |
|---|---|
| mal au cœur | mal au cœur |
| mal à la tête | mal au ventre |
| envie de vomir | envie de vomir |
| a de la fièvre | a soif |
| a chaud | a froid |

## DIALOGUE 2

○ Vous êtes malade. Qu'est-ce qui ne va pas?
■ J'ai mal au cœur et j'ai envie de vomir.
○ Vous avez mal à la tête?
■ Non, mais j'ai mal au ventre.
○ Vous avez soif?
■ Oui, j'ai bu trois ou quatre tasses de tisane ce matin.
○ Vous avez de la fièvre?
■ Oui, mais j'ai froid.
○ Qu'est-ce que vous avez fait hier?
■ Hier soir, j'ai mangé au restaurant avec des amis.
○ Qu'est-ce que vous avez mangé?
■ J'ai pris du poisson avec du riz et une tarte au citron.
○ Vous avez bu beaucoup de vin?
■ Un ou deux verres, c'est tout.

## VOCABULARY

| | |
|---|---|
| (être) malade | (to be) sick, ill |
| avoir mal au cœur | to feel sick |
| vomir | to be sick |
| le ventre | stomach |
| la tisane | herbal tea |
| (avoir de) la fièvre | (to have a) fever, temperature |
| hier | yesterday |
| hier soir | last night |
| le verre | glass |

## ✓ The *passé composé* with *avoir*

The *passé composé* is used to describe a single completed event or action which took place in the past. It can be translated in two different ways.

**J'ai trop mangé.** I ate too much. *or* I have eaten too much.

Most verbs form the *passé composé* with the present tense of **avoir** followed by the past participle of the verb required. All reflexive verbs and a few others form their *passé composé* with **être** rather than **avoir**. See Unit 10.

## ✓ Past participles

Past participles are formed by adding an ending to the stem of the verb. The ending for **-er** verbs is **-é**:

attraper    **attrapé**    Tu as attrapé un rhume/la grippe. You caught a cold/the flu.

appeler    **appelé**    Elle a appelé le médecin. She called the doctor.

The ending for many **-ir** verbs is **-i**:

dormir    **dormi**    Nous avons mal **dormi**. We slept badly.

However, the ending for some **-ir** verbs such as **offrir** ('to offer'), **couvrir** ('to cover'), and **ouvrir** ('to open') is **-ert**:

souffrir    **souffert**    Ils ont **souffert**. They suffered.

The ending for many **-re** verbs such as **vendre** ('to sell'), **attendre** ('to wait'), **entendre** ('to hear'), and **répondre** ('to reply') is **-u**:

attendre    **attendu**    J'ai **attendu**. I waited.

The past participles of other verbs are irregular. See page 127.

---

### ACTIVITY 8

Use the words below to make at least eight correct sentences.

Example: J'ai mangé du chocolat.

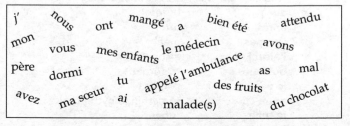

j'   nous    ont    mangé    a    bien été    attendu
mon    vous    mes enfants    le médecin    avons
père    dormi    tu    appelé l'ambulance    as    mal
avez    ma sœur    ai    des fruits    du chocolat
malade(s)

🔊 Now do activities 9 and 10 on the recording.

# Chez le pharmacien

**ACTIVITY 11** is on the recording.

**ACTIVITY 12**

Correct the following summary. There are four errors.

Monsieur Langlois has just seen the doctor, because he's ill. He feels sick and he has a headache. The doctor has prescribed antibiotics, which he has to take twice a day after meals. The pharmacist also suggests Monsieur Langlois eat yoghurt and does not drink any coffee.

**DIALOGUE 3**

- ■ Bonjour, Monsieur Langlois. Vous êtes malade?
- ○ Oui, j'ai mal au ventre et j'ai mal au cœur.
- ■ Vous avez vu le médecin?
- ○ Oui, j'ai une ordonnance. Voilà.
- ■ Alors … il faut prendre ces comprimés trois fois par jour, matin, midi et soir.
- ○ Il faut les prendre avant les repas ou après les repas?
- ■ Avant les repas. Ce sont des antibiotiques, alors ne buvez pas d'alcool. Et n'oubliez pas de manger du yaourt.
- ○ Du yaourt. D'accord.
- ■ Vous avez besoin d'autre chose?
- ○ Oui, je voudrais un tube d'aspirine, s'il vous plaît.

| VOCABULARY | |
|---|---|
| l'ordonnance (f) | prescription |
| l'antibiotique (m) | antibiotic |
| il faut … | you must … , you have to … |
| le comprimé | tablet, pill |
| trois fois par jour | three times a day |
| avant | before |
| après | after |
| le repas | meal |
| l'alcool (m) | alcohol |
| oublier | to forget |
| le yaourt | yoghurt |
| autre chose | something/anything else |
| le tube | tube |
| l'aspirine (f) | aspirin |

## ⊘ *il faut* + infinitive

When it can be translated as 'you must' or 'you have to', **il faut** is usually followed by an infinitive:

**Il faut** vous **reposer**. You must rest.
**Il faut boire** un litre d'eau. You have to drink a litre of water.
**Il faut arrêter** de fumer. You must stop smoking.

## ⊘ Negative imperatives

When instructing someone not to do something, you need to add **ne** before the imperative form of the verb and **pas** afterwards:

**Ne** mangez **pas** de chocolat. Don't eat any chocolate.
**Ne** fumez **pas**. Don't smoke.

## ⊘ Irregular past participles

| avoir | **eu** | Je n'ai pas **eu** mal. It didn't hurt. |
|---|---|---|
| boire | **bu** | Vous avez **bu** un verre d'eau. You drank a glass of water. |
| être | **été** | Tu as **été** très malade. You have been very ill. |
| mettre | **mis** | Il a **mis** son écharpe. He put on his scarf. |
| pouvoir | **pu** | Il n'a pas **pu** manger. He hasn't been able to eat. |
| prendre | **pris** | Elles n'ont pas **pris** d'eau. They didn't take any water. |
| voir | **vu** | Nous n'avons pas **vu** le médecin. We have not seen the doctor. |

---

### ACTIVITY 13

Complete the following list of health tips, using the ideas listed below.

Pour rester en bonne santé, il faut dormir la nuit …

Mais ne travaillez pas trop …

> dormir la nuit
> travailler trop
> boire beaucoup d'eau
> se reposer régulièrement
> faire du sport régulièrement
> fumer vingt cigarettes par jour
> boire dix tasses de café par jour
> boire deux litres de vin par jour
> manger des gâteaux à la crème tous les jours
> manger des fruits et des légumes tous les jours

 Now do activities 14 and 15 on the recording.

# Homeopathy
# L'homéopathie

Despite much criticism from the French Academy of Medicine, homeopathic remedies are available from most French chemists. All French homeopaths are qualified physicians, and 10,000 practitioners prescribe homeopathic treatment either regularly or occasionally. About 20% of the French population has been treated with homeopathy at some stage in their life.

This table lists some of the homeopathic remedies used for colds and shows which one to choose depending on symptoms.

### ACTIVITY 16

Look at the table, and match each of the following French expressions with their English equivalents.

| | | | |
|---|---|---|---|
| 1 | le nez qui coule | a | drinks in sips |
| 2 | a le nez bouché | b | sneezes a lot |
| 3 | a la bouche sèche | c | has a dry mouth |
| 4 | éternue beaucoup | d | runny nose |
| 5 | boit à petites gorgées | e | has a blocked-up nose |

### ACTIVITY 17

From these symptoms, who should take nux vomica and who should take arsenicum album?

A

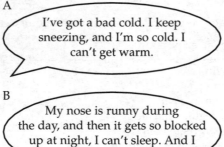

I've got a bad cold. I keep sneezing, and I'm so cold. I can't get warm.

B

My nose is runny during the day, and then it gets so blocked up at night, I can't sleep. And I feel very cold.

| L'Homéopathie contre le rhume | | | | | | |
|---|---|---|---|---|---|---|
| | allium | arsenicum album | belladona | bryonia | nux vomica | pulsatilla |
| bouche | | | | a la bouche sèche | a la bouche sèche | |
| gorge | | | a mal à la gorge | | | |
| nez | • éternue beaucoup<br>• a le nez qui coule | éternue beaucoup | a le nez rouge | a le nez bouché | a le nez bouché la nuit et le nez qui coule le jour | a le nez bouché |
| tête | | | a mal à la tête | a mal à la tête | | |
| yeux | a mal aux yeux | | | a les yeux rouges | | |
| soif | a soif | • a soif<br>• boit à petites gorgées | | • a très soif<br>• boit beaucoup d'eau | | n'a pas soif |
| autres symptômes | | a très froid | a de la fièvre | | a très froid | n'a pas faim |

## ACTIVITY 18

Which remedy would a homoeopath give these people?

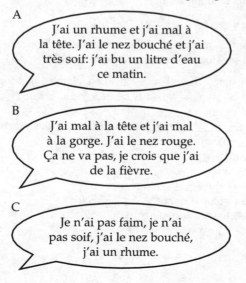

A

J'ai un rhume et j'ai mal à la tête. J'ai le nez bouché et j'ai très soif: j'ai bu un litre d'eau ce matin.

B

J'ai mal à la tête et j'ai mal à la gorge. J'ai le nez rouge. Ça ne va pas, je crois que j'ai de la fièvre.

C

Je n'ai pas faim, je n'ai pas soif, j'ai le nez bouché, j'ai un rhume.

### MALADE
### SICK

Karim Massoud est malade. Il appelle Madame Delaine.

**désolé(e)**    sorry
**au lit**    in bed
**croire (que)**    to believe, think (that)
**pauvre**    poor

### ACTIVITY 19

Listen to the conversation. Which of the following sentences do you hear?

1 Je ne vous ai pas vu ce matin.
2 J'ai préparé votre petit déjeuner.
3 J'ai eu mal au cœur toute la nuit.
4 Je n'ai pas dormi.
5 J'ai très mal à la tête.
6 Je crois que j'ai la grippe.
7 Il faut boire beaucoup d'eau.
8 J'ai appelé le médecin.

### ACTIVITY 20

Complete this transcript of the conversation Madame Delaine had with the doctor about Karim Massoud.

○ Allô? Docteur Botrel? C'est Annie Delaine à la Bonne Étoile. J'ai un client malade. Vous pouvez venir le voir?
○ Qu'est-ce qui ne _____ pas?
○ Il a été _____ toute la nuit. Il n'____ pas dormi. Il a _____ au cœur et il a très mal _____ tête.
○ Il a de la _____?
○ Je crois, oui.
○ Qu'est-ce qu'il ____ mangé hier soir?
○ Je ne sais pas. Il n'a pas _____ ici!
○ Je passe le voir vers deux heures. D'accord?
○ D'accord. Je vous remercie.

## ACTIVITY 21

Imagine Karim Massoud's conversation with the doctor.

## STORY TRANSCRIPT

| | |
|---|---|
| Mme Delaine | Allô? La Bonne Étoile. |
| Karim Massoud | Madame Delaine? C'est Karim Massoud … |
| Mme Delaine | Monsieur Massoud, où êtes-vous? Je ne vous ai pas vu ce matin. Je vous ai attendu pour le petit déjeuner, mais … |
| Karim Massoud | Oui, je suis désolé. Je suis au lit dans ma chambre. |
| Mme Delaine | Ça ne va pas? |
| Karim Massoud | J'ai été malade toute la nuit. Je n'ai pas dormi. |
| Mme Delaine | Qu'est-ce qui ne va pas? |
| Karim Massoud | Je ne sais pas, j'ai mal au cœur et j'ai très mal à la tête. Et puis, par moments, j'ai très froid et par moments, j'ai très chaud. Je crois que j'ai de la fièvre. |
| Mme Delaine | Mon pauvre! Vous avez une bouteille d'eau dans votre chambre? |
| Karim Massoud | Non, je n'en ai plus. |
| Mme Delaine | Je vous apporte une bouteille d'eau tout de suite. Il faut boire beaucoup d'eau. D'accord? |
| Karim Massoud | D'accord. |
| Mme Delaine | Et puis, je vais appeler le médecin. |
| Karim Massoud | Je vous remercie, Madame Delaine. |

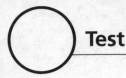

# Test

Now it's time to test your progress in Unit 9.

1 Work out the following anagrams to find ten different parts of the body.

| | | | |
|---|---|---|---|
| les _____ | erisolle | la _____ | reggo |
| les _____ | exchuve | les _____ | stend |
| la _____ | choube | la _____ | mina |
| le _____ | verent | les _____ | exuy |
| la _____ | bamje | le _____ | diep |

**10**

2 Match the following phrases with their English equivalents.

| | | | |
|---|---|---|---|
| 1 | avoir mal aux dents | a | to hurt |
| 2 | avoir mal au ventre | b | to be ill |
| 3 | avoir mal à la gorge | c | to be cold |
| 4 | avoir de la chance | d | to feel sick |
| 5 | avoir mal au cœur | e | to be lucky |
| 6 | avoir la grippe | f | to be thirsty |
| 7 | être malade | g | to have the flu |
| 8 | avoir froid | h | to have a toothache |
| 9 | avoir soif | i | to have a sore throat |
| 10 | faire mal | j | to have a stomachache |

**10**

3 Choose from the words below to complete the following dialogue.

**pris/au/à la/va/aux/ai/avez/j'ai/pris/grippe/mal/êtes**

○ Vous _____ malade. Qu'est-ce qui ne _____ pas?

■ J'_____ attrapé la _____. J'ai _____ à la tête.

○ Vous avez mal _____ gorge?

■ Non, mais j'ai mal _____ ventre et j'ai mal _____ oreilles.

○ Vous _____ de la fièvre?

■ Je ne sais pas. _____ froid et j'ai très soif.

○ Vous avez _____ des médicaments?

■ J'ai _____ de l'aspirine C'est tout.

**12**

4 Use the past participle of the following verbs to complete the dialogue below.

**boire/donner/dormir/être/manger/pouvoir/prendre/voir**

○ Vous avez bien _____ ?

■ Non, je n'ai pas _____ dormir.

○ Pourquoi?

■ Hier soir, j'ai trop _____ et j'ai trop ____. J'ai _____ malade toute la nuit.

○ Vous avez _____ des médicaments?

■ Oui, j'ai _____ le médecin et il m'a _____ une ordonnance.

| 8

5 Find the most appropriate piece of advice for each of following situations.

| 1 J'ai faim. | a Il faut prendre de l'aspirine. |
| 2 J'ai très soif. | b Buvez un grand verre d'eau. |
| 3 Je suis fatigué. | c Ne buvez pas de café le soir. |
| 4 J'ai mal à la tête. | d Il faut appeler le médecin. |
| 5 J'ai mal à la gorge. | e Ne buvez pas d'alcool. |
| 6 Je suis très malade. | f Il faut vous reposer. |
| 7 J'ai envie de dormir. | g Mangez des fruits. |
| 8 Je ne peux pas dormir. | h Il faut aller au lit. |
| | i Il faut manger. |
| 9 J'ai besoin de vitamines. | j Ne parlez pas! |
| 10 Je prends des antibiotiques. | |

| 10

**TOTAL SCORE** | 50

If you scored less than 40, go through the dialogues and the Language Building sections again before completing the Summary on page 134.

# Summary 9

 Now try this final test summarizing the main points covered in this unit.

How would you:
1 say it hurts?
2 say you have caught a cold?
3 say you're ill, you have the flu?
4 say you're hot and you're thirsty?
5 say you're cold and you're hungry?
6 say you have a headache and your back aches?
7 ask some people what they did yesterday?
8 say you ate too much and you drank some red wine?

## REVISION

Think of the last time you – or someone close to you – felt ill. If it were now, would you be able to describe the symptoms in French? Try to be as accurate as possible and say exactly where it hurts and how you (or the patient) feel (cold/hot/thirsty/sleepy, etc.). Also give details of what happened the day before the illness if you think it may be relevant. Finally, think of the advice you (or the patient) were given. Could you say it in French – including suggestions such as taking tablets, not drinking alcohol, resting, etc.?

# 10

# Free time
# Les loisirs

---

**OBJECTIVES**

In this unit you'll learn how to:

- ✅ ask and say what happened
- ✅ talk about likes and dislikes
- ✅ talk about hobbies and interests
- ✅ express frequency
- ✅ talk about the past

And cover the following grammar and language:

- ✅ the *passé composé* with **être**
- ✅ **depuis** ('for', 'since') with the present tense
- ✅ **jouer à/jouer de** ('to play')
- ✅ adverbs of frequency
- ✅ the imperfect tense

---

## LEARNING FRENCH 10

As you progress with your study of French, you will find that the more vocabulary you know the easier it will be to express yourself. It's not possible to learn everything at once, so be discriminating and start by learning the words and phrases which are most useful to *you*.

🎧 Now start the recording for Unit 10.

# What happened?

## Qu'est-ce qui s'est passé?

**ACTIVITY 1** is on the recording.

**ACTIVITY 2**

Correct the statements which are false.

| | | |
|---|---|---|
| 1 | Christine went to the station to meet her friend . | V / F |
| 2 | She arrived at the station at 10.15. | V / F |
| 3 | Martin's train arrived at 8.55. | V / F |
| 4 | They went home for lunch. | V / F |
| 5 | She fell off her bicycle. | V / F |
| 6 | Martin broke his leg. | V / F |
| 7 | He spent 24 hours in hospital. | V / F |
| 8 | He went back to Paris with his arm in plaster. | V / F |

**DIALOGUE 1**

■ Mon copain Martin est venu pour le week-end. Je suis allée le chercher à la gare. Je suis arrivée à la gare à neuf heures moins cinq. Son train est arrivé à dix heures et quart!

○ Oh, là, là! Ma pauvre!

■ Après on est allés déjeuner dans un café.

○ Et vous avez mal mangé?

■ Non, non! Ça s'est bien passé, on a bien mangé. Mais l'après-midi, on est allés se promener à vélo. Martin est tombé de vélo, et il s'est cassé le bras. On est restés douze heures à l'hôpital. Martin est retourné à Paris avec le bras dans le plâtre.

---

### VOCABULARY

| | |
|---|---|
| **chercher** | to collect, to pick up |
| **ça s'est bien passé** | it went well |
| **se promener à vélo** | to go for a bicycle ride |
| **tomber** | to fall |
| **(se) casser** | to break |
| **rester** | to stay |
| **l'hôpital** (*m*) | hospital |
| **retourner** | to go back |
| **le plâtre** | plaster, Band-Aid |

## ✓ *Le passé composé* with *être*

Some verbs form the *passé composé* with **être** rather than **avoir**. The main ones are:

| | | |
|---|---|---|
| aller | **allé** | Je **suis allé** au cinéma. I went to the cinema. |
| arriver | **arrivé** | Je **suis arrivée** en retard. I arrived late. |
| descendre | **descendu** | Tu **es descendu** du train. You got off the train. |
| entrer | **entré** | Tu **es entrée**. You went in. |
| monter | **monté** | Elle **est montée** dans le bus. She got on the bus. |
| mourir | **mort** | Il **est mort** en 1953. He died in 1953. |
| naître | **né** | Il **est né** en 1877. He was born in 1877. |
| partir | **parti** | On **est partis** à midi. We left at 12 o'clock. |
| rester | **resté** | Nous **sommes restés** une heure. We stayed an hour. |
| sortir | **sorti** | Vous **êtes sortis**. You went out. |
| tomber | **tombé** | Elles **sont tombées**. They fell. |
| venir | **venu** | Ils **sont venus** en train. They came by train. |

This also applies to all compound verbs, which are formed by adding a prefix to the original verb, for example <u>de</u>venir ('to become'), <u>rentrer</u> ('to go back'), <u>inter</u>venir ('to intervene').

Reflexive verbs also form the *passé composé* with **être**:

Qu'est-ce qui s'**est passé**? What happened?
Je me **suis levé(e)** de bonne heure. I got up early.

## ✓ Agreements

When the *passé composé* is formed with **être**, the past participle agrees with the subject – an **e** is added when it's feminine and/or an **s** when it's plural. These agreements are generally not heard in spoken French.

Mes parents **sont parti<u>s</u>** ce matin. My parents left this morning.
Mes sœurs **sont resté<u>es</u>** deux jours. My sisters stayed for two days.
Nathalie n'**est** pas **arrivé<u>e</u>** hier. Nathalie didn't arrive yesterday.

There is one exception. If a reflexive verb is followed by a direct object, the past participle does not agree with the subject:

Anne s'**est cassé** le bras. Anne broke her arm.

---

### ACTIVITY 3

Who is speaking – a man or a woman?

1 Je suis née en 1955.   3 Je suis rentré à minuit.
2 Je suis parti à midi.   4 Je suis restée trois heures.

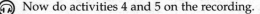 Now do activities 4 and 5 on the recording.

# 10.2 I love reading

## J'adore lire

🔊 **ACTIVITY 6** is on the recording.

**ACTIVITY 7**

Correct this summary. There are six mistakes.

At the age of 88, Madame Lefort is very healthy and dynamic. When asked what her secret is, she says she doesn't know, but she admits she doesn't smoke, and never has. She doesn't drink alcohol, either. She loves doing crosswords, but she hates reading. She prefers sport! She walks regularly, and she goes swimming once a week. She loves water, but she only started swimming ten years ago. That's not all! She also does some yoga – something she started at the age of 38.

**DIALOGUE 2**

○ Madame Lefort, vous avez 88 ans. Vous êtes en pleine forme. Quel est votre secret?

■ Je ne sais pas … Je ne fume pas, je n'ai jamais fumé. Mais je bois du vin. Pas tous les jours, mais souvent.

○ Autrement, vous lisez? Vous faites des mots croisés?

■ J'aime lire, oui, mais je déteste les mots croisés! Je préfère le sport! Je fais de la marche à pied, je fais de la natation, je vais à la piscine trois fois par semaine et je fais du yoga.

○ Vous faites ça depuis longtemps?

■ J'ai toujours fait de la natation. J'adore l'eau! Pour le yoga, je fais du yoga depuis 38 ans. J'ai commencé à l'âge de 50 ans.

○ Eh bien, bravo!

| VOCABULARY | |
|---|---|
| **en pleine forme** | in good shape, very healthy |
| **le secret** | secret |
| **fumer** | to smoke |
| **souvent** | often |
| **autrement** | otherwise |
| **faire des mots croisés** | to do crosswords |
| **détester** | to hate |
| **faire de la marche à pied** | to go walking |
| **la natation** | swimming |
| **bravo!** | congratulations! |

## ✓ *depuis* + present tense

Unlike English, which uses the past tense to express how long something has been going on, the French uses the present tense followed by **depuis**, which can mean either 'for' or 'since' depending on the context:

> Je **joue** aux échecs **depuis** deux ans. I have been playing chess for two years. [*literally* I play chess since two years.]
> Mon père **collectionne** les timbres **depuis** l'âge de douze ans.
> My father has been collecting stamps since the age of twelve.

## ✓ *jouer à/jouer de*

**jouer** is usually followed by **à l'/au/à la/aux**, unless it is used with a musical instrument. In that case, it is followed by **de l'/du/de la/des**.

> Je joue **aux cartes** et tu joues **de la** guitare. I play cards and you play the guitar.
> Il joue **au tennis** et elle joue **du piano**. He plays tennis and she plays the piano.

## ✓ Expressing frequency

The following is a list of common adverbs used to express frequency:

| | | | |
|---|---|---|---|
| **souvent** | often | **une fois par jour** | once a day |
| **toujours** | always | **deux fois par semaine** | twice a week |
| **quelquefois** | sometimes | **trois fois par mois** | three times a month |
| **(ne ... ) jamais** | never | **quatre fois par an** | four times a year |
| | | **de temps en temps** | from time to time |

> Je **ne** vais **jamais** au cinéma, mais je vais **souvent** au théâtre.
> I never go to the cinema, but I often go to the theatre.
> Elle joue au tennis **une ou deux fois par semaine**.
> She plays tennis once or twice a week.

---

### ACTIVITY 8

Read about Monsieur Noah below. Imagine what he would say to someone asking what the secret of his longevity is.

> Casimir Noah, 86 years old
> smokes from time to time (has smoked since the age of 22)
> never drinks alcohol (never has)
> plays chess once or twice a week
> rides a bicycle (has been cycling since the age of 9)

 Now do activities 9 and 10 on the recording.

# 10.3 When I was young
## Quand j'étais jeune

 **ACTIVITY 11** is on the recording.

**ACTIVITY 12**

In what order are the following things mentioned in the conversation?

| | |
|---|---|
| radio | _____ |
| Internet | _____ |
| computer | _____ |
| electricity | _____ |
| television | _____ |
| telephone | _____ |

**DIALOGUE 3**

○ Quand j'étais jeune, Internet n'existait pas et je n'avais pas d'ordinateur. Le soir, je regardais la télévision ou je téléphonais à mes copains.

■ Tu regardais la télévision ou tu téléphonais à tes copains! Tu avais de la chance! Moi, je n'avais pas la télé et je n'avais pas le téléphone.

○ Qu'est-ce que tu faisais alors?

■ Je lisais ou je me disputais avec mon frère ou j'écoutais la radio.

▼ Tu écoutais la radio! Tu avais de la chance! Chez moi, il n'y avait pas de radio, il n'y avait pas l'électricité!

■ Qu'est-ce que vous faisiez alors?

▼ Mon grand-père nous racontait des histoires ou …

△ Vous aviez de la chance!

---

### VOCABULARY

| | |
|---|---|
| **quand** | when |
| **jeune** | young |
| **exister** | to exist |
| **l'ordinateur** (*m*) | computer |
| **se disputer** | to argue |
| **écouter** | to listen to |
| **l'électricité** (*f*) | electricity |
| **raconter** | to tell |
| **l'histoire** (*f*) | story |

## ✅ The imperfect

The imperfect tense has two main uses.

1 It can be used to describe something which used to happen frequently or regularly in the past:

J'**allais** à l'école à pied. I walked/I used to walk to school.

2 It can be used to describe what was happening or what the situation was when something else happened:

Je **dormais** quand elle **est arrivée**. I was asleep when she arrived.
Elle **avait** sept ans quand il **est né**. She was seven when he was born.

To form the imperfect tense, take the **nous** part of the present tense (e.g. **regarder, nous** <u>regardons</u>), remove the **-ons** and add the endings below:

| je **regardais** | nous **regardions** |
|---|---|
| tu **regardais** | vous **regardiez** |
| il/elle/on **regardait** | ils/elles **regardaient** |

There is only one exception. To make the imperfect of **être**, 'to be', you need to add the endings above to the irregular stem **ét-**:

| j'**étais** | nous **étions** |
|---|---|
| tu **étais** | vous **étiez** |
| il/elle/on **était** | ils/elles **étaient** |

---

### ACTIVITY 13

Use the right tense to complete the following dialogue, choosing from the forms listed below.

| | |
|---|---|
| 1  tu as fait/tu faisais | 6  J'ai parlé/Je parlais |
| 2  Tu es allée/Tu allais | 7  j'ai fait/je faisais |
| 3  j'ai travaillé/je travaillais | 8  je suis allée/j'allais |
| 4  J'étais/J'ai été | 9  j'ai fait/je faisais |
| 5  tu es arrivée/tu arrivais | |

○ Qu'est-ce que 1 _____ aujourd'hui? 2 _____ à la piscine?

■ Non, 3 _____ toute la journée. 4 _____ dans le bureau, quand 5 _____. 6 _____ à mon agent. L'année dernière, 7 _____ beaucoup de sport, 8 _____ à la piscine, 9 _____ du vélo. Cette année, je n'ai pas le temps, j'ai trop de travail.

🎧 Now do activities 14 and 15 on the recording.

# 10.4 Leisure

## Les loisirs

### ACTIVITY 16

Before reading the article that follows, decide whether you think the following statements are true or false.

1  Most French people have never been to a zoo.
2  Most French people have never been to a rock concert.
3  Half of the French population has never been to the theatre.
4  Most French people have been to the Opera at least once in their lives.
5  Most French people have been to a classical music concert at least once.
6  Less than a quarter of the French population has never visited a museum.

## LES EXCLUS DU LOISIR

Au cours de leur vie, 83% des Français (15 ans et plus) ne sont jamais allés à l'Opéra.

79% n'ont jamais assisté à un concert de jazz.

75% n'ont jamais assisté à un spectacle de danse professionnelle.

73% n'ont jamais assisté à un concert de rock.

68% n'ont jamais assisté à un concert de musique classique.

60% ne sont jamais allés dans un parc d'attraction.

50% ne sont jamais allés au théâtre.

46% n'ont jamais assisté à un spectacle sportif payant.

39% ne sont jamais allés dans une discothèque.

21% n'ont jamais visité un monument historique.

19% n'ont jamais visité un musée.

13% ne sont jamais allés au cirque.

12% ne sont jamais allés au zoo.

9% ne sont jamais allés au cinéma.

8% ne sont jamais allés dans une fête foraine.

| exclu(e) | excluded |
|---|---|
| **au cours de** | in the course of |
| **la vie** | life |
| **assister à** | to attend |

## ACTIVITY 17

Look through the article, and spot the French equivalents for:

1 show
2 circus
3 funfair
4 museum
5 amusement park
6 sports event for which tickets are required

## ACTIVITY 18

Read through the article and check how accurate your guesses were in activity 16.

## ACTIVITY 19

Say which of the things in the article match your experience and which ones don't. Use the sentences below to help you. You can also use the list of adverbs of frequency on page 139.

**Moi non plus, je ne suis jamais allé(e) à l'Opéra.**
I have never been to the Opera, either.
[*literally* Me neither, I have never been to the Opera.]

**Moi, j'ai souvent assisté à un concert de jazz.**
I have often been to a jazz concert.

**Moi, je suis allé(e) à un concert de rock au moins une fois.**
I have been to a rock concert at least once.

**JE VOULAIS T'INTERVIEWER**
**I WANTED TO INTERVIEW YOU**

Karim Massoud va mieux et il est content de rentrer chez lui. Alexandra vient lui dire au revoir.

| | |
|---|---|
| content(e) | happy |
| ça va mieux? | are you better? |
| inquiet/inquiète | worried |
| demander | to ask |
| interviewer | to interview |
| confidentiel(le) | confidential |
| la série | series |
| étranger/étrangère | foreign |
| chez nous | at/to our home |

**ACTIVITY 20**

Listen to the recording, and tick the sentences you hear.

1 Qu'est-ce qui se passait?
2 Qu'est-ce qui s'est passé?
3 Je restais deux jours au lit.
4 Je suis resté deux jours au lit.
5 Madame Delaine était très inquiète.
6 Madame Delaine a été très inquiète.
7 Elle allait chez le pharmacien.
8 Elle est allée chez le pharmacien.
9 Je voulais t'interviewer.
10 J'ai voulu t'interviewer.
11 Elle arrivait en France.
12 Elle est arrivée en France.

**ACTIVITY 21**

Use the words below to complete this transcript of a previous conversation between Alexandra and Madame Delaine.

a été / avez été / ai appelé / est passé / est resté /
suis allée / avait / avait / étais

| | |
|---|---|
| Mme Delaine | Monsieur Massoud _____ très malade, et il _____ deux jours au lit. |
| Alexandra | Qu'est-ce qui s'_____? |
| Mme Delaine | Il _____ de la fièvre, et il _____ très mal à la tête. J'_____ très inquiète, alors j'_____ le médecin, et puis je _____ chez le pharmacien. |
| Alexandra | Vous _____ très sympa! |

## ACTIVITY 22

Complete Malika Massoud's account of her early years.

«Je _____ au Maroc, et je _____ en France à l'âge de dix ans. Mon père _____ français et ma mère _____ marocaine, mais ils _____ quand j'_____ neuf ans.»

## STORY TRANSCRIPT

| | |
|---|---|
| Karim | Alexandra, tu es venue me dire au revoir? C'est sympa! |
| Alexandra | Ça va mieux? |
| Karim | Oui, merci. |
| Alexandra | Tu as été très malade! Qu'est-ce qui s'est passé? |
| Karim | Je ne sais pas. Je suis resté deux jours au lit, j'avais très mal à la tête, j'avais de la fièvre … |
| Alexandra | Madame Delaine était très inquiète! |
| Karim | Oui, je sais, elle a été très sympa. Elle a appelé le médecin et elle est allée chez le pharmacien pour moi … Maintenant, ça va mieux, et je suis content de rentrer chez moi. |
| Alexandra | Karim, je voulais te demander … Je … je voulais t'interviewer … |
| Karim | Alexandra, je suis désolé, mais je ne peux pas parler de mon travail. C'est confidentiel … |
| Alexandra | Je sais, je ne voulais pas parler de ton travail, je voulais t'interviewer sur tes origines marocaines. C'est pour une série d'articles sur les Français d'origine étrangère. |
| Karim | Ah bon, d'accord! Mais il faut aussi interviewer Malika. |
| Alexandra | Malika? |
| Karim | Oui, Malika, c'est ma femme. Elle est née au Maroc, et elle est arrivée en France à l'âge de dix ans. Son père était français et sa mère était marocaine, mais ils sont morts quand elle avait neuf ans … Viens chez nous. Voici notre numéro de téléphone. |
| Alexandra | Merci. C'est sympa. … Ah, excuse-moi. Allô? … |

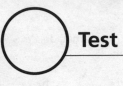

# Test

Now it's time to test your progress in Unit 10.

1 Find the odd one out in each group of phrases.

1 l'équitation/la natation/le yaourt/la marche à pied
2 souvent/tous les jours/cinq fois par semaine/jamais
3 il est parti/tu es sortie/je suis arrivé/elle est restée
4 je travaillais/il jouait/vous regardiez la télé/elles se
   promenaient

**4**

2 Who says what? Note that each speaker/group of speakers says two sentences, and remember that the past participle endings give you important information about gender and number of speakers.

1 Nous sommes montés dans le train.
2 Nous sommes rentrées hier.
3 Nous sommes parties lundi.
4 Nous sommes allés à Paris.
5 Je suis restée deux jours.
6 Je suis arrivée mardi.
7 Je suis tombé du lit.
8 Je me suis réveillé.

a Robert Dion
b Amina Hasna
c Philippe et Céline Waller
d Diane et Caroline Martineau

**8**

3 Use au/à la/aux or du/de l'/de la/des to complete the following sentences.

1 Je faisais _____ vélo.
2 Tu jouais _____ piano.
3 Il faisait _____ natation.
4 Elle jouait _____ cartes.
5 On jouait _____ tennis.
6 Nous faisions _____ équitation.
7 Vous faisiez _____ mots croisés.
8 Elles jouaient _____ guitare.

**8**

4 Use the words in the box below to complete the story.
( * **un saut** = jump † **sauter** = to jump)

**Mon premier saut\* en parachute**

Je _____ à l'aérodrome, j'_____ mon
parachute et je _____ dans l'avion.
J'_____ peur! J'_____ malade! Enfin,
nous _____ en avion. J'_____ par la
fenêtre. C'_____ beau! Et puis le moment de
sauter† _____ . J'_____ de la chance,
mon parachute s'_____ et je _____
dans un jardin ... entre les tomates et les haricots verts.

| | | |
|---|---|---|
| **suis arrivé** | **avais** | **est arrivé** |
| **étais** | **est ouvert** | **était** |
| **suis tombé** | **ai eu** | **ai préparé** |
| **ai regardé** | **suis monté** | **sommes partis** |

12

5 Write down the correct form of the verbs in brackets using
the imperfect tense to complete the dialogue.

○ Dis, grand-père, tu _____(**avoir**) un ordinateur quand
   tu _____(**être**) petit?
■ Non, je n'_____ (**avoir**) pas d'ordinateur.
○ Tes parents _____ (**avoir**) la télé?
■ Non, nous n' _____ (**avoir**) pas la télé.
○ Qu'est-ce que tu _____ (**faire**) après l'école alors?
■ Je m'_____ (**s'amuser**) avec mes copains. On
   _____ (**faire**) du vélo.
○ Et le week-end?
■ Le samedi, il y _____ (**avoir**) école. Le dimanche
   matin, j'_____ (**aller**) à l'église avec mes parents. Le
   dimanche après-midi, je _____ (**jouer**) au foot.
   J'_____ (**adorer**) le foot!

12

TOTAL SCORE  44

If you scored less than 34, go through the dialogues and the
Language Building sections again before completing the
Summary on page 148.

# Summary 10

 Now try this final test summarizing the main points covered in this unit.

How would you:
1 say you love swimming?
2 say you hate crosswords?
3 say you have never smoked?
4 ask what happened?
5 say it went well?
6 say your daughter fell off her bike?
7 say she broke her arm?
8 say she stayed two days in hospital?
9 tell a friend you were asleep when she rang?
10 say your father used to play the piano when he was young?

## REVISION

Don't leave Unit 10 until you feel able to talk about your lifestyle in French. What do you do to stay fit? (Have you ever smoked? Do you walk/swim/play tennis/play football, etc.?) How long have you been doing all this? What else do you like doing in your spare time? (Do you do crosswords? play cards/chess? go to concerts? How often?) Make sure you reuse as much as possible of the language you have learnt so far.

# Review 3

1 Work out the following anagrams to find ten words related to hobbies.

   1 les ---- -------  toms ricosés
   2 l'----------  quiétainot
   3 la ----------  vélotiésin
   4 la --------  aniotant
   5 le ------  cénami
   6 les ------  escart
   7 les ------  séchec
   8 le ------  sinten
   9 le -----  trops .
   10 le ----  lové

2 Rewrite the following words in two separate columns depending on their meanings. One of the words fits in both columns.

   **avion / bateau / cœur / dents / pied / tête / train / ventre / vélo / voiture**

   J'y vais à/en …          J'ai mal au(x)/à la …

3 Find the right response for the following questions.

   1 Elle est née où?
   2 Il y va en voiture?
   3 Tu as une cigarette?
   4 Elle aime la natation?
   5 Tu t'es cassé la jambe?
   6 Qu'est-ce que vous faisiez?
   7 Il ne joue jamais au tennis?
   8 Votre voiture est en panne?

   a Non, je ne fume plus depuis un an.
   b Oui, elle va souvent à la piscine.
   c Non, il préfère la marche à pied.
   d Non, il déteste le sport.
   e Oui, j'ai un pneu crevé.
   f On jouait aux échecs.
   g Oui, ça fait très mal.
   h À Lyon.

4 Choose the correct form of the verb in brackets to complete
Pierre's story of how he gave up smoking.

«Avant, (**je fumais / j'ai fumé**) un paquet de cigarettes par
jour, et je ne (**fais / faisais**) jamais de sport. (**Je détestais /
J'ai détesté**) ça! (**J'ai / J'avais**) souvent mal à la tête et mal
au ventre, et (**je suis / j'étais**) souvent malade, (**j'ai eu /
j'avais**) un rhume tous les mois. Maintenant, (**j'ai arrêté /
j'arrêtais**) de fumer. (**Je fais / J'ai fait**) du sport
régulièrement depuis un an et (**je ne suis / je n'étais**)
jamais malade.»

5 Complete the interview.

| | |
|---|---|
| Interviewer | Qu'est-ce que vous avez comme loisirs? |
| Paul | J'adore aller ____ cinéma. J'____ vais une ou deux fois ____ semaine. J'aime lire, j'écoute ____ radio … |
| Interviewer | Vous regardez ____ télévision? |
| Paul | Non, je ne regarde jamais ____ télé. |
| Interviewer | Qu'est-ce que vous aimez comme musique? |
| Paul | J'adore ____ musique classique, je joue du violon _____ l'âge de quatorze ans. |
| Interviewer | Vous jouez ____ piano aussi? |
| Paul | Non, je préfère ____ violon. |
| Interviewer | Autrement, vous faites ____ sport? Vous jouez ____ tennis? |
| Paul | Non, je ne joue pas ____ tennis, je déteste ____ sport! Je fais _____ marche à pied. C'est tout! |

 **LISTENING**

You're going to hear a tourist guide tell the story of the battle
of Hastings – **la bataille d'Hastings**.

6 How much do you know already? Do this quiz before
listening. (**le roi** king)

1 La femme du roi Édouard s'appelait
   a Édith.
   b Charlotte.
2 Le roi Édouard et sa femme
   a avaient deux filles.
   b n'avaient pas d'enfants.

3 Harold était
   a le frère d'Édith.
   b le cousin d'Édith.
4 Quand Édouard est mort,
   a Harold est devenu roi.
   b Guillaume est devenu roi.
5 Guillaume de Normandie
   a est né à Hastings le 28 septembre 1066.
   b est arrivé à Hastings le 28 septembre 1066.
6 Harold est mort
   a après une mauvaise grippe.
   b pendant la bataille d'Hastings.

7 Listen to the recording and correct your answers to the quiz.

8 Listen to the recording again and complete the following transcript.

Je vais vous raconter l'histoire de la bataille d'Hastings. Alors … Édouard _____ roi d'Angleterre. Sa femme s'appelait Édith. Édouard et Édith n'_____ pas d'enfants. Quand le roi Édouard _____ mort en 1066, le frère d'Édith est _____ roi d'Angleterre. Il s'_____ Harold. Guillaume, le cousin d'Édouard, n'_____ pas content! Il _____ en Normandie, alors il a _____ le bateau et il _____ à Hastings le 28 septembre 1066. La bataille d'Hastings _____. Harold est _____ le 14 octobre 1066, et Guillaume de Normandie _____ devenu roi d'Angleterre.

 **SPEAKING**

9 Here are some of the phrases you have learnt in the last three units. How do you pronounce them? Read them aloud, and then listen to the recording to check your pronunciation.

1 Elle adore le sport.
2 Il faut arrêter de fumer.
3 Qu'est-ce qui s'est passé?
4 Un aller retour, s'il vous plaît.
5 Il apprend le français depuis un an.
6 Quand j'étais jeune, je n'avais pas d'ordinateur.

10 You're ill and the doctor has come to see you. Prepare your side of the conversation using the cues below.

Doctor  Ça ne va pas?
You  (Say you've been ill for two days.)
Doctor  Qu'est-ce qui ne va pas?
You  (Say you're very cold and you have a fever.)
Doctor  Vous avez pris un médicament?
You  (Say you took some aspirin yesterday.)
Doctor  D'accord.
You  (Add that you had a headache yesterday.)
Doctor  Et maintenant?
You  (Say you don't have a headache any more, but you have a sore throat.)

Now try the dialogue on the recording without referring to the book.

12 You're trying to win an award for the most unfit person. Use the cue card to answer the interviewer's questions.

- fume trois paquets de cigarettes par jour
- fume depuis l'âge de 8 ans
- va au bureau en voiture
- déteste le sport
- ne mange jamais de fruits et légumes. Déteste ça!
- ne boit jamais d'eau. Préfère le vin et le café!

# At home
# Chez nous

## LEARNING FRENCH 11

The best way for you to learn and remember vocabulary will depend on the kind of learner you are. If you have a good visual memory, try writing new words on cards or in a small notebook and go through them when you have a spare moment. If, on the other hand, you are better at remembering things you hear, use a cassette to record vocabulary lists and play it whenever you can.

Now start the recording for Unit 11.

# Bienvenue chez moi

(🔊) **ACTIVITY 1** is on the recording.

**ACTIVITY 2**

A Which of the sentences is not spoken by Nathalie, the hostess?

1 Entrez!
2 Asseyez-vous!
3 Vous devez avoir soif.
4 Vous devez être fatigués.
5 Vous avez fait bon voyage?
6 On a mis deux heures et demie.
7 Je suis vraiment contente de vous voir.
8 Vous êtes partis de chez vous à quelle heure?

B In what order do you hear the sentences above?

**DIALOGUE 1**

○ Sophie! Pierre! Bonjour! Entrez! Entrez!
■ Bonjour, Nathalie!
▼ Bonjour!
○ Bienvenue chez moi! Ça va? Vous avez fait bon voyage?
■ Ça a été long, mais ça s'est bien passé. Merci.
○ Vous êtes partis de chez vous à quelle heure?
■ On est partis de chez nous à deux heures, et ... il est quatre heures et demie ... Donc on a mis deux heures et demie!
○ Vous devez être fatigués et vous devez avoir soif. Qu'est-ce que vous prenez? Un jus de fruits? Un thé? Ou ...
■ Oui. Je veux bien un jus de fruits.
▼ Moi aussi.
○ Asseyez-vous! Je vous apporte ça tout de suite. Ah! Je suis vraiment contente de vous voir!

---

| VOCABULARY | |
|---|---|
| **entrez!** | come in! |
| **bienvenue** | welcome |
| **le voyage** | journey, trip |
| **vous avez fait bon voyage?** | did you have a good journey? |
| **mettre** | to take [*time*], [*also* to put] |
| **s'asseoir** | to sit down |

## ✓ *chez* + disjunctive pronouns

The preposition **chez** can be used with either a pronoun or a noun, and it can be translated in a variety of ways depending on the context. For the complete list of disjunctive pronouns, see page 91.

| | |
|---|---|
| chez moi | Je rentre **chez moi**. I'm going home. |
| chez toi | Tu es **chez toi**? Are you at home? |
| chez lui | Il mange **chez lui**. He eats at home. |
| chez elle | Pierre est **chez elle**. Pierre is at her house. |
| chez nous | Venez **chez nous**. Come to our house. |
| chez vous | J'ai téléphoné **chez vous**. I rang your home. |
| chez eux | Ils sont **chez eux**? Are they in? |
| chez Sophie | Il va **chez Sophie**. He's going to Sophie's. |
| chez le médecin | Il est **chez le médecin**. He's at the doctor's. |
| chez mes parents | J'habite **chez mes parents**. I live with my parents. |

### ACTIVITY 3

Match the French with the appropriate English translation.

1  Il est chez lui.
2  On va chez toi?
3  Tu vas chez eux?
4  Elle est chez vous?
5  Vous êtes chez vous?
6  Je vais chez le médecin.
7  Viens manger chez moi.
8  Elle téléphone chez elle.
9  Venez manger chez nous.
10  Elle habite chez ses parents.

a  Are you going to their place?
b  She lives with her parents.
c  Shall we go to your place?
d  I'm going to the doctor's.
e  Come and eat with me.
f  Come and eat with us.
g  She's ringing home.
h  Are you at home?
i  Is she with you?
j  He's at home.

🔊 Now do activities 4 and 5 on the recording.

**Bigger or smaller?**

## Plus grand ou plus petit?

**ACTIVITY 6** is on the recording.

**ACTIVITY 7**

Which of the following conclusions do you agree with?

1 Nathalie, Sophie, and Pierre know each other quite well.
2 Pierre and Sophie have come to this house once before.
3 Nathalie used to live in a place called Arnage.
4 Nathalie has recently moved to this house.
5 Nathalie isn't happy in her new home.
6 Nathalie's new home is quiet.

**DIALOGUE 2**

○ Voilà des jus de fruits. Et j'ai fait une tarte aux poires.
■ Ça a l'air délicieux. Tu nous gâtes!
○ C'est tout naturel. Vous avez fait tout ce trajet pour venir me voir! Au fait, vous avez trouvé la maison facilement?
■ Oui, on a cherché la plus belle maison du village …
▼ Et la plus grande! Et on est arrivés chez toi!
○ Cette maison est moins grande que l'autre …
■ Non! Elle est aussi grande que l'autre!
○ Non, elle est plus petite! Beaucoup plus petite! Mais elle est beaucoup plus agréable. C'est très calme ici, beaucoup moins bruyant qu'à Arnage. J'étais malheureuse là-bas.
■ Voici un petit cadeau pour toi.
○ Ah, c'est gentil! Merci …

| VOCABULARY | |
|---|---|
| avoir l'air | to look [*nice, happy, etc.*] |
| gâter | to spoil |
| naturel(le) | natural, normal |
| c'est tout naturel | it's quite alright |
| au fait | by the way |
| trouver | to find |
| calme | quiet |
| bruyant(e) | noisy |
| malheureux/malheureuse | unhappy |
| là-bas | there |
| gentil(le) | kind, nice |

### ⊘ Comparatives

When making a comparison, you can use one of the following phrases:

**plus ... que**  Une maison est **plus** confortable **qu'**une tente.
A house is **more** comfortable **than** a tent.

**moins ... que**  L'eau est **moins** chère **que** le vin.
Water is **less** expensive **than** wine.

**aussi ... que**  Le métro est **aussi** rapide **que** le bus.
The tube is **as** fast **as** the bus.

When a pronoun is needed after **que**, use the disjunctive pronouns **moi, toi**, etc.

Nous sommes **plus** jeunes **qu'eux**. We are younger than them.
Je suis **moins** grosse **que toi**. I am less fat than you.
Elle est **aussi** mince **que lui**. She is as slim as him.

### ⊘ Superlatives

The equivalent of 'the most ...'/ 'the least ...' in French is **le/la/les plus/moins**:

Il a pris **la plus** grosse pomme. He took the biggest apple.
Elle a choisi les chaussures **les moins** chères. She chose the least expensive shoes.

After a superlative 'in' is translated by **de/d'** and 'in the' by **du/de la/des**:

La Loire est **le plus** long fleuve **de** France.
The Loire is the longest river in France.
C'est l'homme **le plus** célèbre **du** monde.
He's the most famous man in the world.

---

#### ACTIVITY 8

Théo est aussi grand que Diane.
Claire est plus grande que Théo.
Diane est moins grande que Claire.
Matthieu est plus petit qu'Annabelle.
Caroline est moins grande que Diane.
Annabelle est plus petite que Caroline.

1 Qui est le plus grand/la plus grande? _____
2 Qui est le plus petit/la plus petite? _____
3 Qui est le plus grand des garçons? _____
4 Qui est la plus petite des filles? _____

🎧 Now do activities 9 and 10 on the recording.

# 11.3  Feeling better
## Ça va mieux

**ACTIVITY 11** is on the recording.

### ACTIVITY 12

From the dialogue, find the French for:

1 I feel better.
2 It's more beautiful than ours.
3 Yours is bigger than mine!
4 Do you think that Nathalie's garden is smaller than ours?
5 You look much happier than before.
6 That's the most important thing.

### DIALOGUE 3

■ J'étais fatigué après le voyage. Maintenant ça va mieux!
○ Tu reprends de la tarte?
■ Non, merci. J'ai assez mangé.
○ Et toi, Sophie?
▼ Non, merci, je n'ai plus faim, mais ta tarte était délicieuse! Tu es meilleure cuisinière que moi.
■ Et ton jardin est magnifique, Nathalie!
▼ Il est plus beau que le nôtre!
○ Le vôtre est plus grand que le mien!
▼ Ça, je ne sais pas! Pierre, tu crois que le jardin de Nathalie est plus petit que le nôtre?
■ Je ne crois pas! Non!
▼ En tout cas, c'est très agréable ici. Et Nathalie, tu as l'air beaucoup plus heureuse qu'avant. C'est le plus important!

### VOCABULARY

| | |
|---|---|
| **maintenant** | now |
| **ça va mieux** | that's better |
| **reprendre (de la tarte)** | to have some more (tart, pie) |
| **meilleur(e)** | better |
| **le cuisinier/la cuisinière** | cook |
| **magnifique** | magnificent |
| **croire** | to believe, to think |
| **je ne crois pas** | I don't think so |
| **en tout cas** | in any case, anyway |
| **heureux/heureuse** | happy, content |

## ✅ Irregular comparatives and superlatives

The adjective **bon** and the adverbs **bien** and **mal** have irregular comparatives and superlatives.

| | |
|---|---|
| **bon/bonne/bons/bonnes** | good |
| **meilleur/meilleure/meilleurs/meilleures** | better |
| **le meilleur/la meilleure/les meilleurs/les meilleures** | the best |

J'ai une **meilleure** idée. I have a better idea.
Vous êtes **les meilleurs** élèves du lycée. You're the best pupils in the school.

As adverbs, the following are used after verbs:

| | | | |
|---|---|---|---|
| **bien** | well | **mal** | badly |
| **mieux** | better | **pire, plus mal** | worse |
| **le mieux** | the best | **le pire** | the worst |

Il parle **mieux** que toi. He speaks better than you.
Elle chante **plus mal** que moi. She sings worse than me.
Son frère est **pire** que le mien. Her brother is worse than mine.

## ✅ Possessive pronouns

Possessive pronouns ('mine', 'yours', etc.) change depending on whether the noun they refer to is masculine, feminine, singular, or plural. There is no distinction in French between 'his' and 'hers'.

Mon vélo est plus confortable que **le sien**. My bike is more comfortable than his/hers.
Ma voiture est plus rapide que **la sienne**. My car is faster than his/hers.

| | (sing.) | | (pl.) | |
|---|---|---|---|---|
| | (m) | (f) | (m) | (f) |
| mine | **le mien** | **la mienne** | **les miens** | **les miennes** |
| yours | **le tien** | **la tienne** | **les tiens** | **les tiennes** |
| his/hers | **le sien** | **la sienne** | **les siens** | **les siennes** |
| ours | **le nôtre** | **la nôtre** | **les nôtres** | **les nôtres** |
| yours | **le vôtre** | **la vôtre** | **les vôtres** | **les vôtres** |
| theirs | **le leur** | **la leur** | **les leurs** | **les leurs** |

### ACTIVITY 13

Complete the following sentences with **mieux** or **meilleur(e)**.

1 Marie est ma _____ amie.
2 Tu chantes _____ que moi.
3 J'ai été malade, mais ça va _____!
4 Ce gâteau est bon, mais l'autre est _____.

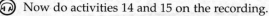 Now do activities 14 and 15 on the recording.

159

DOSSIER

Chère Nathalie,

On a passé un weekend vraiment sympa :
on a très bien mangé et bien bu. On s'est
bien reposés et on a fait de très belles
promenades. Tout ça grâce à toi. Alors, mille
fois merci ! En plus, ta maison et ton jardin
sont vraiment magnifiques. (On peut revenir
bientôt ?)
En attendant, tu es la bienvenue chez nous
quand tu veux, tu le sais.

Grosses bises de nous deux.

Sophie et Pierre

Chère Nathalie,

Mon mari et moi, nous vous remercions
pour une très agréable soirée en votre
compagnie. Le dîner était délicieux, et nous
étions très heureux de faire la connaissance
de vos amis Sophie et Pierre ; ils sont très
gentils et très drôles !

Nous espérons vous revoir bientôt. Chez nous
la prochaine fois !

Amicalement.

Brigitte a Philippe Najac

## ACTIVITY 16

Go through the two thank you notes, and find the French
equivalents of:

1  soon
2  to meet
3  we hope
4  next time
5  meanwhile
6  lots of love
7  kind regards
8  thanks to you

## ACTIVITY 17

Look at the notes again. Who do you think are closest to
Nathalie? Brigitte and Philippe or Sophie and Pierre? How can
you tell?

## ACTIVITY 18

Rewrite Brigitte and Philippe's note using **tu** instead of **vous**.

## ACTIVITY 19

Use the notes to help you write a thank you note to someone
who invited you for dinner last weekend; choose between:

a  a French-speaking friend you have known for many years
b  your new French-speaking neighbours

Your note can be shorter than the examples. All you need is:

- a beginning (bearing in mind that **cher** needs to agree with
  the person it is referring to, e.g. **cher** Pierre, **chère** Nathalie,
  **chers** Pierre et Nathalie)
- a middle (e.g. **On a très bien dîné**, alors mille fois
  merci/**Le dîner était délicieux. Merci pour une agréable
  soirée.**)
- an end (e.g. **grosses bises/amicalement**)

### QU'EST-CE QUE VOUS PRENEZ?
### WHAT WILL YOU HAVE?

Alexandra va à Paris pour interviewer Malika Massoud.

| | |
|---|---|
| **recommander** | to recommend |
| **le thé à la menthe** | mint tea |
| **rafraîchissant(e)** | refreshing |
| **ça vous plaît?** | do you like it? [*literally* does it please you?] |
| **passionnant(e)** | exciting |
| **l'histoire** (*f*) | story |
| **curieux/curieuse** | inquisitive, nosy |
| **bavard(e)** | talkative |
| **gros(se)** | big |
| **le défaut** | fault |

**ACTIVITY 20**

Listen to the recording and put the following summary in the right order.

1 Karim says Malika's mint tea is the best in Paris.
2 Alexandra arrives at Karim and Malika's flat.
3 Malika asks Alexandra a lot of questions.
4 Alexandra agrees to have mint tea.
5 Malika admits she talks too much.
6 Karim tries to stop Malika talking so much.
7 Alexandra asks for water.
8 Malika offers her a drink.
9 Malika asks her in.

## ACTIVITY 21

Later on, Madame Delaine asked Alexandra about Malika.
Complete the conversation.

| | |
|---|---|
| Mme Delaine | Elle est comment? Elle est aussi sympa _____ Karim? |
| Alexandra | Oui, mais elle est _____ bavarde que _____. Elle pose beaucoup de questions, elle est _____ curieuse que moi! Elle dit que ce sont ses _____ gros défauts. |
| Mme Delaine | Tu as bu du thé à la menthe? |
| Alexandra | Oui, il était très bon, très rafraîchissant. Karim dit que c'est le _____ thé à la menthe _____ Paris. |

## ACTIVITY 22

Write a thank you note to Malika on Alexandra's behalf.

## STORY TRANSCRIPT

| | |
|---|---|
| Alexandra | Bonjour! Vous êtes Malika? |
| Malika | Oui. Entrez! Vous êtes Alexandra, c'est ça? |
| Alexandra | Oui. |
| Malika | Ça va? Vous avez trouvé l'appartement facilement? |
| Alexandra | Oui, pas de problème. |
| Malika | Asseyez-vous … Vous avez soif? Qu'est-ce que vous prenez? |
| Alexandra | Je veux bien un verre d'eau, s'il vous plaît. |
| Malika | Vous ne voulez pas de thé à la menthe? Le mien est très rafraîchissant. |
| Karim | Alexandra, bonjour. Ça va? Je te recommande le thé à la menthe de Malika. C'est le meilleur de Paris! |
| Alexandra | J'adore le thé à la menthe, alors je veux bien, oui. |
| Malika | Vous êtes journaliste depuis longtemps? |
| Alexandra | Depuis trois ou quatre ans. |
| Malika | Pourquoi est-ce que vous avez décidé de devenir journaliste? |
| Alexandra | Ah, c'est une longue histoire. |
| Malika | Et ça vous plaît? Ça doit être passionnant comme métier … |
| Karim | Malika, Alexandra est venue t'interviewer, et tu es encore plus curieuse qu'elle! |
| Malika | C'est vrai! Je suis très bavarde et très curieuse. Ce sont mes plus gros défauts. Excusez-moi. Allez, je vous écoute. Qu'est-ce que vous voulez savoir sur moi? |
| Alexandra | Karim me dit que votre histoire est plus intéressante que la sienne. C'est vrai? |
| Malika | Ah, je ne sais pas … |

# Test

Now it's time to test your progress in Unit 11.

1 Rewrite the following words as eight pairs of opposites.

> âgé  bien  calme  bruyant  grand  gros  heureux
> jeune  mal  malheureux  mieux  mince  moins
> petit  pire  plus

2 Find the relevant possessive pronoun from a–p for each phrase 1–16.

| | | | |
|---|---|---|---|
| 1 | ma fille | a | le leur |
| 2 | ta mère | b | la leur |
| 3 | mon fils | c | le sien |
| 4 | ton père | d | le tien |
| 5 | sa maison | e | le mien |
| 6 | son jardin | f | le nôtre |
| 7 | leurs amis | g | la nôtre |
| 8 | nos enfants | h | le vôtre |
| 9 | vos parents | i | la vôtre |
| 10 | notre garage | j | les siens |
| 11 | votre cuisine | k | les leurs |
| 12 | notre voiture | l | les nôtres |
| 13 | leur grand-père | m | les vôtres |
| 14 | leur grand-mère | n | la sienne |
| 15 | ses petits-enfants | o | la tienne |
| 16 | votre appartement | p | la mienne |

3 Look at this information about Nathalie, Pierre, and Sophie. Then complete the sentences which follow comparing the three of them.

| Nathalie | Pierre | Sophie |
|---|---|---|
| née le 20.11.1943 | né le 14.4.1967 | née le 11.7.1962 |
| taille: 1,65m | taille: 1,88m | taille: 1,65m |
| poids: 58 kg | poids: 76 kg | poids: 52 kg |

Sophie est _____ plus mince. Elle est _____ petite que Pierre, mais elle est _____ grande et _____ grosse _____ Nathalie. Pierre est _____ plus grand et le _____ jeune. Il est _____ jeune _____ Sophie. Nathalie est la _____ jeune.

**10**

4 Use the words below to complete the following speech.

> que  pire  moi  mieux  meilleurs  meilleure
> meilleur  de

«Ma _____ amie est italienne, mais elle parle très bien français. _____ que moi! C'est une excellente cuisinière, elle prépare les _____ spaghettis _____ France. En tout cas, il sont meilleurs _____ les miens! Son mari joue très bien du piano. C'est le _____ pianiste de la région. Malheureusement, il chante mal, _____ que _____!»

**8**

5 Find the appropriate response from a–h for the remarks 1–8.

1 Voici un petit cadeau pour toi.
2 Vous avez fait bon voyage?
3 Tu reprends de la tarte?
4 Qu'est-ce que vous prenez?
5 Bienvenue chez moi!
6 Vous n'êtes pas trop fatigués?
7 Tu nous gâtes!
8 Je suis très contente de vous voir!

a Vous avez une très belle maison.
b Je veux bien un jus d'orange.
c Non, merci. Je n'ai plus faim.
d Merci. C'est très gentil.
e C'est tout naturel!
f Très bon. Merci.
g Nous aussi!
h Non, ça va.

**6**

**TOTAL SCORE** **48**

If you scored less than 38, go through the dialogues and the Language Building sections again before completing the Summary on page 166.

# Summary 11

 Now try this final test summarizing the main points covered in this unit.

How would you:
1 invite guests to come in and sit down?
2 ask them about their journey?
3 offer them a fruit juice?
4 ask them if they would like another helping of cake?
5 say 'No, thank you. I've had enough'?
6 say you've brought a small present?
7 tell your hosts that your house is smaller than theirs?
8 tell your hosts that their garden is more beautiful than yours?

## REVISION

Think of the last time you invited someone round to your home. Would you have been able to conduct the conversation in French, making the most of what you have learnt? For example, could you have invited them to come in and sit down, asked about their journey, and offered them refreshments? Alternatively, could you have conducted the conversation as a guest, accepted or declined refreshments, and thanked your hosts?

# Making plans
# Faire des projets

## OBJECTIVES

In this unit you will learn how to:

- ✓ give, accept, or decline invitations
- ✓ arrange to meet
- ✓ talk about the weather and the seasons of the year

And cover the following grammar and language:

- ✓ **il** + impersonal verbs to describe the weather
- ✓ **devoir** ('to have to'), **pouvoir** ('to be able to'), and **vouloir** ('to want') to make plans
- ✓ the conditional
- ✓ the object pronoun **que/qu'** introducing relative clauses
- ✓ the use of **qui** and **que**

## LEARNING FRENCH 12

Between study sessions, spend some time making mental lists of what you have just learnt. What was the topic? What was the activity? What set phrases can you remember? In that way, you're more actively involved in the learning process and you will remember language and vocabulary more easily.

Now start the recording for Unit 12.

## La pluie et le beau temps

(🔊) **ACTIVITY 1** is on the recording.

**ACTIVITY 2**

In Bordeaux …                In Lille …

| | | |
|---|---|---|
| 1 it's windy. | V / F | 6 it's cold. |
| 2 it's raining. | V / F | 7 it's windy. |
| 3 it's rather cold. | V / F | 8 the sky is blue. |
| 4 the sky is grey. | V / F | 9 the sun is shining. |
| 5 it looks like snow. | V / F | 10 the weather is as |

1 it's windy.    V / F    6 it's cold.    V / F
2 it's raining.    V / F    7 it's windy.    V / F
3 it's rather cold.    V / F    8 the sky is blue.    V / F
4 the sky is grey.    V / F    9 the sun is shining.    V / F
5 it looks like snow.    V / F    10 the weather is as
      bad as in Bordeaux.    V / F

**DIALOGUE 1**

○ Ça va? Quel temps fait-il à Bordeaux? Il fait beau?

■ Pas aujourd'hui. Non …

○ Il n'y a pas de soleil?

■ Non, le ciel est gris, il pleut, il y a du vent et il ne fait pas chaud.

○ Oh, là, là! Tu n'as pas de chance!

■ Il y a du soleil à Lille?

○ Oui! Le ciel est bleu … Le soleil brille … Il fait chaud …

■ Arrête! Arrête!

○ Ne t'inquiète pas! Je plaisantais! Il fait aussi mauvais temps qu'à Bordeaux. Il fait froid, il y a de gros nuages … Je crois qu'il va neiger.

| VOCABULARY | |
|---|---|
| **la pluie** | rain |
| **le temps** | weather |
| **quel temps fait-il?** | what's the weather like? |
| **le soleil** | sun |
| **le ciel** | sky |
| **pleuvoir** | to rain |
| **le vent** | wind |
| **briller** | to shine |
| **arrêter** | to stop |
| **plaisanter** | to joke |
| **mauvais(e)** | bad, terrible |
| **le nuage** | cloud |
| **neiger** | to snow |

## ✓ Quel temps fait-il?

Most weather phrases use impersonal verbs, which are only used with **il**:

**Il fait** froid. It's cold.
**Il fait** chaud. It's hot.
**Il fait** beau (temps). The weather's fine.
**Il fait** mauvais (temps). The weather's bad.

**Il y a** du vent. It's windy.
**Il y a** du soleil. It's sunny.
**Il y a** du brouillard. It's foggy.
**Il y a** des nuages. It's cloudy.

**Il pleut**. It's raining.
**Il neige**. It's snowing.

## ✓ Quel temps va-t-il faire?

You can use **aller** + infinitive to say what the weather is going to be like:

Il **va neiger**. It's going to snow.
Il **va pleuvoir**. It's going to rain.
Il **va faire** froid. It's going to be cold.
Il **va y avoir** du soleil. It's going to be sunny.

Note the **t** in the expression **quel temps va-t-il faire?** It has been added for pronunciation reasons to avoid the juxtaposition of two vowels.

## ✓ Les quatre saisons

In French the seasons are masculine.

| | |
|---|---|
| **le printemps** | spring |
| **l'été** | summer |
| **l'automne** | autumn/the fall |
| **l'hiver** | winter |

---

### ACTIVITY 3

Complete the following sentences, and match each description to the right season.

1 Il _____ beau. Il __ __ du soleil. Il _____ chaud.
2 Il _____ froid. Il __ __ des nuages. Quelquefois, ___ neige.
3 Il commence à faire plus froid. Il __ __ du vent et ___ pleut.
4 Il commence à faire moins froid. Il __ __ du soleil. ___
   pleut. ___ __ __ du soleil. ___ pleut ...

a le printemps   b l'automne   c l'hiver   d l'été

🎧 Now do activities 4 and 5 on the recording.

169

# J'aimerais bien

🔊 **ACTIVITY 6** is on the recording.

### ACTIVITY 7

**ce soir, demain,** ou **dimanche prochain?**

1 Valérie doit se lever très tôt …
2 Valérie ne veut pas se coucher tard …
3 Valérie va voir une exposition de peintures …
4 Valérie a rendez-vous à deux heures devant le château …
5 Valérie doit aller chez sa mère …

### DIALOGUE 2

○ Tu veux venir manger chez nous demain midi?
■ Je ne peux pas. Je dois aller chez ma mère.
○ Tu veux dîner avec nous ce soir alors?
■ Ce soir, je ne veux pas me coucher tard, parce que je dois me lever très tôt demain matin. C'est dommage. J'aimerais bien voir Laurent, mais je préférerais le week-end prochain. Vous êtes libres dimanche prochain?
○ Dimanche prochain, on aimerait bien aller à une exposition de peintures au château d'Amboise. Tu veux venir avec nous?
■ D'accord! On pourrait se promener dans les jardins du château après l'exposition. On se retrouve où?
○ Rendez-vous à deux heures devant le château?
■ OK. À dimanche prochain.

| VOCABULARY | |
|---|---|
| **demain** | tomorrow |
| **tard** | late |
| **parce que** | because |
| **tôt** | early |
| **(c'est) dommage** | (that's a) shame, pity |
| **prochain(e)** | next |
| **libre** | free |
| **l'exposition** (f) | exhibition |
| **la peinture** | painting |
| **se promener** | to walk |
| **se retrouver** | to meet |
| **le rendez-vous** | meeting, rendezvous [here = let's meet] |

✅ *devoir* ('to have to'), *pouvoir* ('to be able'), *vouloir* ('to want')

These verbs, often used when making plans, are followed by the infinitive:

> Vous **voulez** dîner avec nous? Do you want to have dinner with us?
> Je ne **peux** pas, je **dois** travailler. I can't, I have to work.
> Je **dois** aller à Strasbourg. Tu **veux** venir avec moi?
> I have to go to Strasbourg. Do you want to come with me?
> Oui, je **veux** bien. Yes, I'd like to.

✅ **The conditional**

The conditional is often used when expressing wishes or preferences, or when making polite requests or suggestions:

> Ils **voudraient** sortir ce soir. They'd like to go out tonight.
> Elle **aimerait** bien aller au théâtre. She'd like to go to the theatre.
> Il **préférerait** aller au cinéma. He'd prefer to go to the cinema.
> Elles **pourraient** aller au restaurant. They could go to a restaurant.
> Ils **devraient** se coucher tôt. They should go to bed early.

To form the conditional of regular verbs, you need to add the imperfect tense endings to the infinitive:

| | |
|---|---|
| j'**aimerais** | nous **aimerions** |
| tu **aimerais** | vous **aimeriez** |
| il/elle/on **aimerait** | ils/elles **aimeraient** |

In the conditional of **pouvoir**, **vouloir**, and **devoir**, the regular endings are added to the following irregular stems:

pouvoir **pourr-**     vouloir **voudr-**     devoir **devr-**

---

### ACTIVITY 8

Complete the conversation using the following words:

**aimerais/dois/pourrais/pourrait/préférerais/veux/voudrais**

| | |
|---|---|
| Laurent | Qu'est-ce qu'on _____ faire ce week-end? |
| Marie | Je _____ aller à l'exposition de peintures d'Amboise. Tu _____ venir avec moi? |
| Laurent | Oui, j' _____ bien, mais c'est le week-end prochain. |
| Marie | Ah, oui. Autrement je _____ voir Valérie. |
| Laurent | Moi, aussi. Je voudrais lui parler. Tu _____ lui demander de venir déjeuner chez nous demain midi. |
| Marie | Je _____ ce soir. |

🎧 Now do activities 9 and 10 on the recording.

## 12.3 The area I like

## La région que j'aime

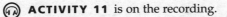 **ACTIVITY 11** is on the recording.

**ACTIVITY 12**

1 Which three chateaux are mentioned in the dialogue?
2 In which one is Mireille's exhibition being held?
3 Which one has her favourite garden?
4 Which one is her favourite?

Quelques châteaux de la Loire:

Amboise, Azay-le-Rideau, Blois, Chambord, Chenonceau, Ussé, Villandry

**DIALOGUE 3**

○ Mireille Kaufman, parlez-nous de l'exposition que vous préparez en ce moment.

■ C'est une exposition qui a lieu au château d'Amboise. Ce sont des tableaux des châteaux de la Loire et de leurs jardins.

○ Et quel est le château de la Loire que vous préférez?

■ Le château que je préfère, c'est le château d'Ussé qui est le château de la Belle au Bois Dormant. Et les jardins que je préfère, ce sont les jardins du château de Villandry.

○ Vous avez d'autres projets après cette exposition?

■ Je vais peindre en Bretagne. C'est une région que j'aime beaucoup. J'ai une tante qui habite à Quimper.

○ Il ne fait pas beau en Bretagne! Il pleut tout le temps!

■ Ce n'est pas vrai! En Bretagne, le ciel est toujours magnifique! La mer aussi! C'est une région qui m'inspire.

---

| VOCABULARY | |
|---|---|
| **avoir lieu** | to take place |
| **le tableau** | painting |
| **la Belle au Bois Dormant** | Sleeping Beauty |
| **le projet** | plan |
| **peindre** | to paint |
| **la tante** | aunt |
| **la mer** | sea |
| **inspirer** | to inspire |

### ✅ que / qu'

**que** ('which', 'that', 'whom') is an object pronoun. Like **qui** (see page 111), it can refer to both people and objects. Unlike its English equivalent, it cannot be omitted in French.

Le livre **que** j'écris. The book (that) I'm writing.
La chanson **qu'**elle chante. The song (that) she's singing.
Le peintre **que** je préfère. The painter (whom) I like best.

### ✅ Using qui and que: subject or object?

Écoute le garçon **qui** chante. Listen to the boy who's singing.

**chante** = verb
who's singing? – the boy
**qui** = subject

Écoute la chanson **que** je chante. Listen to the song I'm singing.

**chante** = verb
who's singing? – I
**je** = subject
what am I singing? – a song
**que** = object

---

### ACTIVITY 13

A  Use **qui** (subject pronoun) and **que** (object pronoun) to complete the following sentences.

1  C'est une artiste _____ a du talent.
2  C'est une artiste _____ j'admire.
3  C'est une région _____ elle aime beaucoup.
4  C'est une région _____ l'inspire.

B  Now complete the following article.

Mireille Kaufman est une artiste _____ a beaucoup de talent et _____ j'admire depuis longtemps. Elle prépare actuellement une exposition _____ va avoir lieu au château d'Amboise. Ce sont des tableaux _____ représentent les châteaux de la Loire et _____ sont riches en couleurs et en émotions. Après Amboise, Mireille doit partir près de Quimper. La Bretagne est une région _____ elle aime beaucoup et _____ l'inspire.

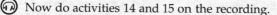 Now do activities 14 and 15 on the recording.

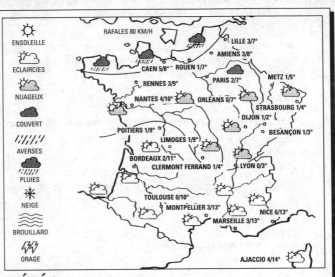

ENSOLEILLE

ECLAIRCIES

NUAGEUX

COUVERT

AVERSES

PLUIES

NEIGE

BROUILLARD

ORAGE

RAFALES 80 KM/H

LILLE 3/7°
AMIENS 3/8°
CAEN 5/8° ROUEN 1/7°
RENNES 3/9° PARIS 2/7° METZ 1/5°
NANTES 4/10° ORLÉANS 0/7°
STRASBOURG 1/4°
DIJON 1/2°
POITIERS 1/9° BESANÇON 1/3°
LIMOGES 1/9°
BORDEAUX 2/11°
CLERMONT FERRAND 1/4° LYON 0/3°
TOULOUSE 0/10°
MONTPELLIER 3/13°
NICE 6/13°
MARSEILLE 3/13°
AJACCIO 4/14°

# MÉTÉO
## LE TEMPS AUJOURD'HUI, RÉGION PAR RÉGION

**Bretagne, Pays de la Loire, Normandie.**
Sur la Bretagne et la Normandie, des pluies faibles gagneront du terrain par le nord-ouest. Sur les Pays de la Loire, malgré quelques éclaircies, les nuages seront nombreux. Le vent de sud-ouest soufflera jusqu'à 90 km/h sur les côtes de la Manche.

**Nord-Picardie, Ile de France.**
Le matin, il pleuvra sur le Nord. Dans l'après-midi, les pluies gagneront la Picardie. Sur l'Ile-de-France, les nuages seront présents, mais on aura tout de même quelques rayons de soleil. Le vent de sud-ouest soufflera jusqu'à 90 km/h sur la côte d'Opale.

**Nord-Est, Bourgogne, Franche-Comté.**
La grisaille sera fortement présente au lever du jour avec des nuages bas, des brumes et des brouillards. L'après-midi, de belles éclaircies se développeront au sud de ces régions.

**Poitou-Charentes, Centre, Limousin.**
Après la dissipation des brouillards matinaux, le soleil brillera généreusement. Toutefois, les passages nuageux seront plus nombreux sur le nord de ces régions.

**Aquitaine, Midi-Pyrénées.**
Les bancs de brume et de brouillard seront nombreux en fin de nuit. Il se dissiperont en cours de matinée et laisseront place à un grand soleil. Les températures, parfois proches de 0°C le matin, seront comprises entre 10°C et 13°C l'après-midi.

**Auvergne, Rhône-Alpes.**
Le matin, le ciel sera souvent nuageux et brumeux. L'après-midi, malgré quelques brouillards parfois tenaces sur le Lyonnais, le soleil sera largement dominant. Les températures resteront fraîches avec 7°C au maximum.

**Pourtout méditerranéen, Corse.**
Les nuages présents le matin sur le Languedoc-Rousillon et la Corse n'empêcheront pas un soleil radieux de briller sur toutes ces régions. Températures agréables comprises entre 11°C et 14°C l'après-midi.

| faible | light |
|--------|-------|
| malgré | in spite of |
| l'éclaircie (f) | bright interval |
| nombreux/nombreuses | numerous |
| souffler | to blow |
| la côte | coast |
| la brume | mist |

## ACTIVITY 16

Look through the weather forecast and spot the French for:

| | | | | | | | |
|---|---------|---|--------|---|------|---|-----|
| 1 | Brittany | 3 | clouds | 5 | wind | 7 | sun |
| 2 | weather | 4 | today | 6 | rain | 8 | fog |

## ACTIVITY 17

A Look through the weather forecast for Brittany/the Loire Valley/Normandy, but do not attempt to understand every word. Concentrate on those you recognize and see how much you can guess from the context. The following activity will help you.

B Choose the most appropriate description for each part of the Brittany/Loire Valley/Normandy area.

1 In Brittany and Normandy, it will
   a be sunny   b snow   c rain.
2 The Loire Valley will be
   a very cloudy   b very sunny   c very foggy.
3 The Channel coast will be
   a hot and sunny   b very windy   c very cold.

## ACTIVITY 18

Find the right description for each of the following areas.
1 Nord-Picardie, Île-de-France
2 Aquitaine, Midi-Pyrénées
3 Auvergne, Rhône-Alpes

A

Ce matin, il pleuvait. Maintenant, il ne pleut plus, mais il y a beaucoup de vent.

B

Ce matin, il y avait des nuages et du brouillard. Maintenant, il y a un peu de soleil, mais il ne fait pas chaud.

C

Ce matin, il y avait du brouillard et il faisait froid. Maintenant ça va mieux, le soleil brille et il fait moins froid.

## ACTIVITY 19

Describe the weather in the Mediterranean area/Corsica. Use the descriptions from activity 18 to help you.

### ⓐ FÉLICITATIONS!
### CONGRATULATIONS!

Aujourd'hui il pleut. Il fait froid. Ça ne va pas …

| | |
|---|---|
| **les nouvelles** (f) | news |
| **le concours** | competition |
| **gagner** | to win [*also* to earn] |
| **le premier prix** | first prize |
| **la remise des prix** | award ceremony |

### ACTIVITY 20

Listen to the recording, then read the following summaries. Which one is the most accurate?

A Today is the first day of spring – Madame Delaine's favourite season – but Alexandra is feeling miserable because she has not heard from Jérôme for a while. Madame Delaine asks her husband to make her a coffee, when Alexandra's mobile phone rings. It's Jérôme calling from Marseille. Alexandra is very pleased. They decide to go and spend a long weekend in Paris in April. Alexandra has a friend who lives near the Eiffel Tower, and they could go and stay with her.

B It's cold and wet today, and Alexandra is feeling miserable. Madame Delaine tries to cheer her up and tells her it's springtime and the weather will get better soon. While Monsieur Delaine makes her a coffee, the phone rings, and Alexandra becomes very excited. Before she has time to ring her parents to tell them she has just won an award, she receives a call from Jérôme and tells him her good news. Alexandra asks Jérôme if he'd like to go to the award ceremony with her, and they make plans to go and stay with a friend of Alexandra's. All is well.

## ACTIVITY 21

Who says each phrase? Alexandra or Jérôme?

1 Félicitations!
2 Je suis à Marseille.
3 Il pleut. Il fait froid.
4 Tu peux venir avec moi?
5 Il y a du soleil, mais il y a du vent.
6 On pourrait passer le week-end à Paris.
7 Je rentre ce soir. Tu veux dîner avec moi?
8 J'ai une copine qui habite près de la tour Eiffel.

## ACTIVITY 22

After speaking to Jérôme, Alexandra called her father. Imagine and practise their conversation. To help you, adapt what she said to Jérôme, and add her father's side of the conversation.

## STORY TRANSCRIPT

| | |
|---|---|
| Mme Delaine | Ça va, Alexandra? |
| Alexandra | Ça ne va pas très bien. Il pleut. Il fait froid et … |
| Mme Delaine | Mais il va bientôt faire beau. C'est le printemps, la saison que je préfère! |
| Alexandra | Et je n'ai pas de nouvelles de Jérôme … |
| Mme Delaine | Ah, ma pauvre Alexandra. Tu veux un café? |
| Alexandra | Oui, je veux bien. Merci. |
| Mme Delaine | Jean-Luc, un café pour Alexandra. |
| Alexandra | Allô? Oui. Ce n'est pas possible! C'est quel jour? À quelle heure? D'accord. Merci et au revoir. |
| | Oh, là, là! Oh, là, là! Je dois appeler mes parents! Vite! Ah, zut! Allô? Jérôme!!! Ça va? Tu es où? À Marseille!!! Il fait beau à Marseille? Il y a du vent, ah! Moi, ça va très, très bien. Tu sais, les articles que j'ai écrits pour le concours de jeunes journalistes … J'ai gagné le premier prix! Je suis super contente! Je dois aller à Paris pour la remise des prix. Tu peux venir avec moi? J'aimerais bien, oui. C'est le 14 avril. J'ai une copine qui habite près de la tour Eiffel. On pourrait aller chez elle. D'accord. À ce soir. Grosses bises. |
| Mme Delaine | Voici ton café. Ça va? |
| Alexandra | Oui, très, très bien! Merci. |

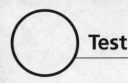

# Test

Now it's time to test your progress in Unit 12.

1 Work out the anagrams to complete the following weather phrases.

|    |           |                  |
|----|-----------|------------------|
| 1  | pulte     | il _____        |
| 2  | genie     | il _____        |
| 3  | aube      | il fait _____   |
| 4  | chadu     | il fait _____   |
| 5  | dorif     | il fait _____   |
| 6  | vaimasu   | il fait _____   |
| 7  | tenv      | il y a du _____ |
| 8  | lesoil    | il y a du _____ |
| 9  | rolubilard| il y a du _____ |
| 10 | eugans    | il y a des _____|

**10**

2 **Vrai ou faux?**

1 Il neige en été.
2 Il fait très chaud en hiver.
3 Quand il pleut, il y a des nuages.
4 Quand il neige, il ne fait pas chaud.
5 En automne, il pleut et il y a du vent.
6 Au printemps, il neige et il fait très froid.
7 À minuit, le ciel est bleu et le soleil brille.
8 Quand il y a du brouillard, il fait très chaud.

**8**

3 Match each of the French phrases below with the right English equivalent.

| 1 il doit …         | a she would like … |
|---------------------|--------------------|
| 2 je peux …         | b I'd quite like … |
| 3 elle veut …       | c she'd rather …   |
| 4 tu devrais …      | d you should …     |
| 5 on pourrait …     | e she wants …      |
| 6 elle voudrait …   | f we could …       |
| 7 j'aimerais bien … | g he must …        |
| 8 elle préférerait …| h I can …          |

**8**

4  Use **qui** or **que** to complete the following sentences.

    1  Écoute la pluie _____ tombe.
    2  Regarde le soleil _____ brille.
    3  J'admire le tableau _____ tu peins.
    4  L'été est la saison _____ je préfère.
    5  Le gâteau _____ j'ai mangé était délicieux.
    6  L'hiver est la saison _____ j'aime le moins.
    7  Picasso est le peintre _____ j'admire le plus.
    8  La Provence est une région _____ j'aime beaucoup.
    9  J'ai une sœur _____ compose des musiques de films.
  10  J'aimerais aller à l'exposition _____ commence
      aujourd'hui.

**10**

5  Put this dialogue back in the right order. The first sentence
   comes first.

    1  Il y a une exposition intéressante au théâtre. Tu veux
      venir avec moi?
    2  Non, samedi je ne peux pas. Je dois aller voir mon père.
    3  J'aimerais bien, oui. Tu veux y aller quand?
    4  À onze heures devant le théâtre?
    5  On se retrouve à quelle heure?
    6  Tu es libre samedi après-midi?
    7  D'accord. À dimanche, alors.
    8  Et dimanche matin?
    9  Dimanche ça va, oui.

**9**

6  In the following text, **que/qu'** is missing in five different
   places. Correct it.

   Richard Lapierre est un cuisinier j'admire depuis
   longtemps. La première fois je suis allée dans son
   restaurant, j'en ai parlé à tous mes amis. Le plat je préfère
   est une soupe de poissons il prépare avec des fruits de mer
   et des petits légumes de son jardin. C'est un plat je trouve
   vraiment délicieux.

**5**

**TOTAL SCORE**    **50**

If you scored less than 40, go through the dialogues and the
Language Building sections again before completing the
Summary on page 180.

# Summary 12

 Now try this final test summarizing the main points covered in this unit.

How would you:
1 say it's hot and sunny?
2 say it's cold and it's snowing?
3 say it's windy and it's raining?
4 say you'd like to go to the cinema?
5 say you'd rather go to the theatre?
6 ask a friend if she wants to come with you?
7 say you can't – you have to work?
8 suggest you meet outside the station?
9 say you could have lunch in the garden?

## REVISION

Before moving on to Unit 13, imagine a telephone conversation with a French-speaking friend living in a different part of the world. How would each of you describe the weather? Make the conversation as long as you can by using as much as possible of the language you have learnt. For example, once you have described the weather where you are, say which season you like best and which you like least. You could also end the conversation by saying where you would like to go and why. (Have another look at the second half of Dialogue 3 to help you.)

# All in the past
# Le passé

---

> **OBJECTIVES**
>
> In this unit you'll learn how to:
> - ✓ talk about past experiences
> - ✓ describe past holidays
> - ✓ express emotions
>
> And cover the following grammar and language:
> - ✓ **en/au/aux** + names of countries
> - ✓ verb + verb constructions
> - ✓ **il y a** + expression of time
> - ✓ the position of pronouns

## LEARNING FRENCH 13

Good language learners take risks and don't mind making mistakes – in gender, verb endings, or word order, for example. This is inevitable, and it often doesn't affect communication. Taking risks and making mistakes is the only way to make progress. When you have completed an activity, it is important you check what you have done. You need to evaluate your strengths and weaknesses regularly so that you know where you need to do more work and can improve accordingly.

 Now start the recording for Unit 13.

# 13.1 I've worked abroad

## J'ai travaillé à l'étranger

**ACTIVITY 1** is on the recording.

**ACTIVITY 2**

Which of the sentences apply to Olivier's stay in Scotland?

1 Il est resté six mois.
2 Il a travaillé dans un café.
3 Il a fait très beau et très chaud.
4 Il a aimé la campagne écossaise.
5 Il n'a pas beaucoup parlé anglais.
6 Il n'a jamais rencontré d'étudiants.
7 Il avait une chambre à l'université.
8 Il a rencontré des gens très sympas.

**DIALOGUE 1**

○ Vous êtes allé aux États-Unis? En Grande-Bretagne?

■ Je ne suis jamais allé aux États-Unis, mais je suis allé au Canada et j'ai passé six mois en Écosse.

○ Qu'est-ce que vous avez fait? Vous avez travaillé?

■ Oui, j'ai travaillé comme serveur dans un café.

○ Vous avez aimé l'Écosse?

■ Je n'ai pas aimé le climat. On a eu beaucoup de neige et il a fait très froid. Mais c'est un très beau pays, la campagne écossaise est très belle, et les Écossais sont très sympas.

○ Vous étiez où exactement?

■ J'étais à Glasgow. Je partageais un appartement avec des étudiants. J'ai rencontré beaucoup de gens très intéressants, et nous avons discuté de choses passionnantes. J'aimerais bien y retourner.

| VOCABULARY | |
|---|---|
| **le climat** | climate |
| **le pays** | country |
| **la campagne** | countryside |
| **partager** | to share |
| **l'étudiant(e)** | student |
| **rencontrer** | to meet |
| **discuter** | to discuss |
| **la chose** | thing |
| **espérer** | to hope |

## ☑ *en/au/aux* + names of countries

When talking about countries, French doesn't differentiate between 'in' and 'to'. Use **en** with feminine country names, **au** with masculine, and **aux** with plural:

| | |
|---|---|
| la Chine | Ma sœur est partie **en** Chine. |
| | My sister went off to China. |
| la Tunisie | Mon frère s'est marié **en** Tunisie. |
| | My brother got married in Tunisia. |
| le Liban | Mon mari est né **au** Liban. |
| | My husband was born in Lebanon. |
| le Danemark | Nous sommes allés **au** Danemark. We went to Denmark. |
| les Antilles | Je pars **aux** Antilles. I am off to the West Indies. |

(*f*)

| | |
|---|---|
| **l'Allemagne** Germany | **la Grande-Bretagne** Great Britain |
| **l'Angleterre** England | **l'Irlande** Ireland |
| **la Belgique** Belgium | **l'Italie** Italy |
| **l'Écosse** Scotland | **la Grèce** Greece |
| **l'Espagne** Spain | **la Suède** Sweden |
| **la France** France | **la Suisse** Switzerland |

(*m*)

**le Canada** Canada
**le Japon** Japan
**le Maroc** Morocco
**le pays de Galles** Wales
**le Portugal** Portugal
**le Sénégal** Senegal

(*pl.*)

**les États-Unis** the United States
**les Pays-Bas** the Netherlands

### ACTIVITY 3

Complete the following sentences.

1 Christophe Colomb est né _____ Italie en 1450 et il est mort _____ Espagne en 1506.

2 Léonard de Vinci est né _____ Italie en 1452 et il est mort _____ France en 1519.

3 Marie Stuart est née _____ Écosse en 1542 et elle est morte _____ Angleterre en 1587.

4 Greta Garbo est née _____ Suède en 1905 et elle est morte _____ États-Unis en 1990.

5 Richard Burton est né _____ pays de Galles en 1925 et il est mort _____ Suisse en 1984.

🎧 Now do activities 4 and 5 on the recording.

## J'adore faire du ski

(🎧) **ACTIVITY 6** is on the recording.

**ACTIVITY 7**

Who does each of the following sentences describe – Thierry or Rachel?

| | |
|---|---|
| 1 loves skiing | 6 had a great holiday |
| 2 hates skiing | 7 didn't like the hotel |
| 3 got very bored | 8 says the pistes were too busy |
| 4 looks very well | 9 has just returned from the Alps |
| 5 had a terrible time | 10 went to the Pyrenees 3 or 4 years ago |

**DIALOGUE 2**

○ Salut! Tu as l'air en pleine forme. Tu rentres de vacances?

■ Oui, je suis allé faire du ski dans les Alpes.

○ C'était bien? Tu as passé de bonnes vacances?

■ Oui, c'était super. J'adore faire du ski. Pas toi?

○ Moi, je déteste ça. Je suis allée dans les Pyrénées il y a trois ou quatre ans. J'ai passé de très mauvaises vacances.

■ Qu'est-ce qui s'est passé? Tu t'es cassé la jambe?

○ Non, mais il y avait beaucoup de monde sur les pistes. Ce n'était pas drôle du tout. Je me suis ennuyée.

■ Qu'est-ce que tu as fait?

○ Je suis restée dans mon hôtel, j'ai dormi, j'ai regardé la télé.

■ C'était un bon hôtel, j'espère!

○ Non, pas vraiment. Les gens de l'hôtel n'étaient pas sympas. Il y avait beaucoup de bruit, et ce n'était pas très propre.

■ C'est dommage! Moi, j'adore aller aux sports d'hiver.

---

| VOCABULARY | |
|---|---|
| **les vacances** (f) | holiday, vacation |
| **faire du ski** | to ski |
| **passer de bonnes vacances** | to have a good holiday |
| **beaucoup de monde** | a lot of people |
| **pas du tout** | not at all |
| **s'ennuyer** | to be bored |
| **le bruit** | noise |
| **propre** | clean |

## ✅ Verb + verb constructions

When two French verbs follow each other directly, the second one is in the infinitive.

J'adore **lire**. I love reading.
Je déteste **conduire**. I hate driving.
Je ne vais pas **faire** la vaisselle. I'm not going to do the washing up.
Je voudrais **téléphoner**. I would like to make a phone call.
Il n'aimait pas **faire** du sport. He didn't like practising sport.

## ✅ *il y a* + expression of time

In French, there is no equivalent of 'ago'. To express this, the phrase **il y a** is used, followed by a time expression:

Je me suis mariée **il y a dix ans**. I got married ten years ago.
Elle a divorcé **il y a six mois**. She got divorced six months ago.
Il est mort **il y a trois semaines**. He died three weeks ago.
Nous sommes arrivés **il y a deux jours**. We arrived two days ago.
Vous avez mangé **il y a une heure**. You ate an hour ago.
Ils ont téléphoné **il y a cinq minutes**. They rang five minutes ago.

---

### ACTIVITY 8

Complete the two lists below to describe what you love and what you hate doing. You can use the verbs in the box and/or add your own.

J'adore ...              Je déteste ...

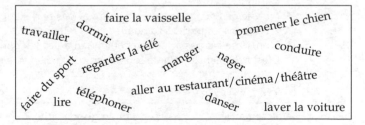

faire la vaisselle
travailler   dormir   promener le chien
          regarder la télé   conduire
faire du sport   manger   nager
lire   téléphoner   aller au restaurant/cinéma/théâtre
   danser   laver la voiture

 Now do activities 9 and 10 on the recording.

## 13.3 I'm feeling depressed
## Je n'ai pas le moral

🎧 **ACTIVITY 11** is on the recording.

**ACTIVITY 12**

Complete the summary.

Pierre feels _____ because he has had an _____ with Rachel. It happened a _____ ago. Pierre was very busy and in a _____ mood. _____ was getting on his nerves, so he told her to _____. And she did. He has not _____ her nor spoken to her since then. His friend thinks the situation is _____ , and Pierre should _____ to her. He advises him to _____ her immediately.

**DIALOGUE 3**

○ Qu'est-ce qu'il y a ? Ça ne va pas?
■ Je n'ai pas le moral.
○ Pourquoi?
■ Parce que je me suis disputé avec Rachel.
○ Quand?
■ Il y a une semaine.
○ Qu'est-ce qui s'est passé?
■ J'avais beaucoup de travail, j'étais de mauvaise humeur. Elle m'énervait. Je lui ai dit de partir, et … elle est partie.
○ Et tu l'as revue?
■ Non, je ne l'ai pas revue et je ne lui ai pas parlé.
○ Tu devrais lui parler! Tu ne lui as pas téléphoné?
■ Non, je ne l'ai pas appelée et elle ne m'a pas téléphoné.
○ C'est ridicule! Appelle-la tout de suite.

---

| VOCABULARY | |
|---|---|
| **avoir le moral** | to be in good spirits |
| **se disputer** | to have an argument |
| **être de mauvaise humeur** | to be in a bad mood |
| **énerver** | to annoy |
| **dire** | to say |
| **revoir** | to see again |
| **ridicule** | ridiculous |

## ✓ The position of pronouns

Both direct and indirect pronouns normally come before the verb:

Vous **le voyez** tous les jours. You see him everyday.
Nous **lui souhaitons** bonne chance. We wish her/him good luck.

When the verb is in a compound tense (like the *passé composé*), the pronoun comes before all parts of the verb:

Nous **leur avons donné** de l'argent. We gave them some money.

When there are two verbs, the pronoun comes before the second verb:

Je **vais lui téléphoner**. I'm going to ring him/her.
Il **devrait les acheter**. He should buy them.

There is one exception. When the verb is in the imperative, the pronoun comes after the verb and a hyphen is added:

**Donne-moi** ton numéro. Give me your number.

## ✓ Ça va!

Je suis en pleine forme. I'm in good shape.
Je suis de bonne humeur. I'm in a good mood.
Je suis heureux/heureuse. I'm happy.
Je suis content(e). I'm pleased.
Je m'amuse bien. I'm having a good time.
C'est drôle. It's funny.

## ✓ Ça ne va pas!

Je suis fatigué(e). I'm tired.
Je suis de mauvaise humeur. I'm in a bad mood.
Je n'ai pas le moral. I'm feeling depressed.
Je suis triste. I'm sad.
Je m'ennuie. I'm bored.
C'est énervant. It's annoying.

---

### ACTIVITY 13

Find the right place in the sentences for each of the pronouns.

1 (lui)      (Tu/as/écrit?)
2 (lui)      (Non, je/ne/ai/pas/écrit.)
3 (lui)      (Tu/devrais/écrire! Tu/as/son/adresse?)
4 (la/l')    (Non, je/ne/ai/pas.)
5 (lui) (te)  (Téléphone-/Je/vais/donner/son/numéro!)
6 (le/l') (la)  (Oui, je/ai. Appelle-/tout/de/suite.)

 Now do activities 14 and 15 on the recording.

DOSSIER

# La France

## PREMIÈRE DESTINATION MONDIALE

La France a accueilli 67 millions de touristes étrangers en 1997. [ … ] La France serait donc toujours la première destination mondiale, devant l'Espagne, les États-Unis, l'Italie et la Chine. Ce résultat s'explique bien sûr par les atouts propres à la France en matière touristique et culturelle, mais aussi par sa situation géographique, qui en fait un passage obligé pour les nombreux touristes qui se rendent en Espagne ou en Italie. La France est cependant dépassée par l'Espagne en ce qui concerne le nombre de longs séjours effectués (quatre nuits et plus) et par les États-Unis en ce qui concerne les recettes touristiques.

L'Île-de-France a accueilli à elle seule 36,2 millions de touristes, soit 8% de plus qu'en 1996. 55% étaient des étrangers; les Britanniques représentaient 17%, les Américains 12%, les Allemands 10%, les Italiens 8% et les Japonais 8%. [ … ]

| | |
|---|---|
| **mondial(e)** | world |
| **accueillir** | to welcome, to receive |
| **le résultat** | result |
| **s'explique** | [*here* =] can be explained |
| **l'atout** (*m*) | asset |
| **propre à** | characteristic of |
| **en matière touristique et culturelle** | as far as tourism and culture are concerned |
| **un passage obligé** | a necessary route |
| **se rendre** | to go |
| **cependant** | however |
| **dépassé(e)** | overtaken |
| **en ce qui concerne le nombre de …** | as far as the number of … is concerned |
| **le séjour** | stay |
| **effectué(e)** | made, undertaken |
| **la recette** | revenue [*also* recipe] |
| **l'Île-de-France** | the Paris area |
| **soit** | that is [*from* être] |

**ACTIVITY 16**

Look through the article and spot the names of:

1 five countries   2 five nationalities

**ACTIVITY 17**

Choose the right explanation for each of the following points.

1 La France a accueilli 67 millions de touristes étrangers en 1997.
   a 67 million French people travelled abroad in 1997.
   b 67 million foreign tourists came to France in 1997.

2 La France serait donc toujours la première destination mondiale.
   a More tourists visit France than any other country in the world.
   b France has finally become the most popular holiday destination.

3 Ce résultat s'explique [ … ] par sa situation géographique qui en fait un passage obligé pour les [ … ] touristes qui se rendent en Espagne ou en Italie.
   a Many tourists come to France because they have to go through it on their way to Spain or Italy.
   b Many tourists would rather go to France than to Spain or Italy.

4 La France est dépassée par l'Espagne en ce qui concerne le nombre de longs séjours effectués (quatre nuits et plus).
   a More tourists stay in Spain for at least four days than in France.
   b More tourists stay in France for at least four days than in Spain.

5 La France est dépassée [ … ] par les États-Unis en ce qui concerne les recettes touristiques.
   a The United States makes more money from tourism than France.
   b France makes more money from tourism than the United States.

6 L'Île-de-France a accueilli 36,2 millions de touristes, soit 8% de plus qu'en 1996.
   a More tourists than the previous year visited the Paris area in 1997.
   b In 1996, 8% more tourists visited Paris than any other area.

## LA REMISE DES PRIX
## THE AWARD CEREMONY

C'est le 14 avril. Alexandra est à Paris pour la remise des prix.

| | |
|---|---|
| fier/fière | proud |
| encourager | to encourage |
| le rédacteur/la rédactrice en chef | editor in chief |
| raconter (des histoires) | to tell (stories) |
| savoir | to know |
| découvrir | to discover |
| répondre | to answer |
| poser des questions | to ask questions |

### ACTIVITY 18

Do this activity first without listening to the story again. Which of the following sentences do you think Alexandra said? Then listen again to check your answers.

1 Je suis très heureuse.
2 Je voudrais les remercier.
3 J'ai toujours été très curieuse.
4 Mon père ne m'a jamais aidée.
5 Je ne voulais pas être journaliste.
6 J'aimais raconter des histoires à mes copines.
7 À l'âge de dix ans, je voulais être rédactrice en chef.
8 Je voudrais dire que j'ai beaucoup de chance.
9 Je ne pose jamais de questions indiscrètes.
10 J'adore écrire et c'est mon métier!

## ACTIVITY 19

Complete this article about Alexandra.

Alexandra Coubard dit qu'elle a beaucoup de chance. Elle adore _____ des gens, elle _____ poser des _____, elle adore _____, et c'est son _____!

Elle a toujours voulu _____ journaliste. Quand elle _____ petite, elle _____ raconter des _____ à ses copines. À dix ans, elle _____ rédactrice en chef du magazine de son école. Elle _____ toujours tout savoir: elle _____ ses copains et copines, ses professeurs et les parents. Et elle découvrait déjà des secrets ...

Hier soir, Alexandra _____ ses parents, ses professeurs, son rédacteur en chef et toutes les personnes qu'elle a interviewées. Elle est très sympathique, et en plus c'est une bonne journaliste. Nous _____ souhaitons bonne chance!

## ACTIVITY 20

Imagine some of the things Alexandra said to the editor in chief when she was interviewed for her first job in journalism.

## STORY TRANSCRIPT

Alexandra   Je vous remercie pour ce prix. Je suis très heureuse et très fière. Ce soir, je pense à toutes les personnes qui m'ont aidée et encouragée: mes parents, mes professeurs et mon rédacteur en chef. Je voudrais les remercier.

J'ai toujours été très curieuse, et j'ai toujours voulu être journaliste. Quand j'étais petite, j'aimais raconter des histoires à mes copines. À l'âge de dix ans, j'étais rédactrice en chef du magazine de mon école. Je voulais toujours tout savoir et tout comprendre: j'interviewais mes copains et copines, les professeurs et les parents. Et je découvrais déjà des secrets!

Ce soir, je pense aussi à toutes les personnes que j'ai interviewées, à toutes les personnes qui ont répondu à mes questions. Je les remercie.

Pour terminer, je voudrais dire que j'ai beaucoup de chance. J'adore rencontrer des gens, j'adore poser des questions, j'adore écrire, et c'est mon métier! Merci, tout le monde!

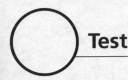

# Test

Now it's time to test your progress in Unit 13.

1 Put the names of each of the following countries in the appropriate column. ($^1/_2$ point for each correct answer.)

| On va en … | On va au … | On va aux … | |
| --- | --- | --- | --- |
| l'Angleterre | l'Écosse | l'Inde | le Pakistan |
| les Antilles | l'Espagne | l'Irlande | les Pays-Bas |
| la Belgique | les États-Unis | le Kenya | le pays de Galles |
| le Canada | la France | le Japon | la Suisse |
| le Chili | la Grande-Bretagne | le Maroc | la Tunisie |

**10**

2 Find the pairs of opposites.

| | |
| --- | --- |
| né | de bonne humeur |
| bon | être triste |
| arriver | partir |
| adorer | mauvais |
| vacances | divorcer |
| se marier | s'amuser |
| s'ennuyer | détester |
| avoir le moral | fatigué |
| en pleine forme | travail |
| de mauvaise humeur | mort |

**10**

3 Insert the words below in the right places to complete the following episode of Pierre and Rachel's story.

**l' / l' / l' / la / le / leur / lui / lui / lui / lui**

Ça va mieux entre Pierre et Rachel.
Il/ne/a/pas/encore/revue, mais/il/a/parlé au téléphone.
Ce n'est pas Pierre qui/a/appelée, c'est Rachel
qui/a/téléphoné.
Elle/a/dit/qu'elle/voulait/voir.
Il/a/dit/qu'il/voulait/voir.
Alors, il/a/invitée/au/restaurant/ce/soir.
Je/souhaite/bonne/chance!

**10**

4 What did Halima Bedoui say to the hospital nurse at 11.10 on 10 February 2000? Complete the text.

le 10 février 1990: Halima Bedoui arrive en France.
le 10 février 1997: elle rencontre son mari.
le 10 août 1999: elle se marie.
le 3 février 2000: elle arrive dans les Alpes.
le 8 février 2000: elle se casse la jambe.
à 10 heures 10, le 10 février 2000: elle téléphone à son mari.
à 11 heures, le 10 février 2000: son mari arrive à l'hôpital.

Je suis arrivée en France _____ dix ans. J'ai
rencontré mon mari _____ trois ans. Je me suis
mariée _____ six mois. Je _____ arrivée dans
les Alpes _____ . Je _____ cassé la jambe
_____ . J'_____ à mon mari
_____ . Mon mari _____ à l'hôpital
_____ .

| 11 |

5 Find the right reply from a–h for the questions 1–8.

1 Vous avez travaillé à l'étranger?
2 Qu'est-ce que vous avez fait?
3 C'était bien comme travail?
4 Vous étiez où exactement?
5 Le café était bon?
6 Vous avez rencontré beaucoup d'Américains?
7 Vous avez aimé les États-Unis?
8 Vous aimeriez y retourner?

a J'étais à Seattle.
b C'est un pays passionnant.
c Oui, mais pas pour travailler.
d J'ai travaillé dans un bureau.
e J'ai passé un an aux États-Unis.
f Je ne sais pas, parce que je n'en bois jamais.
g Ce n'était pas très intéressant, je me suis ennuyée.
h Oui, je partageais un appartement avec des étudiants qui avaient beaucoup d'amis.

| 9 |

TOTAL SCORE | 50 |

If you scored less than 40, go through the dialogues and the
Language Building sections again before completing the
Summary on page 194.

# Summary 13

 Now try this final test summarizing the main points covered in this unit.

How would you:
1  say you've never been to Wales?
2  say you spent three months in France?
3  say your sister was born in the United States?
4  ask a friend whether she had a good holiday?
5  say you were bored because you didn't meet any nice people?
6  say your son got married six months ago?
7  say you had an argument with your mother?
8  say it's because you were in a bad mood?

## REVISION

Before moving on, imagine telling a friend about the last time you went away. Where did you go? How long did you stay? What was the weather like? Did you have a good time? What did you do? Make sure you make the most of the language you have learnt so far, and pay particular attention to past tenses, dates, and lengths of time. Also add a few sentences describing how you felt (were you tired? in a good/bad mood? were you happy/sad/depressed, etc.?).

# The world of work
## Au travail

---

**OBJECTIVES**

In this unit you'll learn how to:

- ✓ make telephone calls
- ✓ leave a message
- ✓ introduce yourself
- ✓ explain why you're calling
- ✓ arrange a meeting

And cover the following grammar and language:

- ✓ ways of expressing the future (the present tense + time expression; **aller** + infinitive; the future tense)
- ✓ the future of regular **-er** and **-ir** verbs
- ✓ the future of **être**
- ✓ **venir de** + infinitive
- ✓ the future of regular **-re** verbs
- ✓ the future of irregular verbs

---

### LEARNING FRENCH 14

Now you have acquired the basics of French, you need to learn to make the most of what you know in order to extend your listening and reading skills. For example, always try to see how much the context can help you understand. Train yourself to ignore unimportant words so that you can get the gist of what you're hearing or reading. Learn to recognize common patterns between French and English to help you guess unfamiliar words.

Now start the recording for Unit 14.

## Can I leave a message?

## Je peux laisser un message?

🔊 **ACTIVITY 1** is on the recording.

**ACTIVITY 2**

Complete the following sentences using 'Nathalie Pavy' or 'Philippe Perrin'.

1 _____ travaille pour les éditions du Bertin.
2 _____ téléphone aux éditions du Bertin.
3 _____ voudrait parler à _____ .
4 _____ est en réunion.
5 _____ ne sera pas là cet après-midi.
6 _____ sera de retour demain matin.
7 _____ laisse un message pour _____.
8 _____ rappellera demain.

**DIALOGUE 1**

▼ Allô? Les éditions du Bertin, bonjour.
○ Bonjour. Je voudrais parler à Nathalie Pavy, s'il vous plaît.
▼ Ne quittez pas, je vous la passe.
■ Allô?
○ Bonjour. Est-ce que je pourrais parler à Nathalie Pavy?
■ Je regrette. Madame Pavy est en réunion. C'est de la part de qui?
○ Je m'appelle Philippe Perrin. Elle sera là cet après-midi?
■ Non, pas cet après-midi. Elle sera de retour demain matin. Vous voulez laisser un message?
○ Je la rappellerai demain, mais vous pouvez lui dire que j'ai appelé?
■ D'accord, je lui dirai.
○ C'est très gentil. Merci. Au revoir.

---

| VOCABULARY | |
|---|---|
| l'édition (f) | publication |
| ne quittez pas | hold the line |
| passer | to put through |
| la réunion | meeting |
| être en réunion | to be in a meeting |
| c'est de la part de qui? | who's calling? |
| de retour | back |
| rappeler | to call back |

## ✓ The future tense

In French, the idea of future can be expressed in different ways.

1 You can use the present tense with an appropriate time expression when talking about plans:

Je ne **suis** pas libre demain. I'm not/I won't be available tomorrow.
Nous **partons** en vacances lundi. We're going on holiday on Monday.

2 You can use **aller** + infinitive to express what's about to happen:

Elle **va téléphoner** au patron. She's going to ring the boss.

3 You can use the future tense – especially when making predictions (as in weather forecasts or horoscopes) or stating a fact about the future:

Il **neigera** toute la journée. It'll snow all day.
Je **gagnerai** beaucoup d'argent. I will earn a lot of money.

## ✓ The future of regular -er and -ir verbs

To form the future of regular -er and -ir verbs, you need to add the following endings to the infinitive:

| **laisser**, 'to leave' | | **finir**, 'to finish' | |
|---|---|---|---|
| je **laisserai** | nous **laisserons** | je **finirai** | nous **finirons** |
| tu **laisseras** | vous **laisserez** | tu **finiras** | vous **finirez** |
| il/elle/on **laissera** | ils/elles **laisseront** | il/elle/on **finira** | ils/elles **finiront** |

## ✓ The future of être

To form the future of **être**, add the regular endings to the stem **ser-**:

| je **serai** | nous **serons** |
|---|---|
| tu **seras** | vous **serez** |
| il/elle/on **sera** | ils/elles **seront** |

### ACTIVITY 3

Complete the conversation using the future tense.

| | |
|---|---|
| Secrétaire | Vous pouvez rappeler Madame Ledantec? |
| Nathalie Pavy | Je la _____ plus tard. Les Américains sont là et nous _____ en réunion jusqu'à midi et demi. |
| Secrétaire | Vous _____ là cet après-midi? |
| Nathalie Pavy | Non, je ne _____ pas là. |
| Secrétaire | Vous _____ de retour demain matin? |
| Nathalie Pavy | Oui. Vous pouvez finir ces lettres pour ce soir? |
| Secrétaire | Oui, je les _____ cet après-midi. |

🎧 Now do activities 4 and 5 on the recording.

# Ici Nathalie Pavy

**ACTIVITY 6** is on the recording.

**ACTIVITY 7**

Correct the statements which are false.

| | | |
|---|---|---|
| 1 | Philippe Perrin is a translator. | V / F |
| 2 | He wrote to Nathalie Pavy last month. | V / F |
| 3 | Nathalie Pavy never received his letter. | V / F |
| 4 | Nathalie Pavy now deals with illustrators. | V / F |
| 5 | Philippe Perrin's file is with the new arts director. | V / F |

**DIALOGUE 2**

▼ Allô. Les éditions du Bertin. Bonjour.

■ Bonjour. Je voudrais parler à Nathalie Pavy, s'il vous plaît.

▼ Son poste est occupé. Vous voulez patienter?

■ Oui, bien sûr.

○ Allô. Ici Nathalie Pavy.

■ Allô, bonjour. Je m'appelle Philippe Perrin. Je suis illustrateur, et je vous ai écrit le mois dernier …

○ Monsieur Perrin, oui, j'ai bien reçu votre courrier, mais je ne m'occupe plus des illustrateurs. Je viens de transmettre votre dossier au nouveau directeur artistique. Je vais vous donner ses coordonnées. Il s'appelle Thierry Martinez, et vous pouvez le contacter au 01 43 42 55 77.

■ Le 01 43 42 55 77. Je vous remercie.

○ Je vous en prie.

---

### VOCABULARY

| | |
|---|---|
| **le poste** | extension |
| **occupé(e)** | busy, engaged |
| **patienter** | to hold (the line) |
| **l'illustrateur** (*m*) | illustrator |
| **recevoir** | to receive |
| **le courrier** | letter |
| **transmettre** | to pass on |
| **le dossier** | file |
| **le directeur artistique** | art director, artistic director |
| **contacter** | to contact |
| **les coordonnées** (*f pl.*) | details |
| **je vous en prie** | you're welcome |

## ✓ *venir de* + infinitive

You can use **venir de** + infinitive to say that something has just happened:

> Je **viens de transmettre** votre dossier au nouveau directeur artistique.
> I've just passed your file to the new art director.
> Elle **vient de sortir**. She has just gone out.

## ✓ Useful telephone phrases

> **Je lui dirai.** I'll tell him/her.
> **Ne quittez pas.** Hold on.
> **C'est noté.** I've made a note.
> **C'est de la part de qui?** Who's calling?
> **Je vous le/la passe.** I'll put you through.
> **Merci d'avoir appelé.** Thank you for calling.
> **Son poste est occupé.** His/Her line is busy.
> **Il/Elle est en réunion.** He/She is in a meeting.
> **Vous voulez patienter?** Do you wish to hold?
> **Je voudrais parler à X.** I'd like to speak to X.
> **Je peux laisser un message?** Can I leave a message?
> **J'ai bien reçu votre courrier.** I have received your letter.
> **Je vais vous donner ses coordonnées.** I'll give you his/her details.
> **Vous voulez laisser un message?** Do you want to leave a message?

### ACTIVITY 8

Put the following dialogue back in the right order.

1 Société BGL. Bonjour.
2 Je lui dirai. C'est noté.
3 Non merci. Je peux laisser un message?
4 Bien sûr. C'est de la part de qui?
5 Son poste est occupé. Vous voulez patienter?
6 Je voudrais parler à Monsieur Sandoz, s'il vous plaît.
7 Je m'appelle Nina Santini et j'ai bien reçu son courrier.

### ACTIVITY 9

Complete the exchanges between two stressed office workers.

1 'Il est sorti?'                 'Il vient de sortir.'
2 'Elle a appelé?'         _____
3 'Ils ont reçu mon courrier?'    _____
4 'Vous avez noté mon message?' _____
5 'Vous lui avez dit?'        _____

Now do activities 10 and 11 on the recording.

# Which day would suit you?
# Quel jour vous conviendrait?

🔊 **ACTIVITY 12** is on the recording.

**ACTIVITY 13**

Correct the five mistakes in the following summary.

Thierry Martinez, le rédacteur en chef des éditions du Bertin,
téléphone à Philippe Perrin. Il lui dit qu'il vient d'examiner
son dossier et qu'il aimerait le rencontrer. Philippe Perrin ira
donc voir Thierry Martinez le mardi 27 avril. Il arrivera vers
dix heures, et il rencontrera les collègues de Nathalie Pavy qui
lui parleront de leurs projets. Ensuite Martinez et Perrin iront
prendre un café et ils pourront discuter.

**DIALOGUE 3**

○ Allô?

■ Est-ce que Philippe Perrin est là, s'il vous plaît?

○ Oui, c'est moi.

■ Bonjour. Ici Thierry Martinez. Je travaille pour les éditions
du Bertin, où je suis directeur artistique …

○ Bonjour.

■ Madame Pavy m'a transmis votre dossier que je viens
d'examiner. Votre travail m'intéresse et j'aimerais vous
rencontrer. Quel jour vous conviendrait?

○ Je serai à Paris la semaine prochaine, et j'aurai un peu de
temps le mardi 27 et le mercredi 28 avril.

■ J'ai une réunion mardi toute la journée, mais je serai libre
mercredi. Venez mercredi matin, vers 11 heures.

○ D'accord. C'est noté.

■ Je vous présenterai à mes collègues, ils vous parleront de
nos projets. Ensuite on ira déjeuner et on pourra discuter.

○ Très bien. Merci d'avoir appelé. À mercredi prochain.

---

### VOCABULARY

| | |
|---|---|
| **convenir** | to suit |
| **intéresser** | to interest |
| **présenter** | to introduce |
| **le collègue** | colleague |
| **ensuite** | then |
| **discuter** | to discuss |

## ✓ The future of regular *-re* verbs

To form the future of regular **-re** verbs, you need to remove the final **e** from the infinitive and add the usual endings:

**vendre**, 'to sell'

| | |
|---|---|
| je **vendrai** | nous **vendrons** |
| tu **vendras** | vous **vendrez** |
| il/elle/on **vendra** | ils/elles **vendront** |

Other regular **-re** verbs include: **attendre** ('to wait'), **descendre** ('to go down'), **entendre** ('to hear'), **répondre** ('to answer').

## ✓ The future of irregular verbs

The endings are always the same, only the stem can be irregular.

| aller | to go | j'**irai**, tu **iras**, etc. |
|---|---|---|
| avoir | to have | j'**aurai**, etc. |
| faire | to make, to do | je **ferai**, etc. |
| venir | to come | je **viendrai**, etc. |
| voir | to see | je **verrai**, etc. |
| pleuvoir | to rain | il **pleuvra** |
| pouvoir | to be able to | je **pourrai**, etc. |
| vouloir | to want | je **voudrai**, etc. |
| savoir | to know | je **saurai**, etc. |
| recevoir | to receive | je **recevrai**, etc. |
| devoir | to have to | je **devrai**, etc. |

You will also need these stems to form the conditional: **j'irais**, **j'aurais**, **je ferais**, **je viendrais**, etc.

### ACTIVITY 14

A French friend has had the following prediction from an English-speaking fortune teller. Translate it into French.

> You will meet a millionaire (**un millionnaire**) who will call you every day. You will go to the theatre with him, he will introduce you to his friends, and you will speak about interesting things. One day, he will invite you to a restaurant, you'll wait for him, but he won't come. You'll never see him again and you'll be very sad.

 Now do activities 15 and 16 on the recording.

## Correspondance

---

### Curriculum Vitae

**Perrin Philippe**
35 ans

adresse: 6 rue Rubens 44000 Nantes
téléphone: 02 40 53 55 56

**Diplômes – Formation**
- Baccalauréat scientifique – 1983
- Diplôme supérieur d'arts appliqués – 1986

**Expérience professionelle**
- Aide-maquettiste, éditions Milan à Toulouse (1986–1989)
- Illustrateur publicitaire, agence MGP à Nantes
(1990–1995)
- Illustrateur indépendant (depuis 1996)

**Langues**
anglais lu, parlé, écrit

**Sports pratiqués**
natation, cerf-volant de compétition

---

Philippe Perrin
6 rue Rubens
44000 Nantes

Madame Nathalie Pavy
Éditions du Bertin
55 rue Amelot
75011 Paris

Nantes, le 15 avril 2000

Madame,

J'ai appris à la foire du livre de Bologne que vous
recherchiez de nouveaux illustrateurs, et je me permets
donc de vous proposer mes services.

Vous trouverez ci-joint mon curriculum vitae ainsi que des
photocopies de mon travail. En espérant que mon dossier
retiendra votre attention, je reste à votre disposition pour
vous fournir les renseignements complémentaires que vous
pourriez souhaiter.

Je vous prie de croire à mes sentiments respectueux.

*Perrin*

| les arts appliqués | applied arts |
| **publicitaire** | advertising |
| **le cerf-volant** | kite |
| **ci-joint(e)** | herewith |
| **ainsi que** | as well as |
| **en espérant** | while hoping |
| **fournir** | to provide |
| **les renseignements** | information |

## ACTIVITY 17

Find in the CV the French equivalents of:

1 A levels
2 career history
3 assistant designer
4 freelance illustrator
5 qualifications and training
6 read, spoken, and written

## ACTIVITY 18

Find in the letter the French equivalents of:

1 I'd be happy to provide any further information you may require
2 I heard … that you were looking for new illustrators
3 Please find herewith my CV and photocopies of my work
4 I hope you will find my work of interest
5 I would like to offer you my services
6 the Bologna Book Fair
7 Yours sincerely

## ACTIVITY 19

**Vrai ou faux?**

1 Philippe Perrin can speak English.
2 He flies kites at competition level.
3 He has formal arts qualifications.
4 He has always worked freelance.
5 He has worked in advertising.
6 He is looking for work.
7 He lives in Toulouse.

# 14.5 La Bonne Étoile

 **LE NOUVEAU STAGIAIRE**
**THE NEW TRAINEE**

Alexandra s'occupe d'un nouveau stagiaire, Raphaël Lacase.

| | |
|---|---|
| **tranquillement** | quietly |
| **le/la stagiaire** | trainee |
| **la patronne** | (female) boss, owner |
| **servir** | to serve |
| **passer** | to spend |

### ACTIVITY 20

Who's speaking: Madame Delaine, Alexandra, or Raphaël?

1  J'espère qu'Alexandra s'occupera bien de vous.
2  Je vous présente mon nouveau stagiaire.
3  On pourra discuter tranquillement.
4  Quel jour vous conviendrait?
5  Elle passe sa vie au téléphone.
6  Un instant, je vous le passe.
7  Merci d'avoir appelé.
8  On prendra un café.
9  Ce sera intéressant.
10  OK.

### ACTIVITY 21

Use the words below to complete the conversation that took place later between Alexandra and Jérôme.

**allés / arrivé / présenté / Raphaël Lacase / rencontrer /**
**stagaire / sympa**

Alexandra:  Mon nouveau _____ est _____ ce matin.
Jérôme      Il s'appelle comment?
Alexandra   _____.
Jérôme      Vous êtes _____ à La Bonne Étoile?
Alexandra   Oui, je l'ai _____ à Monsieur et Madame
            Delaine.
Jérôme      Il est _____?
Alexandra   Oui, et il voudrait te _____ !
Jérôme      Moi!!!

## ACTIVITY 22

Imagine the full conversation between Raphaël and the person who called him on Alexandra's mobile. He introduced himself as Jean Hureau and said he wanted to meet Raphaël. He first suggested the afternoon, which was not convenient for Raphaël, so they finally agreed to meet at 8.30 the next morning.

## STORY TRANSCRIPT

| | |
|---|---|
| Alexandra | Excuse-moi, Raphaël ... Allô? Oui, c'est moi. Oui, c'est ça. Je m'occupe du dossier de Najouah Abdel et j'aimerais vous rencontrer. Quel jour vous conviendrait? À quinze heures cet après-midi? D'accord. Au revoir et ... merci d'avoir appelé. Raphaël, j'ai une réunion importante cet après-midi. Tu pourras venir avec moi. Tu verras, ce sera intéressant! |
| Raphaël | OK. |
| Alexandra | Mais on va d'abord à La Bonne Étoile. Je te présenterai aux patrons, ils sont très sympas. On prendra un café et puis on pourra discuter tranquillement. |
| Raphaël | OK. |
| | |
| Mme Delaine | Bonjour, Alexandra. Ça va? |
| Alexandra | Bonjour ... Je vous présente mon nouveau stagiaire, Raphaël Lacase. Raphaël, je te présente Madame Delaine, la patronne de La Bonne Étoile, le meilleur café de la région! |
| Mme Delaine | Tu es trop gentille, Alexandra! Bonjour, Raphaël. |
| Raphaël | Bonjour. |
| Mme Delaine | Qu'est-ce que je vous sers? |
| Alexandra | Deux cafés, s'il vous plaît. |
| Mme Delaine | Jean-Luc, deux cafés pour Alexandra et Raphaël. |
| Alexandra | Alors, qu'est-ce que tu penses de ... |
| Mme Delaine | Deux cafés. Voilà ... Raphaël, j'espère qu'Alexandra s'occupera bien de vous. Son plus gros défaut, vous verrez, c'est qu'elle passe sa vie au téléphone! |
| Alexandra | Ce n'est pas vrai! Vous ... Ah, excusez-moi! Allô? ... Oui, bien sûr. C'est de la part de qui? ... Un instant, je vous le passe ... Raphaël, c'est pour toi ... |
| Raphaël | Allô? |

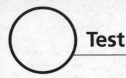

# Test

Now it's time to test your progress in Unit 14.

1 Match the French with its English equivalent.

| ici … | I've written it down |
| libre | I'll put you through … |
| gentil | to hold the line |
| occupé | free, available |
| patienter | in a meeting |
| c'est noté | letter, mail |
| le courrier | … speaking |
| en réunion | engaged |
| les coordonnées | details |
| je vous le/la passe | kind |

**10**

2 Complete the sentences with the correct pronoun.

| Il | serai en réunion jusqu'à onze heures |
| Je | serons de retour demain matin. |
| Tu | auront pas le temps ce soir. |
| Nous | pourrez discuter avec eux. |
| Vous | pleuvra toute la journée. |
| Ils n' | l'attendront pour dîner. |
| Elle ne | ne la reverras jamais. |
| Elles | viendra pas. |

**8**

3 Who's saying each sentence? The caller or the receptionist?

1 Je lui dirai.
2 Ne quittez pas.
3 Je vous le passe.
4 Il est en réunion.
5 Son poste est occupé.
6 C'est de la part de qui?
7 Vous voulez patienter?
8 Je rappellerai plus tard.
9 Je peux laisser un message?
10 Est-ce que je pourrais parler à Monsieur Lebrun?

**10**

4 Use the future tense to complete the following sentences.

1 Je n' _____ pas le moral. (**avoir**)
2 Tu ne _____ pas contente. (**être**)
3 Ça n' _____ pas. (**aller**)
4 Il _____ pleuvoir. (**aller**)
5 Nous ne _____ pas en vacances. (**partir**)
6 Vous _____ malade. (**être**)

6

5 Choose the right words to complete the following dialogue.

**appelé / dirai / est / occupé / parler / part / patienter / prie
/ rappellerai / réunion / sera / vous**

▼ Allô. Société Norbert. Bonjour.
○ Bonjour, je voudrais _____ à Laurent Lamy, s'il
vous plaît.
▼ Son poste est _____. Vous voulez _____?
■ Oui, bien sûr.
Une minute plus tard.
○ Allô?
■ Est-ce que Laurent Lamy _____ là?
○ Je regrette. Il est en _____.
■ Est-ce qu'il _____ là cet après-midi?
○ Oui, je crois. C'est de la _____ de qui?
■ Colette Cadogan. Je _____ cet après-midi, mais
vous pouvez lui dire que j'ai _____?
○ Bien sûr. Je lui _____.
■ Je _____ remercie.
○ Je vous en _____.

12

**TOTAL SCORE**   46

If you scored less than 36, go through the dialogues and the
Language Building sections again before completing the
Summary on page 208.

# Summary 14

 Now try this final test summarizing the main points covered in this unit.

How would you:
1 ask if you can speak to Madame Dupont?
2 ask if she'll be in this afternoon?
3 ask if you can leave a message?
4 say 'can you tell her I called?'
5 say you'll call back tomorrow?
6 say 'I wrote to you last week'?
7 say 'I have not received your letter'?
8 say you're looking after this file?
9 say 'I'd like to meet you'?
10 ask 'what day would suit you?'
11 say you have a meeting all day?
12 say you'll be free on Friday morning?

## REVISION

Before leaving Unit 14, think of the last time you had difficulty reaching someone on the phone. Can you work out how the conversation would have gone in French? See how you can make the most of all the language you have learnt in this course. You can of course change or embellish what actually happened. You could, for example, pretend that the person who answered your call was very chatty and gave you unnecessary information, e.g. 'Mrs X is not in this afternoon. She has gone to the hospital to see her husband. He fell off his bike yesterday and broke his leg. Tomorrow morning she'll be in a meeting until 11', etc.

# Review 4

1 Which word is the odd one out in each group?

    1 l'automne / l'été / l'étranger / l'hiver / le printemps
    2 le ciel / l'humeur / le nuage / la pluie / le vent
    3 l'Allemagne / l'Écosse / la Foire / la Grèce / le Japon
    4 énervant / grand / gros / mince / petit
    5 adorer / aimer / détester / préférer / rencontrer
    6 aller / arriver / dormir / partir / sortir

2 Find the pairs of opposites.

| | |
|---|---|
| bruyant | adorer |
| détester | s'amuser |
| s'ennuyer | arriver |
| froid | bon |
| l'hiver | calme |
| mauvais | chaud |
| moins | content |
| mort | l'été |
| partir | grand |
| petit | né |
| le travail | plus |
| triste | les vacances |

3 Match each question 1–9 with the appropriate answer a–i.

| | | | |
|---|---|---|---|
| 1 | Tu lui as parlé? | a | J'aimerais bien, mais je dois travailler. |
| 2 | Quel temps fait-il? | b | Nous sommes allés en Australie. |
| 3 | C'est de la part de qui? | c | Non, merci. Je n'ai plus faim. |
| 4 | Qu'est-ce que tu as fait? | d | Non, elle était en réunion. |
| 5 | Ils se sont mariés quand? | e | Je suis allée au cinéma. |
| 6 | Vous reprenez de la tarte? | f | Je crois qu'il va neiger. |
| 7 | Vous êtes allés à l'étranger? | g | Bernard Lefort. |
| 8 | Quel jour vous conviendrait? | h | Jeudi ou vendredi. |
| 9 | Vous voulez dîner avec nous? | i | Il y a quatre ans. |

## GRAMMAR AND USAGE

4 Choose the right words to complete the speech bubble.

Une grand-mère parle à son petit-fils:

> Tu (**as/es**) né à sept heures du matin, et ton papa
> m'(**a/ai**) téléphoné à sept heures et demie pour me dire
> que tu (**étais/êtes**) un garçon et que tu
> t'(**appelais/appellez**) Thomas. Je (**voulais/voulaient**)
> te voir tout de suite, alors (**j'ai pris/je prenais**) un taxi
> et (**j'ai/je suis**) allée à l'hôpital. C'(**est/était**) l'hiver,
> mais il (**faisait/font**) beau. Le ciel (**a été/était**) bleu.
> J'(**étais/avais**) heureuse. Quand (**j'étais/je suis**)
> arrivée dans la chambre, tu (**étais/êtes**) dans les bras
> de ta maman et tu (**as dormi/dormais**) tranquillement.
> Ta maman (**ai/avait**) l'air fatiguée, mais très heureuse.

5 Choose from the words in the box to complete the weather forecast.

Il ne _____ pas beau aujourd'hui: de gros nuages
noirs _____ ce matin. Cet après-midi, vous n'
_____ pas envie de sortir: il _____, il y
_____ du vent, et il ne _____ pas chaud.
Demain matin, il ne _____ plus, mais il _____
encore froid et il y _____ du brouillard. Ne vous
inquiétez pas, ça _____ beaucoup mieux après-
demain: le ciel _____ bleu, le soleil _____,
les températures _____ très agréables et vous
_____ aller vous promener!

> arriveront  aura  aura  aurez  brillera  fera  fera
> ira  pleuvra  pleuvra  pourrez  sera  seront  fera

## 🔊 LISTENING

You're going to hear a quiz show about the life of Vincent Van Gogh.

6 A How much do you know already? Do the following quiz before listening.

| | |
|---|---|
| **le tournesol** | sunflower |
| **couper** | to cut |

1 Vincent Van Gogh est né
   a en France   b aux Pays-Bas.
2 Théo, le frère de Vincent Van Gogh, habitait
   a Paris.   b Arles, dans le sud de la France.
3 À Paris, Vincent Van Gogh a peint
   a environ 20 tableaux.   b plus de 200 tableaux.
4 À Arles, Vincent Van Gogh a travaillé avec
   a Paul Gauguin.   b Henri Matisse.
5 C'est   a à Paris   b à Arles
   que Van Gogh a peint «la chambre» et «les tournesols».
6 En 1888, Vincent Van Gogh n'allait pas bien
   a et il s'est cassé la main.   b et il s'est coupé l'oreille.
7 Quand Van Gogh est mort,
   a il avait 37 ans   b il avait 57 ans.

B Now listen to the recording and correct your answers to the quiz.

7 Listen to the recording again and complete the following summary.

Vincent Van Gogh _____ né _____ Pays-Bas le 30 mars 1853. Il _____ un frère _____ s'appelait Théo et qui _____ Paris. Van Gogh est allé voir Théo en 1886, et il est _____ deux ans à Paris. Pendant cette période, il a peint _____ de 200 tableaux. Ensuite, Van Gogh est _____ à Arles dans le sud de la France. C'est à Arles qu'il a peint «les tournesols» et «la chambre», par exemple. Le peintre Paul Gauguin était un ami de Van Gogh, il est venu le voir, et les deux hommes ont _____ ensemble pendant trois ou quatre mois. Mais Van Gogh était malade, les deux hommes se sont _____ et Van Gogh s'est coupé l'oreille. En mai 1890, Van Gogh est _____ habiter à Auvers-sur-Oise, dans la région parisienne. Il n'allait pas bien, il était triste et malheureux. Il est _____ le 29 juillet 1890. Il _____ seulement 37 ans.

8 Here are some of the phrases you have learnt in the last three units. How do you pronounce them? Read them aloud, and then listen to the recording to check your pronunciation.

1 Mon grand-père est né en France.
2 Ils ne sont jamais allés aux États-Unis.
3 Il était de mauvaise humeur et il avait l'air fatigué.
4 Je voudrais parler au directeur, s'il vous plaît.
5 Vous pouvez lui dire que j'ai appelé?
6 Je lui ai écrit la semaine dernière.

9 You're trying to ring someone in France. Use the cues to help you with your side of the conversation.

Recept.: Allô? Société Lavigne. Bonjour.
You: (Ask if you can speak to Monsieur Kelif.)
Recept.: Je regrette. Il n'est pas là ce matin.
You: (Ask if he'll be in this afternoon.)
Recept.: Non, il sera de retour demain après-midi.
You: (Ask if you can leave a message.)
Recept.: Bien sûr. C'est de la part de qui?
You: (Say your name is Jo Ross. You're working for LPC in Scotland.)
Recept.: Je lui dirai. C'est noté.

Now try the dialogue again without referring to the book.

10 Imagine you've just come back from a holiday in Australia. Look at the postcard you wrote while you were there and answer your friend's questions.

Salut!
Le voyage a été difficile (j'étais fatigué, il y avait beaucoup de monde, et l'avion n'était pas très propre ...), mais maintenant ça va!

Je passe de très bonnes vacances. L'Australie est un très beau pays, j'ai rencontré des gens très sympas, et on s'amuse bien. En plus, ici c'est l'été, le ciel est bleu, le soleil brille, il fait beau et chaud.

Je suis ici depuis trois semaines. Déjà! Je serai triste de rentrer en France la semaine prochaine. J'espère revenir bientôt ...

Bises.

Ch.

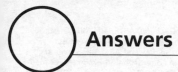

# Answers

## Unit 1

**2**   1 meeting; 2 parting (saying good night);
3 parting; 4 parting; the key phrase is **à
demain**, 'see you tomorrow'; 5 meeting (in
the evening)

**3**   1 d; 2 a; 3 c; 4 b

**7**   A 1, 3, 5, 6; B a 4; b 1; c 5

**8**   *Food*: un gâteau ('cake'), un hamburger,
une omelette, une pizza; *Drink*: un jus
d'orange ('orange juice'), un thé '((cup of)
tea'), une bière ('beer'), une limonade
('lemonade')

**9**   *Example*: Un gâteau et un café, s'il vous
plaît.

**13**   tea 3€; coca cola 3,25€; coffee 2,15€;
sandwich 5€. They pay 4,30€ in total.

**14**   2 **deux**; 12 **douze**; 20 **vingt**; 3 **trois**;
13 **treize**; 30 **trente**; 4 **quatre**; 14 **quatorze**;
40 **quarante**; 5 **cinq**; 15 **quinze**

**15**   sept euros; neuf euros; dix euros; onze
euros; seize euros; dix-huit euros; vingt et
un euros; vingt-six euros; vingt-neuf euros

**18**   1 yes (**bière**, 9 euros); 2 no (they have
omelettes, pizzas, and a dish of the day –
**plat du jour**); 3 yes (they have omelettes);
4 plat du jour (32 euros).

**19**   *Example*: Waiter: Monsieur?/Madame? Une
salade niçoise et une eau minérale, s'il
vous plaît. You: Une salade niçoise et une
eau minérale. D'accord.

**20**   1 F (it's Madame Delaine); 2 V; 3 F (a
sandwich and a Perrier); 4 V; 5 V; 6 F (she
says **à demain** – 'see you tomorrow')

**21**   1 Alexandra; 2 Madame Delaine;
3 Alexandra; 4 Madame Delaine;
5 Alexandra; 6 Alexandra

**Test**

*1*   1 d; 2 b; 3 g; 4 h; 5 e; 6 c; 7 a; 8 f

*2*   1 f; 2 c; 3 e; 4 b; 5 a; 6 d

*3*   **une** omelette; **une** bière; **un** sandwich; **un**
jus d'orange; **une** pizza; **un** café

*4*   1 trois; 2 huit; 3 vingt et un; 4 trente-six;
5 trente; 6 vingt-quatre (2 + 11 = 13 + 11 =
24 + 11 = 35); 7 treize; 8 douze; 9 dix-huit

*5*   1 Une pizza, six euros trente. 2 Une salade
et un café, s'il vous plaît. 3 Un sandwich et
une bière, s'il vous plaît. 4 Au revoir. 5
Bonsoir, tout le monde. 6 Bonjour,
Madame. 7 Merci, Monsieur. 8 Bonne nuit.
À demain.

## Summary 1

*1* Bonjour. Bonsoir. *2* Au revoir. Bonne nuit. *3*
Monsieur. Madame. Mademoiselle. *4* S'il vous
plaît. Merci. *5* Un sandwich et un café, s'il vous
plaît. *6* Bon appétit. *7* un, deux, trois, quatre,
cinq, six, sept, huit, neuf, dix

## Unit 2

**2**   Plan B

**3**   Il y a un bureau de poste. Il y a des
distributeurs de billets. Il y a un jardin
public. Il y a des restaurants. Il y a des
toilettes. Il y a un cinéma. Il y a une salle
de concert. Il y a un centre culturel. Il y a
une gare. Il y a une cathédrale. Il y a une
église. Il y a une banque. Il y a un hôtel. Il
y a un musée.

**4**   *Example*:
○ Là, il y a un café. En face, il y a un
jardin public. Et à côté, il y a une
banque.
■ Et là, qu'est-ce qu'il y a ?
○ Le château.
■ Il y a un cinéma?
○ Oui, il y a un cinéma là.
■ Où est l'hôtel?
○ L'hôtel est là.

**8**   Sketch A

**9**   A Tournez à droite. B Tournez à gauche.
C Continuez tout droit. D Je ne sais pas.
E Allez jusqu'à la banque.

**13**   1 Café des Amis, 46 rue de Bordeaux;
2 Chez Abdel, 55 boulevard de la gare;
3 Chez Nicole, 69 rue Victor-Hugo;
4 Restaurant du Jardin, 37 avenue de la
liberté

**14**   vingt et un, trente-deux, trente-trois,
quarante-quatre, quarante-neuf,
cinquante-huit, soixante-six, soixante-sept

**18**   1 F; 2 V; 3 F; 4 V; 5 F; 6 V; 7 F; 8 V; 9 F; 10 F;
11 V; 12 F

**19**   1 Le café est en face de la banque. 3 Le
musée est dans l'avenue de la liberté. 5 Le
cinéma ABC est en face de l'église Saint-
Bernard. 7 La gare SNCF est dans la rue
Victor-Hugo. 9 Le château est dans
l'avenue de la liberté. 10 L'église Saint-
Bernard est dans l'avenue de la liberté.
12 Le restaurant Chez Halim est dans la
rue Charles-de-Gaulle.

**20**   *Example*: Continuez tout droit jusqu'à la
banque. Tournez à gauche. La gare est
dans la rue Victor-Hugo.

**21**   1 a; 2 b; 3 b; 4 a; 5 b

**22** Alexandra; 44 rue de la liberté; à la gare tournez à gauche; continuez tout droit jusqu'au pont; tournez à droite dans la rue de la liberté; en face de La Bonne Étoile; à côté de la banque

**Test**

*1* a 2; b 9; c 7; d 6; e 3; f 8; g 1; h 4; i 5

*2* 1 alors; 2 jusqu'à; 3 une église; 4 treize; 5 d'accord; 6 les feux

*3* 1 café **de la** gare; 2 hôtel **du** port; 3 avenue **de la** plage; 4 rue **de la** cathédrale; 5 musée **du** château; 6 boulevard **des** Anglais

*4* 1 quarante; 2 cinquante-cinq; 3 soixante et un; 4 trente-sept; 5 trente-trois; 6 quarante-trois; 7 cinquante; 8 soixante-sept

*5* 1 Pour aller à la gare, s'il vous plaît? 2 Il y a des distributeurs de billets? 3 Allez jusqu'au pont. 4 Continuez tout droit. 5 Tournez à droite aux feux. (or) Aux feux tournez à droite. 6 Tournez à gauche après la banque. (or) Après la banque tournez à gauche. 7 Il y a un café à côté du jardin public. (or) Il y a un jardin public à côté du café. 8 Il y a une église en face du restaurant.

**Summary 2**

*1* Pour aller à la gare, s'il vous plaît? *2* Il y a un bureau de poste à côté du cinéma. *3* Il y a un téléphone en face des toilettes. *4* Tournez à gauche. *5* Tournez à droite. *6* Continuez tout droit. *7* Allez jusqu'aux feux. *8* Trente, quarante, cinquante, soixante.

# Unit 3

*2* 1 at 8.00; 2 at 8.30; 3 at 10.15; 4 at 11.45

*3* 1 dînez (9.00); 2 commence (12.15); 3 jouent (1.10), 4 travailles (1.45)

*7* There are three mistakes in the phone numbers. The first one should end in **82 98** (instead of 92 98), the second one should start with **01 64 75** (instead of 01 64 95), and the third one should end in 91 (instead of 71). Otherwise, the club is open until 10 o'clock during the week (**de 8 heures à 22 heures**), and until six o'clock on Saturdays (**de 10 heures à 18 heures le samedi**). It doesn't open on Sundays.

*8* 96 – quatre-vingt-seize; 70 soixante-dix; 82 – quatre-vingt-deux; 84 – quatre-vingt-quatre; 74 – soixante-quatorze; 99 – quatre-vingt-dix-neuf; 105 – cent cinq – 80 – quatre-vingts; 91 – quatre-vingt-onze; 71 – soixante et onze

*12* 1 is working until ten o'clock; 2 has an English class; 3 is looking after the children; 4 is going away; 5 is coming back

*13* 1 c; 2 e; 3 b; 4 d; 5 a

*16* A The seven channels mentioned are TF1, F2, F3, C+, la 5e, ARTE, and M6. (C+ stands for Canal Plus. La 5e only broadcasts during the day, and ARTE takes over at 19.00.) As one of the programmes is called DIMANCHE SOIR and another L'ÉQUIPE DU DIMANCHE, we can assume this is a Sunday broadcast.
B A film buff might want to watch the documentary about the Cannes Film Festival (F2: 22.55–0.30), or the Robert Altman special with two films directed by Robert Altman and a documentary about the same director (ARTE: 20.40–1.45). A sports fanatic may want to watch the Formule 1 Grand Prix race in Monaco (TF1: 14.25–16.25), or the football magazine (C+: 22.45–23.15). A current affairs enthusiast may be interested in the debate about education (F3: 22.25–23.35) or a programme about the anti-smoking campaign (M6: 22.55–23.25).

*17* 1 F (il commence à 11 heures moins 20 et finit à 11 heures 35); 2 F (il commence à 2 heures 25 et finit à 4 heures 25); 3 V; 4 V; 5 V; 6 V

*18* *Example*: On regarde Formule 1? C'est sur TF1. Ça commence à 14 heures 25 et ça finit à 16 heures 25.

*19* Alexandra is having a coffee with Jérôme, and suggests they go out for dinner on **Monday** night. Unfortunately Jérôme is leaving for Spain on **Monday** morning and may not be back until **eleven thirty** or **midnight** on Wednesday night. He has a Spanish class which finishes at ten o'clock on Thursday nights and Alexandra plays basketball on **Friday** nights. Jérôme suggests they go out on **Saturday** instead, but Alexandra takes a call on her mobile, and leaves immediately without giving Jérôme an answer.

*20* 2, 4, 5, 8, 10

*21* 1 Alexandra; 2 Jérôme; 3 Jérôme; 4 Alexandra; 5 Alexandra; 6 Madame Delaine

**Test**

*1* mardi, jeudi, lundi, samedi, mercredi, vendredi, dimanche. And in the right order: lundi, mardi, mercredi, jeudi, vendredi, samedi, dimanche.

*2* a 00.00; b 11.00; c 03.15; d 10.25; e 02.30; f 03.50; g 04.45

*3* 1 garde; 2 prépar**es**; 3 joue; 4 dîn**e**; 5 travaill**ons**; 6 rentr**ez**; 7 regard**ent**

*4* soixante et un 61, soixante et onze 71, soixante-quatorze 74, soixante-dix-sept 77, quatre-vingt-un 81, quatre-vingt-huit 88, quatre-vingt-onze 91, quatre-vingt-treize 93, quatre-vingt-dix-neuf 99, cent 100

*5* 1 c; 2 f; 3 b; 4 i; 5 h; 6 d; 7 a; 8 e; 9 g

## Summary 3

*1* lundi, mardi, mercredi, jeudi, vendredi, samedi, dimanche; *2* Il est quelle heure? *3* Il est dix heures. *4* Il est quatre heures et demie. *5* Il est huit heures moins le quart. *6* Ça commence à quelle heure? *7* Ça finit à quatre heures et quart. *8* Je ne travaille pas le samedi. *9* soixante-dix, quatre-vingts, quatre-vingt-dix, cent

## Review 1

**1** 1 merci; 2 s'il vous plaît; 3 d'accord; 4 un musée; 5 une étoile

**2** le château; l'église; la gare; le musée

**3** 1 V; 2 F (c'est mercredi soir); 3 F (il travaille au musée); 4 V; 5 F (c'est vendredi soir); 6 V; 7 V

**4** Le musée; au musée; aux feux; à la gare; la rue; Le musée; du café; des jardins; du jardin public

**5** dînes, travaille, commence, finit, part, rentrent, partez, travaillons, joue, regardent

**6** 1 soixante-douze 72; 2 soixante-cinq 65; 3 cinquante-cinq 55; 4 seize 16; 5 cent 100; 6 quatre-vingt-quatre 84; 7 quatre-vingt-treize 93; 8 soixante-dix-neuf 79

**7** Before coming to the class, I saw my friend Julie. She suggested we had a cup of **coffee**, but I said it was not possible because I had an English class at half past **six**. We agreed to meet at a quarter **past** six tomorrow. Julie asked me if I knew the Grand Café, and I said '**no**'. It's next to a **bank** in Paris Street, opposite the **park**.

**8** travaille; gare; mardi; jeudi; cours; as; vendredi; dimanche; ne; pas; quelle; commence; moins; finis; demie; samedi; heures; minuit

**10** 1 Bonjour. Ça va? 2 Ce n'est pas possible. Je travaille jusqu'à minuit. 3 D'accord. Où? 4 C'est en face du jardin public? 5 À huit heures et demie? 6 Au revoir. À samedi.

**11** Je recommande le restaurant Bienvenue. C'est dans la rue de la République. Numéro quatre-vingt-douze. Oui, c'est ça. Oui, c'est ouvert le dimanche. C'est le zéro deux, quarante, soixante et un, soixante-treize, quatre-vingt-quatorze.

# Unit 4

**2** 1 V; 2 F (129 euros for a night); 3 F (it's a single room); 4 V; 5 F (it's on the 3rd floor)

**3** 1 145 euros, 2 3600 dollars, 3 470 euros, 4 22500 livres, 5 1 euros, 6 999 dollars

**4** 109 cent neuf; 654 six cent cinquante-quatre; 345 trois cent quarante-cinq; 4700 quatre mille sept cents; 590 cinq cent quatre-vingt-dix; 33600 trente-trois mille six cents; 2345 deux mille trois cent quarante-cinq; 9999 neuf mille neuf cent quatre-vingt-dix neuf

**8** 1 Yes. 2 Yes. 3 Yes. 4 The cost per day is €4.25 for the site + €4.25 for the car + €5.90 per person. 5 It's free for children under the age of eight.

**9** 1 15/08/2016; 2 20/02/2002; 3 30/06/2025; 4 08/05/1945; 5 14/07/1789; 6 27/01/1995

**13** 1 the left; 2 2; 3 a living room, a bathroom, and a toilet

**14** 1 d C'est un hôtel **agréable**. 2 b C'est un camping **confortable**. 3 c Nous avons un **petit** jardin. 4 a Les ascenseurs sont **modernes**. 5 e Tu as une **belle** cuisine.

**17** 1 The first, second, and fourth properties are in Paris. 2 The last two properties are for sale. 3 The first three properties are for rent. 4 The third and fifth properties are houses. 5 The first, second, and fourth properties are flats. 6 The second, third, and fifth properties have at least two bedrooms. 7 The first and fourth properties have only one bedroom. 8 The third property is for holiday rent. 9 The first property is the smallest (30m2). 10 The third property has a swimming pool. 11 The fifth property has a study. 12 The fourth property has a lift.

**18** 1 The fifth property is a house for sale in Nantes, and it has three bedrooms. 2 The third property is a villa in the South of France. It has 5 or 6 bedrooms and a pool, and is available for rent in July and August. 3 The fourth property is a flat for sale in Paris, and there is a lift. 4 The second property is a flat for rent in Paris, and it has two bedrooms. 5 The first property is a flat for rent in Paris, and it has one bedroom.

**19** *Example*: (first property) Voici le séjour. La cuisine est là à droite. Alors, il y a tout, cuisinière, four, réfrigérateur, lave-linge. Là, vous avez la chambre à droite et la salle de bains à gauche.

**20** 8; 50; 6,40; 7; 11; 7; 60; 02 47 81 92 75

**21** 1 Le Château. 2 La Bonne Étoile. 3 Le Château. 4 La Bonne Étoile. 5 Le Château. 6 La Bonne Étoile.

## Test

*1* 1 voici; 2 juin; 3 l'ascenseur; 4 la nuit; 5 la clé; 6 l'escalier; 7 la piscine; 8 mars

*2* 1 123; 2 2002; 3 456; 4 789; 5 9876; 6 4567; 7 9999

*3* 1 juillet; 2 décembre; 3 février; 4 avril; 5 juin; 6 janvier; 7 novembre; 8 mai; 9 août; 10 septembre; 11 mars; 12 octobre

*4* bonnes; vieille; confortable; belle; grand; petit; jolie; moderne; beaux; grande

*5* J'ai une réservation. Tu as une tente ou une caravane? Je m'appelle Jacqueline Simon. Ils ont un beau jardin. Elle a une grande maison. Vous avez une piscine? Nous avons une belle chambre.

*6* 1 f; 2 b; 3 e; 4 a; 5 c; 6 d

**Summary 4**

*1* Je m'appelle Chris Martin. Ça s'écrit C-H-R-I-S M-A-R-T-I-N. *2* janvier, février, mars, avril, mai, juin, juillet, août, septembre, octobre, novembre, décembre; *3* Je voudrais réserver une chambre. *4* Où est la salle de bains? *5* Le séjour est petit. *6* La cuisine est grande. *7* Vous avez un beau jardin.

# Unit 5

**2** A

B *Example*: Bonjour! Je m'appelle Sylvie et j'ai 35 ans. Je suis originaire de Nice, mais en ce moment j'habite Lille. Je suis infirmière. J'ai 1 enfant (Diane, 7 ans), mais je suis séparée. À bientôt!

Or: Bonjour! Je m'appelle Linda et j'ai quarante ans. Je suis portugaise et j'habite Paris. J'ai un petit appartement près de la tour Eiffel.

Je suis interprète de conférence. C'est un métier passionnant. Je parle français, portugais et anglais. Je comprends l'espagnol et l'italien, et j'apprends le japonais.

Je suis divorcée, mais je n'ai pas d'enfants. En ce moment, je suis seule et je cherche l'âme sœur. À bientôt!

Or: Bonjour! Je m'appelle Karima, j'ai 38 ans, je suis divorcée, et j'ai deux enfants. J'habite Marseille, et je suis professeur d'espagnol. Je parle français, espagnol et anglais. En ce moment, j'apprends le japonais, c'est passionnant!

**3** Bonjour. Je m'appelle ... J'ai ... ans. Je suis ... J'habite ... Je parle ... et j'apprends ...

**7** 1 a; 2 b; 3 a; 4 b; 5 b

**8** Son; Jean; sa; Thérèse; Son; Laurent; ses; Madeleine; Paul; leur; leur

**12** 1 V; 2 V; 3 F (until six o'clock); 4 F (she takes her dog out for a walk, and she has something to eat); 5 F (around three o'clock); 6 F (she listens to music, buys records, and chooses music for her next session)

**13** beaucoup; est; occupe; se; lève; s'; couche

**16** 1 d; 2 c; 3 g (it comes from the strong-smelling French cheese called camembert); 4 b (it is a literal translation of 'to have the blues'); 5 e; 6 a; 7 f

**17** 71, soixante et onze; 77, soixante-dix-sept; 85, quatre-vingt-cinq; 88, quatre-vingt-huit; 90, quatre-vingt-dix; 99, quatre-vingt-dix-neuf

**18** 1; 2; 4; 7; 8; 9

**19** comment; appelle; est; français; sont; où; habite; quel; ans; est; s'

**20** *Example*: Je m'appelle Karim Massoud. J'ai 28/29/30 ans. J'habite Paris. Je suis architecte.

**Test**

*1* 1 g; 2 b; 3 e; 4 f; 5 a; 6c; 7 d
*2* 1 e; 2 d; 3 f; 4 b; 5 c; 6 a
*3* Je m'occupe d'ordinateurs. Tu t'inquiètes beaucoup. Elle se lève à trois heures. Nous ne nous ennuyons pas. Vous vous lavez dans la salle de bains. Ils s'amusent dans le jardin.
*4* vos; Mon; ma; Son; mes; leur; leurs; votre; sa
*5* 1 Ma sœur est journaliste. 2 Elle aime beaucoup son métier. 3 Mon beau-frère est américain. 4 Mes beaux-parents sont irlandais. 5 Le chien de mes enfants s'appelle Tintin. 6 Vos enfants apprennent l'allemand? 7 Tu te lèves à quelle heure? 8 Vous vendez des ordinateurs?

**Summary 5**

*1* Mes parents sont divorcés. *2* Mon père a quatre-vingt-huit ans, et il habite New York. *3* Ma sœur parle anglais, français et allemand. *4* Mon frère apprend le japonais. *5* Le mari de ma sœur est au chômage. *6* J'aime beaucoup mes petits-enfants. Ils sont très drôles. *7* Ils lèvent à six heures et demie.

# Unit 6

**2** 1 F (for her friend); 2 V; 3 F (scarves, not hats); 4 F (they cost between 41.90 and 48 euros); 5 F; 6 V

**3** 1 c; 2 d; 3 b; 4 a

**7** He's looking for onions, carrots, turnips, tomatoes, garlic, and basil, which are the ingredients for the **soupe au pistou** (a speciality of Provence).

**8** A Je voudrais des aubergines, des poivrons, des tomates, des courgettes, des oignons et de l'ail.

**12** 1 F (a pair of trousers); 2 F (size 40); 3 V; 4 F (they cost 114 euros); 5 V; 6 V

**13** Je cherche **une jupe**.
Nous avons **celle-ci** en **noir** ou **celle-là** en **gris**.
Je n'aime pas **la grise**, mais **la noire** est très **jolie**. **Elle** est en coton?
**Elle** coûte combien?
Non, **elle** est trop **grande**.
En 38, je l'ai en **bleu**, mais pas en **noir**.
Ça va? **Elle** est assez **longue**.
Oui, c'est **parfait**. Je **la** prends.

**16** Je fais du .... Mon mari fait du ... /Ma femme fait du ... /Mon père fait du ... /Ma mère fait du ... /Mon frère fait du .../Ma sœur fait du ...

**18** 1, 10, 4, 9, 6, 5, 8, 3, 2, 7

**19** 1 Karim; 2 shop assistant; 3 Alexandra; 4 shop assistant; 5 Karim; 6 shop assistant

20 *Example*: Je cherche un pull pour mon copain. Il fait quelle taille? Il fait du 44. J'ai celui-ci en bleu ou celui-là en gris. Celui-ci coûte combien? Celui-ci coûte 65,30 euros. D'accord, je le prends. Vous voulez un paquet-cadeau? Oui, je veux bien. Merci.

**Test**

1   1 g; 2 a; 3 c; 4 h; 5 d; 6 f; 7 e; 8 b
2   1 un cadeau; 2 une fleur; 3 une pomme; 4 carré; 5 une fraise
3   des; en; de; des; en; d'; de; du; de l'; de la; de
4   Cet; ces; celui-ci; celui-là; ces; Celles-ci; celles-là; Ces; ceux-ci; ceux-là; ce; cette
5   1 a; 2 b; 3 a; 4 b; 5 b; 6 a
6   1 sales assistant; 2 customer; 3 customer; 4 sales assistant; 5 sales assistant; 6 sales assistant; 7 customer; 8 sales assistant

**Summary 6**

*1* Je cherche un cadeau pour ma sœur. *2* Cette assiette coûte combien? *3* C'est trop cher. *4* Je voudrais un kilo de pommes de terre. *5* Vous avez du lait? *6* J'en voudrais un litre. *7* Ces chaussures coûtent combien? *8* Je peux les essayer? *9* Je fais du 42. *10* Elles sont trop grandes.

# Unit 7

2   Table 3
3   *Possible answers*: Moi, je vais choisir la salade. Toi, tu vas prendre le steak. Lui, il va prendre la tarte. Elle va choisir le poisson. Lui, il va prendre la soupe. Nous allons choisir la salade. Vous allez prendre la salade. Eux, ils vont prendre le steak. Elles vont choisir le poisson.
7   1, 3, 5
8   1 On peut avoir de l'eau? 2 Nous n'avons plus de pain. 3 Elle ne peut pas manger d'œufs. 4 Je peux avoir une bouteille de vin? 5 Le chef peut me faire une omelette? 6 Vous pouvez leur apporter le menu? 7 Vous pouvez m'apporter un couteau? 8 Vous pouvez lui donner une fourchette?
12  1 V; 2 F (strawberries with cream); 3 V; 4 V; 5 F (they order two espressos); 6 V
13  1 Qu'est-ce que vous avez comme sandwiches / soupes / poisson / viande / glaces / sorbets / tartes / gâteaux / desserts? 2 *Example*: Pour moi, une sandwiche au poulet et une glace à la fraise, s'il vous plaît.
16  1 You can have fish soup, salmon pâté, or prawns with avocado. 2 You can have prawns with avocado. 3 You can have an onion tart. 4 You can have the **poulet basquaise** (chicken cooked with red and green peppers). 5 You can have the **côte d'agneau aux herbes de Provence** (lamb

chop cooked with herbs). 6 You can have the **risotto aux champignons** (rice cooked with mushrooms). 7 You can have the **glace à l'ananas** (pineapple ice cream). 8 You can have the **crème caramel**, the **glace à l'ananas** (pineapple ice cream), or the **gâteau à l'orange** (orange cake). 9 You can have the **tarte aux fraises** (strawberry tart) or the **gâteau à l'orange** (orange cake).

18  When describing the flavours or fillings, make sure you use **au/à l'/à la/aux** correctly. If in doubt, have another look at the relevant Language Building section on page 95.
19  Jérôme had **onion soup** and **a fillet of pork**. He left the restaurant **at a quarter past nine**.
20  1 V; 2 V; 3 F (elle prend le poulet basquaise); 4 F (elle adore le poulet basquaise); 5 F (il prend la soupe à l'oignon); 6 F (il prend le filet de porc)

**Test**

1   1 la soupe; 2 la tarte; 3 le poulet; 4 le jambon; 5 les fraises; 6 la vanille; 7 le fromage; 8 le poisson
2   je, me; il, lui; tu, te; elle, lui; ils, leur
3   1 d; 2 e; 3 f; 4 b; 5 c; 6 a
4   à la; au; au; à l'; aux; à la; au; à la
5   1 a; 2 a; 3 b; 4 b; 5 b; 6 b; 7 a; 8 a
6   1 waiter; 2 diner; 3 waiter; 4 waiter; 5 diner; 6 diner; 7 diner; 8 waiter; 9 diner; 10 waiter

**Summary 7**

*1* Je n'ai pas de couteau. *2* Le poulet est délicieux. *3* Je n'ai plus de pain. *4* Le plat du jour, qu'est-ce que c'est? *5* Qu'est-ce que vous avez comme glaces? *6* Je vais prendre la glace à la vanille. *7* Vous pouvez m'apporter un café, s'il vous plaît? *8* L'addition, s'il vous plaît.

**Review 2**

1   1 poisson; 2 août; 3 laine; 4 crevette; 5 juin; 6 poire
2   un vendeur; une vendeuse; un serveur; une serveuse; un gardien; une gardienne; un fermier; une fermière; un(e) réceptionniste; un professeur; un(e) journaliste; un directeur; une directrice; un informaticien; une informaticienne; un(e) secrétaire; un technicien; une technicienne; un infirmier; une infirmière; un comédien; une comédienne
3   1 f; 2 h; 3 e; 4 c; 5 a; 6 b; 7 g; 8 d
4   528; 641; 234; 1252; 999; 7777; 8396
5   voudrais; avez; faites; fais; avons; voulez; veux; peux; va; vais; fait
6   des; du; des; des; de la; aux; de la; à la

**7** avez; avons; comprennent; comprend; apprends; vendez; vend; apprends; prends; apprend; vous réveillez; nous réveillons; se lève; se lave; s'habille; te lèves; me lève; m'occupe; se lèvent; se lèvent; prend

**8** 1; 2; 4; 6; 8; 9; 10

**9** The second article.

**11** 1 Bonsoir. Vous avez une chambre? 2 Pour deux personnes. 3 Pour une nuit. 4 Il y a la télévision dans la chambre? 5 Quel est le prix de la chambre? 6 Très bien. Je la prends.

# Unit 8

**2** Summary B

**3** elle **y** va **en** voiture; elle ne peut pas **y** aller à pied ou à vélo; elle va peut-être **y** aller en train ou **en** avion

**7** Ticket 2

**12** Nom: Antoine Beaufort
Voiture: Renault blanche
Numéro d'immatriculation: 3454 CP 93
Problème: freins

**16** You should know words such as **le billet, la gare, le voyage, acheter, le mois, payer, le téléphone, l'horaire.**

**17** 1 les boutiques SNCF; 2 les agences de voyage; 3 les guichets; 4 les billeteries automatiques

**18** 1 Tous les billets sont vendus dans les gares, les boutiques SNCF et les agences de voyage; 2 ils sont valables 2 mois; 3 Vous pouvez payer par carte bancaire.

**19** 1 08 36 35 35 35. 2 It is available seven days a week from 07.00 until 22.00. 3 Yes. The Internet address is http://www.sncf.fr.

**20** 1 Minitel. 2 Yes. 3 24 hours a day.

**21** 1; 9; 3; 2; 7; 8; 6; 4; 5

**22** See the transcript on page 117.

**23** *Example:* – Allô? – Jérôme. Allô, c'est moi. – Bonjour. – Ça va? – Ça va. – Moi, ça ne va pas. Je suis en panne d'essence. – Tu es en panne d'essence. – Tu peux m'aider? – Malheureusement, je ne peux pas. Je vais à Tours, je dois y être à dix-sept heures. – Il est quinze heures. J'ai une réunion à Châteauroux. Je dois y être à quinze heures trente. S'il te plaît, Jérôme! – Téléphone à Karim Massoud! – Oh, tu n'es pas sympa.

**Test**

*1* 1 k; 2 h; 3 a; 4 f; 5 j; 6 d; 7 e; 8 b; 9 c; 10 g; 11 i

*2* 1 en car; 2 en bus; 3 à vélo; 4 à pied; 5 à moto; 6 en métro; 7 en bateau; 8 en voiture

*3* 1 f; 2 d; 3 e; 4 c; 5 a; 6 b

*4* 1 c; 2 e; 3 b; 4 d; 5 a

*5* Je dois aller à Lille. Vous voulez voyager quand? Aujourd'hui. Je dois y être à 18 heures. Il y a un train qui part de Lyon à 14 heures 38. Il arrive à Lille à quelle heure? Il arrive à Lille à 17 heures 45. Quel est le prix du billet? Première classe ou seconde? Seconde. Un aller simple coûte 63 euros.

**Summary 8**

*1* Tu vas travailler en voiture ou en bus? *2* Vous y allez à pied ou à vélo? *3* Je dois aller à Marseille. *4* J'y vais en bateau ou en avion. *5* Le train part à quelle heure? *6* Le train arrive à quelle heure? *7* Un aller retour, s'il vous plaît. *8* Ma voiture est en panne. *9* J'ai un pneu crevé.

# Unit 9

**2** A 1, 2, 3, 5, 6, 8, 9; B Only Madame Lenoir mentions backache as one of her husband's problems (**il a mal au dos**).

**3** à la gorge; **au** pied; à **la** main droite et **au** bras gauche; **aux** pieds et **aux** mains; **au** dos

**7** B

**8** *Example:* j'ai mangé du chocolat; tu as bien dormi? mon père a attendu l'ambulance; mes enfants ont été malades; nous avons appelé le médecin; j'ai mal dormi; ma sœur a attendu le médecin; vous avez mangé des fruits?

**12** Monsieur Langlois has just seen the doctor, because he's ill. He feels sick and he has a **stomachache**. The doctor has prescribed antibiotics, which he has to take **three** times a day **before** meals. The pharmacist also suggests Monsieur Langlois eat yoghurt and not drink any **alcohol**.

**13** Il faut dormir la nuit, boire beaucoup d'eau, se reposer régulièrement, faire du sport régulièrement et manger des fruits et des légumes tous les jours. Mais ne travaillez pas trop, ne fumez pas vingt cigarettes par jour, ne buvez pas dix tasses de café par jour, ne buvez pas deux litres de vin par jour et ne mangez pas de gâteaux à la crème tous les jours.

**16** 1 d; 2 e; 3 c; 4 b; 5 a

**17** A arsenicum album; B nux vomica

**18** A bryonia; B belladona; C pulsatilla

**19** 1, 4, 5, 7

**20** va; malade; a; mal; à la; fièvre; a; mangé

**Test**

*1* les oreilles; les cheveux; la bouche; le ventre; la jambe; la gorge; les dents; la main; les yeux; le pied

*2* 1 h; 2 j; 3 i; 4 e; 5 d; 6 g; 7 b; 8 c; 9 f; 10 a

*3* êtes; va; ai; grippe; mal; à la; au; aux; avez; J'ai; pris; pris

*4* dormi; pu; mangé; bu; été; pris; vu; donné

*5* 1 i; 2 b; 3 f; 4 a; 5 j; 6 d; 7 h; 8 c; 9 g; 10 e

**Summary 9**

*1* Ça fait mal. *2* J'ai attrapé un rhume. *3* Je suis malade, j'ai la grippe. *4* J'ai chaud et j'ai soif. *5* J'ai froid et j'ai faim. *6* J'ai mal à la tête et j'ai mal au dos. *7* Qu'est-ce que vous avez fait hier? *8* J'ai trop mangé et j'ai bu du vin rouge.

# Unit 10

**2** 1 V; 2 F (at 8.55); 3 F (at 10.15); 4 F (they went to a café); 5 F (Martin fell off his bicycle); 6 F (he broke his arm); 7 F (12 hours); 8 V

**3** 1 une femme; 2 un homme; 3 un homme; 4 une femme

**7** At the age of 88, Madame Lefort is very healthy and dynamic. When asked what her secret is, she says she doesn't know, but she admits she doesn't smoke, and never has. **She often drinks wine.** She loves **reading**, but she hates **doing crosswords**. She prefers sport! She walks regularly, and she goes swimming **three times** a week. She loves water, **she has always swum.** That's not all! She also does some yoga – something she started at the age of **50**.

**8** Je m'appelle Casimir Noah. J'ai 86 ans. Je fume de temps en temps (j'ai commencé à l'âge de 22 ans). Je ne bois jamais d'alcool (je n'ai jamais bu d'alcool). Je joue aux échecs une ou deux fois par semaine. Je fais du vélo depuis l'âge de 9 ans.

**12** radio 1; Internet 1; computer 2; electricity 6; television 3; telephone 4

**13** 1 tu as fait; 2 Tu es allée; 3 j'ai travaillé; 4 j'étais; 5 tu es arrivée; 6 Je parlais; 7 je faisais; 8 j'allais; 9 je faisais

**17** 1 un spectacle; 2 le cirque; 3 une fête foraine; 4 un musée; 5 un parc d'attraction; 6 un spectacle sportif payant

**18** 1 F (only 12% have never been to a zoo); 2 V; 3 V; 4 F (83% have never been to the Opera); 5 F (68% have never been to a classical music concert); 6 V

**19** Follow the examples given.

**20** 2, 4, 5, 8, 9, 12

**21** a été; est resté; est passé; avait; avait; étais; ai appelé; suis allée; avez été

**22** suis née; suis arrivée; était; était; sont morts; avais

**Test**

*1* 1 le yaourt; 2 jamais; 3 elle est restée (no movement); 4 je travaillais (all the others describe leisure activities)

*2* 1 c; 2 d; 3 d; 4 c; 5 b; 6 b; 7 a; 8 a

*3* 1 du vélo; 2 du piano; 3 de la natation; 4 aux cartes; 5 au tennis; 6 de l'équitation; 7 des mots croisés; 8 de la guitare

*4* suis arrivé; ai préparé; suis monté; avais; étais; sommes partis; ai regardé; était; est arrivé; ai eu; est ouvert; suis tombé

*5* avais; étais; avais; avaient; avions; faisais; amusais; faisait; avait; allais; jouais; adorais

**Summary 10**

*1* J'adore la natation. *2* Je déteste les mots croisés. *3* Je n'ai jamais fumé. *4* Qu'est-ce qui s'est passé? *5* Ça s'est bien passé. *6* Ma fille est tombée de vélo. *7* Elle s'est cassé le bras. *8* Elle est restée deux jours à l'hôpital. *9* Je dormais quand tu as téléphoné. *10* Mon père jouait du piano quand il était jeune.

**Review 3**

**1** 1 les mots croisés; 2 l'équitation; 3 la télévision; 4 la natation; 5 le cinéma; 6 les cartes; 7 les échecs; 8 le tennis; 9 le sport; 10 le vélo

**2** J'y vais en avion; en bateau; à pied; en train; à vélo; en voiture
J'ai mal au cœur; aux dents; au pied; à la tête; au ventre

**3** 1 h; 2 c; 3 a; 4 b; 5 g; 6 f; 7 d; 8 e

**4** je fumais; je ne faisais jamais; je détestais; j'avais; j'étais; j'avais; j'ai arrêté; je fais; je ne suis jamais

**5** **au** cinéma; J'**y** vais; **par** semaine; **la** radio; **la** télévision; **la** télé; **la** musique classique; **depuis** l'âge; **du** piano; **le** violon; **du** sport; **au** tennis; **au** tennis; **le** sport; **de la** marche à pied

**7** 1 a; 2 b; 3 a; 4 a; 5 b; 6 b

**8** Je vais vous raconter l'histoire de la bataille d'Hastings. Alors... Édouard **était** roi d'Angleterre. Sa femme s'appelait Édith. Édouard et Édith n'**avaient** pas d'enfants. Quand le roi Édouard **est** mort en 1066, le frère d'Édith est **devenu** roi d'Angleterre. Il s'**appelait** Harold. Guillaume, le cousin d'Édouard, n'**était** pas content! Il **habitait** en Normandie, alors il a **pris** le bateau et il **est arrivé** à Hastings le 28 septembre 1066. La bataillle d'Hastings **a commencé**. Harold est **mort** le 14 octobre 1066, et Guillaume **est** devenu roi d'Angleterre.

**10** 1 Je suis malade depuis deux jours. 2 J'ai très froid et j'ai de la fièvre. 3 Ma voiture était en panne. 4 Non. J'y suis allé en bus. 5 Oui, et j'ai attendu le bus une demi-heure. 6 J'ai pris de l'aspirine hier. 7 J'avais mal à la tête hier. 8 Je n'ai plus mal à la tête, mais j'ai mal à la gorge.

# Unit 11

**2** A 6; B 1, 5, 8, 6, 4, 3, 2, 7

**3** 1 j; 2 c; 3 a; 4 i; 5 h; 6 d; 7 e; 8 g; 9 f; 10 b

**7** 1, 3, 4, 6

**8** 1 Claire; 2 Matthieu; 3 Théo; 4 Annabelle

**12** 1 ça va mieux; 2 il est plus beau que le nôtre; 3 le vôtre est plus grand que le mien; 4 tu crois que le jardin de Nathalie est plus petit que le nôtre? 5 tu as l'air beaucoup plus heureuse qu'avant; 6 c'est le plus important

**13** 1 ma meilleure amie; 2 mieux que moi; 3 ça va mieux; 4 l'autre est meilleur

**16** 1 bientôt; 2 faire la connaissance de; 3 nous espérons; 4 la prochaine fois; 5 en attendant; 6 grosses bises; 7 amicalement; 8 grâce à toi

**17** Sophie and Pierre are closest to Nathalie. They say **tu** to her, and end their note with **grosses bises**, which is less formal than **amicalement**.

**18** Mon mari et moi **te** remercions pour une très agréable soirée en **ta** compagnie. Le dîner était délicieux, et nous étions très heureux de faire la connaissance de **tes** amis Sophie et Pierre; ils sont très gentils et très drôles! Nous espérons **te** revoir bientôt. Chez nous la prochaine fois!

**19** *Example* a: Mille fois merci pour le dîner de samedi soir. Le repas était délicieux, et j'étais très contente de te voir. On a passé une soirée très sympa. Grosses bises
*Example* b: Nous vous remercions pour une très agréable soirée en votre compagnie. Votre maison est magnifique, le dîner était délicieux, et nous étions très heureux de faire la connaissance de vos enfants. Ils sont très sympathiques.
Amicalement

**20** 2, 9, 8, 7, 1, 4, 3, 6, 5

**21** aussi sympa **que** Karim; **plus** bavarde que **lui**; **plus** curieuse que moi; ses **plus** gros défauts; le **meilleur** thé à la menthe **de** Paris

**22** Chère Malika, Merci pour l'interview; j'étais très heureuse de faire votre connaissance, et votre histoire est très intéressante. Merci aussi pour le thé à la menthe, il était délicieux et très rafraîchissant!
Amicalement. Alexandra

## Test

*1* âgé–jeune; bien–mal; calme–bruyant; grand–petit; gros–mince; heureux–malheureux; mieux–pire; moins–plus

*2* 1 p; 2 o; 3 e; 4 d; 5 n; 6 c; 7 k; 8 l; 9 m; 10 f; 11 i; 12 g; 13 a; 14 b; 15 j; 16 h

*3* Sophie est **la** plus mince. Elle est **plus** petite que Pierre, mais elle est **aussi**

grande et **moins** grosse **que** Nathalie. Pierre est **le** plus grand et le **plus** jeune. Il est **plus** jeune **que** Sophie. Nathalie est la **moins** jeune.

*4* Ma **meilleure** amie; **Mieux** que moi; les **meilleurs** spaghettis **de** France; meilleurs **que** les miens; le **meilleur** pianiste; **plus mal** que **moi**

*5* 1 d; 2 f; 3 c; 4 b; 5 a; 6 h; 7 e; 8 g

## Summary 11

*1* Entrez! Asseyez-vous! *2* Vous avez fait bon voyage? *3* Vous prenez du jus de fruits? *4* Vous reprenez du gâteau? *5* Non, merci. J'ai assez mangé. *6* J'ai apporté un petit cadeau. *7* Notre maison est plus petite que la vôtre. *8* Votre jardin est plus beau que le nôtre.

# Unit 12

**2** 1 V; 2 V; 3 V; 4 V; 5 F; 6 V; 7 F; 8 F; 9 F; 10 V

**3** 1 Il **fait** beau. Il y a du soleil. Il **fait** chaud. (d) 2 Il **fait** froid. Il **y a** des nuages. Quelquefois, **il** neige. (c) 3 Il **y a** du vent et **il** pleut. (b) 4 Il **y a** du soleil. **Il** pleut. Il y a du soleil. Il pleut (a)

**7** 1 demain; 2 ce soir; 3 dimanche prochain; 4 dimanche prochain; 5 ce soir

**8** pourrait; dois/voudrais; veux; aimerais; voudrais/dois; pourrais; préférerais

**12** 1 Amboise; Ussé; Villandry; 2 Amboise; 3 Villandry; 4 Ussé

**13** A 1 **qui** a du talent; 2 **que** j'admire; 3 **qu'**elle aime beaucoup; 4 **qui** l'inspire; B **qui** a beaucoup de talent; et **que** j'admire; une exposition **qui** va avoir lieu; des tableaux **qui** représentent; **qui** sont riches; une région **qu'**elle aime beaucoup et **qui** l'inspire

**16** 1 la Bretagne; 2 le temps; 3 les nuages; 4 aujourd'hui; 5 le vent; 6 la pluie; 7 le soleil; 8 le brouillard

**17** B 1 c (**pluies**); 2 a (**nuages**); 3 b (**le vent**)

**18** 1 A; 2 C; 3 B

**19** *Example*: Ce matin, il y avait des nuages. Maintenant, le soleil brille, et il ne fait pas trop froid.

**20** Summary B

**21** 1 Jérôme; 2 Jérôme; 3 Alexandra; 4 Alexandra; 5 Jérôme; 6 Jérôme; 7 Jérôme; 8 Alexandra

**22** *Example*: – Allô, Papa? C'est moi. Ça va? – Oui, merci. Et toi? – Ça va très bien. – Qu'est-ce qui se passe? – Tu sais, les articles que j'ai écrits pour le concours de jeunes journalistes … – Oui, et alors? – J'ai gagné le premier prix! Je suis super contente! – Félicitations, ma chérie! – Je dois aller à Paris pour la remise des prix. – C'est quand? – C'est le 14 avril. J'y vais avec Jérôme. – Je suis très content pour toi.

**Test**

*1* 1 il pleut; 2 il neige; 3 il fait beau; 4 il fait chaud; 5 il fait froid; 6 il fait mauvais; 7 il y a du vent; 8 il y a du soleil; 9 il y a du brouillard; 10 il y a des nuages

*2* 1 F (il neige en hiver); 2 F (il fait très chaud en été); 3 V; 4 V; 5 V; 6 F (en hiver); 7 F (à midi); 8 F (il ne fait pas très chaud)

*3* 1 g; 2 h; 3 e; 4 d; 5 f; 6 a; 7 b; 8 c

*4* 1 qui; 2 qui; 3 que; 4 que; 5 que; 6 que; 7 que; 8 que; 9 qui; 10 qui

*5* 1, 3, 6, 2, 8, 9, 5, 4, 7

*6* Richard Lapierre est un cuisinier **que** j'admire depuis longtemps. La première fois que je suis allée dans son restaurant, j'en ai parlé à tous mes amis. Le plat **que** je préfère est une soupe de poissons **qu'**il prépare avec des fruits de mer et des petits légumes de son jardin. C'est un plat **que** je trouve vraiment délicieux.

**Summary 12**

*1* Il fait chaud et il y a du soleil. *2* Il fait froid et il neige. *3* Il y a du vent et il pleut. *4* J'aimerais bien aller au cinéma. *5* Je préférerais aller au théâtre. *6* Tu veux venir avec moi? *7* Je ne peux pas. Je dois travailler. *8* Rendez-vous devant la gare. *9* On pourrait déjeuner dans le jardin.

# Unit 13

*2* 1, 2, 4, 8

*3* 1 en Italie; **en** Espagne; 2 **en** Italie; **en** France; 3 **en** Écosse; **en** Angleterre; 4 **en** Suède; **aux** États-Unis; 5 **au** pays de Galles; **en** Suisse

*7* 1 Thierry; 2 Rachel; 3 Rachel; 4 Thierry; 5 Rachel; 6 Thierry; 7 Rachel; 8 Rachel; 9 Thierry; 10 Rachel

*8* *Example*: J'adore nager, aller au théâtre et téléphoner.
Je déteste faire la vaisselle, conduire et laver la voiture.

*12* Pierre feels **depressed** because he has had an **argument** with Rachel. It happened a **week** ago. Pierre was very busy and in a **bad** mood. **She** was getting on his nerves, so he told her to **leave**. And she did. He has not **seen** her nor spoken to her since then. His friend thinks the situation is **ridiculous**, and Pierre should **speak** to her. He advises him to **ring** her immediately.

*13* Tu **lui** as écrit? Non, je ne **lui** ai pas écrit. Tu devrais **lui** écrire! Non je ne **l'**ai pas. Téléphone-**lui**. Je vais **te** donner son numéro! Oui, je **l'**ai. Appelle-**la** tout de suite.

*16* 1 la France; l'Espagne; les États-Unis; l'Italie; la Chine
2 les Britanniques; les Américains; les Allemands; les Italiens; les Japonais

*17* 1 b; 2 a; 3 a; 4 a; 5 a; 6 a

*18* 1, 2, 3, 6, 8, 10

*19* [...] Elle adore **rencontrer** des gens, elle **adore** poser des **questions**, elle adore **écrire**, et c'est son **métier**! Elle a toujours voulu **être** journaliste. Quand elle **était** petite, elle **adorait** raconter des **histoires** à ses copines. À dix ans, elle **était** rédactrice en chef du magazine de son école. Elle **voulait** toujours tout savoir: elle **interviewait** ses copains et copines, ses professeurs et les parents. [...] Alexandra a **remercié** ses parents [...] Nous **lui** souhaitons bonne chance!

*20* She could have said some of the things she mentioned in her speech. For example: J'ai toujours été très curieuse, et j'ai toujours voulu être journaliste. Quand j'étais petite, j'aimais raconter des histoires à mes copines. À l'âge de dix ans, j'étais rédactrice en chef du magazine de mon école. Je voulais toujours tout savoir et tout comprendre: j'interviewais mes copains et copines, les professeurs et les parents. Et je découvrais déjà des secrets! J'adore rencontrer des gens, j'adore poser des questions, j'adore écrire.

**Test**

*1* en Angleterre; en Belgique; en Écosse; en Espagne; en France; en Grande-Bretagne; en Inde; en Irlande; en Suisse; en Tunisie
au Canada; au Chili; au Kenya; au Japon; au Maroc; au pays de Galles; au Pakistan
aux Antilles; aux États-Unis; aux Pays-Bas

*2* né–mort; bon–mauvais; arriver–partir; adorer–détester; vacances–travail; se marier–divorcer; s'ennuyer–s'amuser; avoir le moral–être triste; en pleine forme–fatigué; de mauvaise humeur–de bonne humeur

*3* Il ne l'a pas encore revue, mais il **lui** a parlé au téléphone. Ce n'est pas Pierre qui **l'**a appelée, c'est Rachel qui **lui** a téléphoné. Elle **lui** a dit qu'elle voulait **le** voir. Il **lui** a dit qu'il voulait **la** voir. Alors, il **l'**a invitée au restaurant ce soir. Je **leur** souhaite bonne chance!

*4* Je suis arrivée en France **il y a** dix ans. J'ai rencontré mon mari **il y a** trois ans. Je me suis mariée **il y a** six mois. Je **suis** arrivée dans les Alpes **il y a une** semaine. Je me **suis** cassé la jambe **il y a deux** jours. J'ai **téléphoné** à mon mari **il y a une** heure. Mon mari **est arrivé** à l'hôpital **il y a dix** minutes.

*5* 1 e; 2 d; 3 g; 4 a; 5 f; 6 h; 7 b; 8 c

## Summary 13

*1* Je ne suis jamais allé(e) au pays de Galles. *2* J'ai passé trois mois en France. *3* Ma sœur est née aux États-Unis. *4* Tu as passé de bonnes vacances? *5* Je me suis ennuyé(e) parce que je n'ai pas rencontré de gens sympas. *6* Mon fils s'est marié il y a six mois. *7* Je me suis disputé(e) avec ma mère. *8* C'est parce que j'étais de mauvaise humeur.

# Unit 14

**2** 1 Nathalie Pavy; 2 Philippe Perrin; 3 Philippe Perrin – Nathalie Pavy; 4 Nathalie Pavy; 5 Nathalie Pavy; 6 Nathalie Pavy; 7 Philippe Perrin – Nathalie Pavy; 8 Philippe Perrin

**3** Je la **rappellerai**; nous **serons**; Vous **serez**; je ne **serai** pas; Vous **serez**; je les **finirai**;

**7** 1 F (he's an illustrator); 2 V; 3 F; 4 F (she doesn't any more); 5 V

**8** 1, 6, 5, 3, 4, 7, 2

**9** 1 Il vient de sortir. 2 Elle vient d'appeler. 3 Ils viennent de recevoir votre courrier. 4 Je viens de noter votre message. 5 Je viens de lui dire.

**13** Thierry Martinez, le **directeur artistique** des éditions du Bertin, téléphone à Philippe Perrin. Il lui dit qu'il vient d'examiner son dossier et qu'il aimerait le rencontrer. Philippe Perrin ira donc voir Thierry Martinez **le mercredi 28** avril. Il arrivera vers **onze** heures, et il rencontrera les collègues de **Thierry Martinez** qui lui parleront de leurs projets. Ensuite Martinez et Perrin iront **déjeuner** et ils pourront discuter.

**14** Vous rencontrerez un millionnaire qui vous téléphonera tous les jours. Vous irez au théâtre avec lui, il vous présentera à ses amis, et vous discuterez de choses intéressantes. Un jour, il vous invitera au restaurant, vous l'attendrez, mais il ne viendra pas. Vous ne le reverrez jamais et vous serez très triste.

**17** 1 baccalauréat; 2 expérience professionnelle; 3 aide-maquettiste; 4 illustrateur indépendant; 5 diplômes – formation; 6 lu, parlé, écrit

**18** 1 je reste à votre disposition pour vous fournir les renseignements complémentaires que vous pourriez souhaiter; 2 J'ai appris … que vous recherchiez de nouveaux illustrateurs; 3 Vous trouverez ci-joint mon curriculum vitae ainsi que des photocopies de mon travail; 4 En espérant que mon dossier retienra votre attention; 5 je me permets donc de vous proposer mes services; 6 la foire du livre de Bologne; 7 Je vous prie de croire à mes sentiments respectueux

**19** 1 V; 2 V; 3 V; 4 F (only since 1996); 5 V; 6 V; 7 F (he lives in Nantes)

**20** 1 Madame Delaine; 2 Alexandra; 3 Alexandra; 4 Alexandra; 5 Madame Delaine; 6 Alexandra; 7 Alexandra; 8 Alexandra; 9 Alexandra; 10 Raphaël

**21** stagiaire; arrivé; Raphaël Lacase; allés; présenté; sympa; rencontrer

## Test

*1* ici–speaking; libre–free, available; gentil–kind; occupé– engaged; patienter–to hold the line; c'est noté–I've written it down; le courrier–letter, mail; en réunion–in a meeting; les coordonnées–details; je vous le/la passe–I'll put you through

*2* Il pleuvra toute la journée; Je serai en réunion jusqu'à onze heures; Tu ne la reverras jamais; Nous serons de retour demain matin; Vous pourrez discuter avec eux; Ils n'auront pas le temps ce soir; Elle ne viendra pas; Elles l'attendront pour dîner

*3* 1 the receptionist; 2 the receptionist; 3 the receptionist; 4 the receptionist; 5 the receptionist; 6 the receptionist; 7 the receptionist; 8 the caller; 9 the caller; 10 the caller

*4* 1 aurai; 2 seras; 3 ira; 4 pleuvra; 5 partirons; 6 serez

*5* parler; occupé; patienter; est; réunion; sera; part; rappellerai; appelé; dirai; vous; prie

## Summary 14

*1* Est-ce que je pourrais parler à Madame Dupont, s'il vous plaît? *2* Elle sera là cet après-midi? *3* Je peux laisser un message? *4* Vous pouvez lui dire que j'ai appelé? *5* Je rappellerai demain. *6* Je vous ai écrit la semaine dernière. *7* Je n'ai pas reçu votre courrier. *8* Je m'occupe de ce dossier. *9* J'aimerais vous rencontrer. *10* Quel jour vous conviendrait? *11* J'ai une réunion toute la journée. *12* Je serai libre vendredi matin.

## Review 4

**1** 1 l'étranger; 2 l'humeur; 3 la Foire; 4 énervant; 5 rencontrer; 6 dormir

**2** bruyant–calme; détester–adorer; s'ennuyer–s'amuser; froid–chaud; l'hiver–l'été; mauvais–bon; moins–plus; mort–né; partir–arriver; petit–grand; le travail–les vacances; triste–content

**3** 1 d; 2 f; 3 g; 4 e; 5 i; 6 c; 7 b; 8 h; 9 a

**4** Tu es né; m'a téléphoné; tu étais; tu t'appelais; je voulais; j'ai pris; je suis allée; C'était; il faisait beau; le ciel était; j'étais heureuse; je suis arrivée; tu étais; tu dormais; avait l'air

**5** fera; arriveront; aurez; pleuvra; aura; fera; pleuvra; fera; aura; ira; sera; brillera; seront; pourrez

**6** B 1 b; 2 a; 3 b; 4 a; 5 b; 6 b; 7 a

**7** Vincent Van Gogh **est** né **aux** Pays-Bas le
30 mars 1853. Il **avait** un frère **qui**
s'appelait Théo et qui **habitait** Paris. Van
Gogh est allé voir Théo en 1886, et il est
**resté** deux ans à Paris. Pendant cette
période, il a peint **plus** de 200 tableaux.
Ensuite, Van Gogh est **parti** à Arles dans le
sud de la France. C'est à Arles qu'il a peint
«les tournesols» et «la chambre», par
exemple. Le peintre Paul Gauguin était un
ami de Van Gogh, il est venu le voir et les
deux hommes ont **travaillé** ensemble
pendant trois ou quatre mois. Mais Van
Gogh était malade, les deux hommes se
sont **disputés** et Van Gogh s'est coupé
l'oreille. En mai 1890, Van Gogh est **parti**
habiter à Auvers-sur-Oise, dans la région
parisienne. Il n'allait pas bien, il était triste
et malheureux. Il est **mort** le 29 juillet
1890. Il **avait** seulement 37 ans.

**9** 1 Je voudrais parler à Monsieur Kelif. 2 Il
sera là cet après-midi? 3 Je peux laisser un
message? 4 Je m'appelle Jo Ross, je
travaille pour LPC en Écosse.

**10** Oui, je suis allé(e) en Australie. Pas
vraiment, il y avait beaucoup de monde et
l'avion n'était pas très propre. Oui
beaucoup. J'ai passé de très bonnes
vacances. Oui, j'ai rencontré des gens très
sympas et on s'est bien amusés. Je suis
resté un mois. C'était l'été. Le ciel était
bleu, le soleil brillait, il faisait beau et
chaud. J'espère!

# Grammar summary

## Nouns

*Gender*

All French nouns are either masculine or feminine.

    (*m*)  **le Canada** Canada    **le train** train    **un ami** friend

    (*f*)   **la France** France    **la voiture** car    **une amie** friend

*Plurals*

French nouns add **-s** in the plural, unless they end in **-s**, **-z**, or **-x**.

| (*sing.*) | (*pl.*) |
| --- | --- |
| **la chaussure** shoe | **les chaussures** shoes |
| **le prix** price | **les prix** prices |

Most words ending in **-eu**, **-au** and **-eau** add **-x** instead of **-s**.

    **le gâteau** cake    **les gâteaux** cakes

A few nouns have an irregular plural form.

    **un œil** eye          **des yeux** eyes

    **un journal** newspaper    **des journaux** newspapers

## The definite article

The French for 'the' is **le** with a masculine noun, and **la** with a feminine noun. **le** and **la** change to **l'** before a noun starting with a vowel or – in some cases – an **h** and to **les** in the plural.

    **l'Angleterre** England    **l'ordinateur** computer    **l'hôtel** hotel

    **les États-Unis** the United States    **les ordinateurs** computers

*à + definite article*

    **à + le → au**      Un sandwich **au** jambon. A ham sandwich.

    **à + les → aux**    Une tarte **aux** pommes. An apple tart.

*de + definite article*

    **de + le → du**      C'est en face **du** café. It's opposite the café.

    **de + les → des**    C'est à côté **des** toilettes. It's next to the toilet.

## The indefinite article

The French for 'a' is **un** with a masculine noun, and **une** with a feminine noun. **un** and **une** change to **des** in the plural.

    <u>**un**</u> **chien** a dog      <u>**des**</u> **chiens** dogs

    <u>**une**</u> **chaise** a chair    <u>**des**</u> **chaises** chairs

## Adjectives

*Agreement*

Adjectives agree in number and gender with the noun they qualify.

|  | (sing.) |  | (pl.) |  |
|---|---|---|---|---|
|  | (m) | (f) | (m) | (f) |
| small | **petit** | **petite** | **petits** | **petites** |
| young | **jeune** | **jeune** | **jeunes** | **jeunes** |
| pretty | **joli** | **jolie** | **jolis** | **jolies** |
| modern | **moderne** | **moderne** | **modernes** | **modernes** |

Some adjectives are irregular. For example:

|  | (sing.) |  | (pl.) |  |
|---|---|---|---|---|
|  | (m) | (f) | (m) | (f) |
| beautiful | **beau** | **belle** | **beaux** | **belles** |
| old | **vieux** | **vieille** | **vieux** | **vieilles** |
| good | **bon** | **bonne** | **bons** | **bonnes** |
| new | **nouveau** | **nouvelle** | **nouveaux** | **nouvelles** |

*Position*

Adjectives are usually placed after the noun they describe.

> Vous avez une maison **confortable**. You have a comfortable house.

However, a few common adjectives are placed before the noun.

> Ils ont une **belle** cuisine. They have a beautiful kitchen.

## Possessive adjectives

Possessive adjectives agree in number and gender with the noun they qualify. There is no distinction in French between 'his', 'her', and 'its'.

| **mon** mari | my husband | **notre** chat | our cat |
|---|---|---|---|
| **ma** femme | my wife | **notre** maison | our house |
| **mes** enfants | my children | **nos** animaux | our pets |

| **ton** copain | your (boy)friend | **votre** chemise | your shirt |
|---|---|---|---|
| **ta** copine | your (girl)friend | **votre** veste | your jacket |
| **tes** amis | your friends | **vos** vêtements | your clothes |

| **son** nez | her/his nose | **leur** père | their father |
|---|---|---|---|
| **sa** tête | her/his head | **leur** mère | their mother |
| **ses** cheveux | her/his hair | **leurs** frères | their brothers |

## Demonstrative adjectives

In French, the demonstrative adjectives (the words for 'this', 'that', 'these', or 'those' used before a noun) are:

| (m) | (f) | (pl.) |
|---|---|---|
| **ce/cet** | **cette** | **ces** |

## Interrogative adjectives

**quel** is an interrogative adjective meaning 'which?' or 'what?' It changes to **quelle** with a feminine noun. Both masculine and feminine forms add an **-s** in the plural.

## Subject pronouns

| | |
|---|---|
| **je** I | **nous** we |
| **tu** you | **vous** you |
| **il** he | **ils** they |
| **elle** she | **elles** they |
| **on** we | |

**Je** mange un croissant. I'm eating a croissant.

**Remember!**
1 The **tu** form is only used when speaking to a child or someone you know well.
2 The **vous** form is used when speaking to a person you don't know well or to a group of people – including children.
3 When in doubt, use the **vous** form.
4 In everyday conversation, **on** is often used instead of **nous**.
5 **ils** refers to a group of males or a mixed group.
6 **elles** refers to a group of females only.

## Disjunctive pronouns

| | (*sing.*) | | (*pl.*) |
|---|---|---|---|
| je | **moi** | nous | **nous** |
| tu | **toi** | vous | **vous** |
| il | **lui** | ils | **eux** |
| elle | **elle** | elles | **elles** |

Disjunctive pronouns can be used in different ways.

1 For emphasis, when used before the subject pronoun:
   **Lui**, il est végétarien. <u>He</u>'s a vegetarian.

2 After prepositions such as **pour**, **avec**, or **sans**:
   Je travaille pour **lui**. I work for him.

3 With **et** for the equivalent of 'and you?', etc.
   Moi, je n'aime pas la viande. **Et vous**? I don't like meat. And you?

## Object pronouns

*Direct object pronouns*

| | (*sing.*) | | (*pl.*) |
|---|---|---|---|
| je | **me/m'** me | nous | **nous** us |
| tu | **te/t'** you | vous | **vous** you |
| il | **le/l'** him/it | ils | **les** them |
| elle | **la/l'** her/it | elles | **les** them |

*Indirect object pronouns*

|  | (sing.) |  |  | (pl.) |
|---|---|---|---|---|
| je | **me/m'** to/at me | nous | **nous** to/at us |
| tu | **te/t'** to/at you | vous | **vous** to/at you |
| il | **lui** to/at him | ils | **leur** to/at them |
| elle | **lui** to/at her | elles | **leur** to/at them |

Indirect object pronouns are used with verbs which are normally followed by **à**, such as **apporter à** ('to bring'), **donner à** ('to give'), **envoyer à** ('to send'), **téléphoner à** ('to telephone'):

> Il parle à Eve. Il **lui** parle. He's talking to Eve. He's talking to her.

Both direct and indirect object pronouns come before the verb:

> Ce pull est joli. Je **le** prends. This sweater is pretty. I'll take it.
> Nous **leur avons donné** de l'argent. We gave them some money.

When there are two verbs, and the second is in the infinitive, the pronoun comes after the first verb:

> Il **devrait les acheter**. He should buy them.
> Je **vais lui téléphoner**. I'm going to ring him/her.

With the imperative, the pronoun comes after the verb:

> **Regarde-le**. Look at him!     **Téléphone-moi**. Ring me.

### The pronoun *y*

The pronoun **y** ('there') is used to avoid repeating a phrase describing a location. It usually comes before the verb.

> Je pars en Écosse. I am leaving for Scotland.
> Vous **y** allez comment? How are you going there?

### The pronoun *en*

The pronoun **en** is used to avoid repeating **de/du/de la/de l'/des** + noun. It usually comes before the verb.

> Je voudrais **des** pommes. I would like some apples.
> Vous **en** voulez combien? How many (of them) do you want?

## Possessive pronouns

Possessive pronouns agree in number and gender with the noun they qualify.

|  | (m) | | (f) | |
|---|---|---|---|---|
|  | (sing.) | (pl.) | (sing.) | (pl.) |
| mine | **le mien** | **les miens** | **la mienne** | **les miennes** |
| yours | **le tien** | **les tiens** | **la tienne** | **les tiennes** |
| his/hers | **le sien** | **les siens** | **la sienne** | **les siennes** |
| ours | **le nôtre** | **les nôtres** | **la nôtre** | **les nôtres** |
| yours | **le vôtre** | **les vôtres** | **la vôtre** | **les vôtres** |
| theirs | **le leur** | **les leurs** | **la leur** | **les leurs** |

Mon chien est plus petit que **le tien**. My dog is smaller than yours.

## Demonstrative pronouns

Demonstrative pronouns are the words for 'this (one)/that (one)' used in place of nouns. **ce/c'** is used with **être** and **cela/ça** is used with all other verbs.

**C'est combien?** How much is it? **Ça fait combien?** How much is it?

## Relative pronoun *qui*

The relative subject pronoun **qui** ('who', 'which', or 'that') is used to refer to either people or objects mentioned earlier in the sentence.

J'ai un ami **qui** habite là-bas. I have a friend who lives there.

## Relative pronoun *que*

**que** ('which', 'that', 'whom') is an object pronoun used to refer to both people and objects mentioned earlier in the sentence. Unlike its English equivalent, it cannot be omitted in French.

Le livre **que** j'écris. The book (that) I'm writing.

## Prepositions

*en/au/aux + name of country*

French doesn't differentiate between 'in' and 'to' when referring to countries. Use en with feminine names of countries, **au** with masculine names, and **aux** with plural.

Ma sœur est partie **en** Chine. My sister went to China.
Mon mari est né **au** Liban. My husband was born in Lebanon.
Je pars **aux** Antilles. I am off to the West Indies.

*en/à + means of transport*

en is used to introduce means of transport.

**en voiture** by car          **en car** by coach

However, à is used in the following cases:

**à pied** on foot              **à moto** by motorbike
**à vélo/à bicyclette** by bike  **à cheval** on horseback

*de*

de is used to express possession. Remember that the word order is different in French and in English.

le mari **d'**Anne Anne's husband

Use **du** instead of **de** + **le** and **des** instead of **de** + **les**.

le bureau **du** professeur the teacher's office

## Adverbs

Many French adverbs end in **-ment**. They are usually formed by adding **-ment** to the feminine form of the relevant adjective.

| Adjective | | | Adverb | |
|---|---|---|---|---|
| (m) | (f) | | | |
| facile | **facile** | easy | **facilement** | easily |
| heureux | **heureuse** | happy | **heureusement** | fortunately |

There are a few exceptions. For example:

| gentil | **gentille** | kind | **gentiment** | kindly |
|---|---|---|---|---|
| vrai | **vraie** | true | **vraiment** | really |

## Comparatives and superlatives

*Comparatives*

| **plus ... que** | Une maison est **plus** confortable **qu'**une tente. |
|---|---|
| | A house is more comfortable than a tent. |
| **moins ... que** | L'eau est **moins** chère **que** le vin. |
| | Water is less expensive than wine. |
| **aussi ... que** | Le métro est **aussi** rapide **que** le bus. |
| | The tube is as fast as the bus. |

Superlatives

Il a pris **la plus** grosse pomme. He took the biggest apple.
Elle a choisi **les moins** chères. She chose the least expensive ones.

*Irregular comparatives and superlatives*

| **bon/bonne/bons/bonnes** | good |
|---|---|
| **meilleur/meilleure/meilleurs/meilleures** | better |
| **le meilleur/la meilleure/les meilleurs/les meilleures** | the best |

J'ai une **meilleure** idée. I have a better idea.

| **bien** | well | **mal** | badly |
|---|---|---|---|
| **mieux** | better | **pire, plus mal** | worse |
| **le mieux** | the best | **le pire** | the worst |

Il parle **mieux** que toi. He speaks better than you.
Elle chante **plus mal** que moi. She sings worse than me.
Son frère est **pire** que le mien. Her brother is worse than mine.

## Asking questions

1  The formal way is to change the sentence word order, so that the verb comes before the subject:

    **Travaillez-vous** le lundi? Do you work on Mondays?

2  A more common way is to keep the same word order and raise the intonation at the end of the sentence:

    **Vous travaillez** le lundi? Do you work on Mondays?

3  You can also add **est-ce que** at the beginning of a sentence:

**Est-ce que** vous travaillez le lundi? Do you work on Mondays?

## Negatives

The most common negatives are **ne/n' ... pas** ('not'), **ne/n' ... plus** ('not any more', 'no ... left'), and **ne/n' ... jamais** ('never'). **ne** comes before the verb, and **pas/plus/jamais** after the verb.

Je **ne** comprends **pas**. I don't understand.
Ce **n'**est **pas** possible. It's not possible.

Negatives are followed with **de/d'** rather than **un/une, du/de l'/de la/des.**

Il n'y a pas **de** marché. There is no market.
Je n'ai pas **d'**eau. I have no water.

## Verbs

*The infinitive*
Dictionaries and glossaries list verbs in the infinitive, which ends in **-er, -ir, -re**, or **-oir**. Verbs within each group take the same endings.

*Reflexive verbs*
A verb whose object refers to the same person as its subject. The verb form contains an object pronoun, to indicate this reflexive action.

| [*verb starts with a consonant*] | [*verb starts with a vowel*] |
|---|---|
| **se réveiller**, 'to wake up' | **s'amuser**, 'to enjoy oneself' |
| je **me** réveille | je **m'**amuse |
| tu **te** réveilles | tu **t'**amuses |
| il/elle/on **se** réveille | il/elle/on **s'**amuse |
| nous **nous** réveillons | nous **nous** amusons |
| vous **vous** réveillez | vous **vous** amusez |
| ils/elles **se** réveillent | ils/elles **s'**amusent |

*The present tense*
French only has one form of the present tense, so **je travaille** is the equivalent of both 'I work' and 'I am working'.

*The imperative*
The imperative is used to give orders and instructions or to make requests. It has three forms: **tu** (informal 'you'), **nous**, and **vous**. The **nous** and **vous** forms are the same as the present tense. The **tu** form drops the final **s** of the present.

Tourne/Tournez à droite. Turn right.
Tournons à droite. Let's turn right.

*The imperfect tense*
The imperfect tense has two main uses. It is used to describe:

1  Something which used to happen regularly in the past:

J'**allais** à l'école à pied. I walked/I used to walk to school.

2 What the situation was when something else happened:

Je **dormais** quand elle **est arrivée**. I was sleeping when she arrived.

To form the imperfect tense, take the **nous** part of the present tense (e.g. **regarder, nous regardons**), remove the **-ons** and add the endings below:

| | |
|---|---|
| je **regard<u>ais</u>** | nous **regard<u>ions</u>** |
| tu **regard<u>ais</u>** | vous **regard<u>iez</u>** |
| il/elle/on **regard<u>ait</u>** | ils/elles **regard<u>aient</u>** |

*The passé composé*

The *passé composé* is used to describe single events that took place in the past. To form the *passé composé*, you need – in most cases – the present tense of **avoir** followed by the past participle of the verb.

J'**ai** trop **mangé**. I ate too much/I have eaten too much.

Some verbs form their *passé composé* with **être** rather than **avoir**. See the verb tables on pages 232–6 for details

Je **suis allé(e)** au cinéma. I went to the cinema.

*Past participles*

Past participles are formed by adding an ending to the stem of the verb.

**-é** for regular **-er** verbs:
**appeler → appel<u>é</u>**
**-i** for some **-ir** verbs:
**choisir → chois<u>i</u>**
**-u** for some **-ir, -re**, or **-oir** verbs:
**venir → ven<u>u</u>** come

For irregular past participles, see the verb tables on pages 232–6.

When using a *passé composé* with **être**, you need to make the past participle agree with the subject: add an **-e** when it's feminine, and/or an **-s** when it's plural.

Nathalie **est arrivée** hier. Nathalie arrived yesterday.

*The future*

In French, the idea of future can be expressed in different ways.

1 You can use the present tense with an appropriate time expression when talking about plans (as in English):

Je ne **suis** pas libre demain. I'm not/I won't be available tomorrow.

2 You can use **aller** + infinitive to express what's about to happen:

Elle **va téléphoner** au patron. She's going to ring the boss.

3  You can use the future tense:

Il **neigera** toute la journée. It will snow all day.

To form the future of regular -**er** and -**ir** verbs, add the following endings to the infinitive:

| | |
|---|---|
| **laisser** ('to leave') | **finir** ('to finish') |
| je **laisserai** | je **finirai** |
| tu **laisseras** | tu **finiras** |
| il/elle/on **laissera** | il/elle/on **finira** |
| nous **laisserons** | nous **finirons** |
| vous **laisserez** | vous **finirez** |
| ils/elles **laisseront** | ils/elles **finiront** |

To form the future of regular -**re** verbs, remove the final -**e** from the infinitive and add the endings above.

*The conditional*
The conditional is often used when expressing wishes or preferences, or making polite requests or suggestions.

Ils **voudraient** sortir ce soir. They'd like to go out tonight.
Il **préférerait** aller au cinéma. He'd rather go to the cinema.

To form the conditional, take the future tense, remove the endings, and replace them with those of the imperfect.

| | |
|---|---|
| j'**aimerais** | nous **aimerions** |
| tu **aimerais** | vous **aimeriez** |
| il/elle/on **aimerait** | ils/elles **aimeraient** |

## Regular -*er* verbs

| | present | future | imperfect | passé composé | |
|---|---|---|---|---|---|
| je/j' | **travaille** | **travaillerai** | **travaillais** | ai travaillé | |
| tu | **travailles** | **travailleras** | **travaillais** | as travaillé | |
| il/elle/on | **travaille** | **travaillera** | **travaillait** | a travaillé | |
| nous | **travaillons** | **travaillerons** | **travaillions** | avons travaillé | |
| vous | **travaillez** | **travaillerez** | **travailliez** | avez travaillé | |
| ils/elles | **travaillent** | **travailleront** | **travaillaient** | ont travaillé | |

## Regular -*ir* verbs

| | present | future | imperfect | passé composé |
|---|---|---|---|---|
| je/j' | **finis** | **finirai** | **finissais** | ai fini |
| tu | **finis** | **finiras** | **finissais** | as fini |
| il/elle/on | **finit** | **finira** | **finissait** | a fini |
| nous | **finissons** | **finirons** | **finissions** | avons fini |
| vous | **finissez** | **finirez** | **finissiez** | avez fini |
| ils/elles | **finissent** | **finiront** | **finissaient** | ont fini |

## Regular -re verbs

|  | present | future | imperfect | passé composé |
|---|---|---|---|---|
| je/j' | vend<u>s</u> | vendr<u>ai</u> | vend<u>ais</u> | ai vendu |
| tu | vend<u>s</u> | vendr<u>as</u> | vend<u>ais</u> | as vendu |
| il/elle/on | vend | vendr<u>a</u> | vend<u>ait</u> | a vendu |
| nous | vend<u>ons</u> | vendr<u>ons</u> | vend<u>ions</u> | avons vendu |
| vous | vend<u>ez</u> | vendr<u>ez</u> | vend<u>iez</u> | avez vendu |
| ils/elles | vend<u>ent</u> | vendr<u>ont</u> | vend<u>aient</u> | ont vendu |

**prendre** ('to take') is slightly irregular.
**je prend, tu prends, il prend, nous <u>prenons</u>, vous <u>prenez</u>, ils <u>prennent</u>**
**apprendre** ('to learn') and **comprendre** ('to understand') also follow this pattern.

## Irregular verbs

*avoir* ('to have')
**avoir** is also an auxiliary verb, used to form tenses such as the *passé composé*.

|  | present | future | imperfect | passé composé |
|---|---|---|---|---|
| je/j' | ai | aurai | avais | ai eu |
| tu | as | auras | avais | as eu |
| il/elle/on | a | aura | avait | a eu |
| nous | avons | aurons | avions | avons eu |
| vous | avez | aurez | aviez | avez eu |
| ils/elles | ont | auront | avaient | ont eu |

*être* ('to be')
**être** is also an auxiliary verb, used to form the *passé composé* of certain verbs.

|  | present | future | imperfect | passé composé |
|---|---|---|---|---|
| je/j' | suis | serai | étais | ai été |
| tu | es | seras | étais | as été |
| il/elle/on | est | sera | était | a été |
| nous | sommes | serons | étions | avons été |
| vous | êtes | serez | étiez | avez été |
| ils/elles | sont | seront | étaient | ont été |

## Other irregular verbs

*aller* ('to go')

|  | present | future | imperfect | passé composé |
|---|---|---|---|---|
| je/j' | vais | irai | allais | suis allé(e) |
| tu | vas | iras | allais | es allé(e) |
| il/elle/on | va | ira | allait | est allé(e) |
| nous | allons | irons | allions | sommes allé(e)s |
| vous | allez | irez | alliez | êtes allé(e)(s) |
| ils/elles | vont | iront | allaient | sont allé(e)s |

### dormir ('to sleep')

|  | present | future | imperfect | *passé composé* |
|---|---|---|---|---|
| je | **dors** | **dormirai** | **dormais** | **ai dormi** |
| nous | **dormons** | **dormirons** | **dormions** | **avons dormi** |

### ouvrir ('to open')

|  | present | future | imperfect | *passé composé* |
|---|---|---|---|---|
| je/j' | **ouvre** | **ouvrirai** | **ouvrais** | **ai ouvert** |
| nous | **ouvrons** | **ouvrirons** | **ouvrions** | **avons ouvert** |

### partir ('to leave')

|  | present | future | imperfect | *passé composé* |
|---|---|---|---|---|
| je/j' | **pars** | **partirai** | **partais** | **suis parti(e)** |
| tu | **pars** | **partiras** | **partais** | **es parti(e)** |
| il/elle/on | **part** | **partira** | **partait** | **est parti(e)** |
| nous | **partons** | **partirons** | **partions** | **sommes parti(e)s** |
| vous | **partez** | **partirez** | **partiez** | **êtes parti(e)(s)** |
| ils/elles | **partent** | **partirent** | **partaient** | **sont parti(e)s** |

### sortir ('to go out')

|  | present | future | imperfect | *passé composé* |
|---|---|---|---|---|
| je/j' | **sors** | **sortirai** | **sortais** | **suis sorti(e)** |
| nous | **sortons** | **sortirons** | **sortions** | **sommes sorti(e)s** |

### venir ('to come')

|  | present | future | imperfect | *passé composé* |
|---|---|---|---|---|
| je/j' | **viens** | **viendrai** | **venais** | **suis venu(e)** |
| tu | **viens** | **viendras** | **venais** | **es venu(e)** |
| il/elle/on | **vient** | **viendra** | **venait** | **est venu(e)** |
| nous | **venons** | **viendrons** | **venions** | **sommes venu(e)s** |
| vous | **venez** | **viendrez** | **veniez** | **êtes venu(e)(s)** |
| ils/elles | **viennent** | **viendront** | **venaient** | **sont venu(e)s** |

### connaître ('to know [a person, place]')

|  | present | future | imperfect | *passé composé* |
|---|---|---|---|---|
| je/j' | **connais** | **connaîtrai** | **connaissais** | **ai connu** |
| tu | **connais** | **connaîtras** | **connaissais** | **as connu** |
| il/elle/on | **connaît** | **connaîtra** | **connaissait** | **a connu** |
| nous | **connaissons** | **connaîtrons** | **connaissions** | **avons connu** |
| vous | **connaissez** | **connaîtrez** | **connaissiez** | **avez connu** |
| ils/elles | **connaissent** | **connaîtront** | **connaissaient** | **ont connu** |

### croire ('to believe')

|  | present | future | imperfect | *passé composé* |
|---|---|---|---|---|
| je/j' | **crois** | **croirai** | **croyais** | **ai cru** |
| nous | **croyons** | **croirons** | **croyions** | **avons cru** |
| ils/elles | **croient** | **croirons** | **croyaient** | **ont cru** |

### dire ('to say')

|           | present | future | imperfect | passé composé |
|-----------|---------|--------|-----------|---------------|
| je/j'     | **dis**     | **dirai**  | **disais**    | **ai dit**        |
| tu        | **dis**     | **diras**  | **disais**    | **as dit**        |
| il/elle/on | **dit**    | **dira**   | **disait**    | **a dit**         |
| nous      | **disons**  | **dirons** | **disions**   | **avons dit**     |
| vous      | **dites**   | **direz**  | **disiez**    | **avez dit**      |
| ils/elles | **disent**  | **diront** | **disaient**  | **ont dit**       |

### écrire ('to write')

|        | present    | future     | imperfect   | passé composé |
|--------|------------|------------|-------------|---------------|
| je/j'  | **écris**      | **écrirai**    | **écrivais**    | **ai écrit**      |
| nous   | **écrivons**   | **écrirons**   | **écrivions**   | **avons écrit**   |

### faire ('to do', 'to make')

**faire** is used in a variety of phrases, such as:

> Quel temps **fait**-il? What is the weather like? Il **faisait** froid. It was cold.
>
> Ça **fait** combien? How much does it cost?
>
> Vous **faites** quelle taille? What size do you take?

|           | present   | future  | imperfect | passé composé |
|-----------|-----------|---------|-----------|---------------|
| je/j'     | **fais**      | **ferai**   | **faisais**   | **ai fait**       |
| tu        | **fais**      | **feras**   | **faisais**   | **as fait**       |
| il/elle/on | **fait**     | **fera**    | **faisait**   | **a fait**        |
| nous      | **faisons**   | **ferons**  | **faisions**  | **avons fait**    |
| vous      | **faites**    | **ferez**   | **faisiez**   | **avez fait**     |
| ils/elles | **font**      | **feront**  | **faisaient** | **ont fait**      |

### lire ('to read')

|           | present  | future  | imperfect | passé composé |
|-----------|----------|---------|-----------|---------------|
| je/j'     | **lis**      | **lirai**   | **lisais**    | **ai lu**         |
| tu        | **lis**      | **liras**   | **lisais**    | **as lu**         |
| il/elle/on | **lit**     | **lira**    | **lisait**    | **a lu**          |
| nous      | **lisons**   | **lirons**  | **lisions**   | **avons lu**      |
| vous      | **lisez**    | **lirez**   | **lisiez**    | **avez lu**       |
| ils/elles | **lisent**   | **liront**  | **lisaient**  | **ont lu**        |

### mettre ('to put')

|           | present   | future    | imperfect | passé composé |
|-----------|-----------|-----------|-----------|---------------|
| je/j'     | **mets**     | **mettrai**   | **mettais**   | **ai mis**        |
| tu        | **mets**     | **mettras**   | **mettais**   | **as mis**        |
| il/elle/on | **met**     | **mettra**    | **mettait**   | **a mis**         |
| nous      | **mettons**  | **mettrons**  | **mettions**  | **avons mis**     |
| vous      | **mettez**   | **mettrez**   | **mettiez**   | **avez mis**      |
| ils/elles | **mettent**  | **mettront**  | **mettaient** | **ont mis**       |

### falloir ('to be necessary')

|     | present | future  | imperfect | passé composé |
|-----|---------|---------|-----------|---------------|
| il  | **faut**    | **faudra**  | **fallait**   | **a fallu**       |

**pleuvoir** ('to rain')

|       | present | future   | imperfect | *passé composé* |
|-------|---------|----------|-----------|-----------------|
| il    | pleut   | pleuvra  | pleuvait  | a plu           |

**savoir** ('to know [a fact]')

|           | present | future   | imperfect | *passé composé* |
|-----------|---------|----------|-----------|-----------------|
| je/j'     | sais    | saurai   | savais    | ai su           |
| tu        | sais    | sauras   | savais    | as su           |
| il/elle/on| sait    | saura    | savait    | a su            |
| nous      | savons  | saurons  | savions   | avons su        |
| vous      | savez   | saurez   | saviez    | avez su         |
| ils/elles | savent  | sauront  | savaient  | ont su          |

**voir** ('to see')

|           | present | future   | imperfect | *passé composé* |
|-----------|---------|----------|-----------|-----------------|
| je/j'     | vois    | verrai   | voyais    | ai vu           |
| tu        | vois    | verras   | voyais    | as vu           |
| il/elle/on| voit    | verra    | voyait    | a vu            |
| nous      | voyons  | verrons  | voyions   | avons vu        |
| vous      | voyez   | verrez   | voyiez    | avez vu         |
| ils/elles | voient  | verront  | voyaient  | ont vu          |

**devoir** ('to have to')

|           | present | future   | imperfect | *passé composé* |
|-----------|---------|----------|-----------|-----------------|
| je/j'     | dois    | devrai   | devais    | ai dû           |
| tu        | dois    | devras   | devais    | as dû           |
| il/elle/on| doit    | devra    | devait    | a dû            |
| nous      | devons  | devrons  | devions   | avons dû        |
| vous      | devez   | devrez   | deviez    | avez dû         |
| ils/elles | doivent | devront  | devaient  | ont dû          |

**pouvoir** ('to be able to')

|           | present | future   | imperfect | *passé composé* |
|-----------|---------|----------|-----------|-----------------|
| je/j'     | peux    | pourrai  | pouvais   | ai pu           |
| tu        | peux    | pourras  | pouvais   | as pu           |
| il/elle/on| peut    | pourra   | pouvait   | a pu            |
| nous      | pouvons | pourrons | pouvions  | avons pu        |
| vous      | pouvez  | pourrez  | pouviez   | avez pu         |
| ils/elles | peuvent | pourront | pouvaient | ont pu          |

**vouloir** ('to want')

|           | present | future   | imperfect | *passé composé* |
|-----------|---------|----------|-----------|-----------------|
| je/j'     | veux    | voudrai  | voulais   | ai voulu        |
| tu        | veux    | voudras  | voulais   | as voulu        |
| il/elle/on| veut    | voudra   | voulait   | a voulu         |
| nous      | voulons | voudrons | voulions  | avons voulu     |
| vous      | voulez  | voudrez  | vouliez   | avez voulu      |
| ils/elles | veulent | voudront | voulaient | ont voulu       |

# Vocabulary glossary

## A

| | | |
|---|---|---|
| | à | in, to, at, with |
| d' | abord | first |
| l' | abricot (m) | apricot |
| d' | accord | OK |
| | accueillir | to welcome |
| | acheter | to buy |
| | adorer | to love |
| l' | aéroport (m) | airport |
| | agréable | pleasant |
| | aider | to help |
| l' | ail (m) | garlic |
| | aimer | to like |
| | ainsi que | as well as |
| l' | Allemagne (f) | Germany |
| | allemand(e) | German |
| | aller | to go |
| l' | aller simple (m) | single ticket, one-way ticket |
| l' | aller retour (m) | return ticket, roundtrip ticket |
| | allô? | hello [on the telephone] |
| | alors | so |
| | américain(e) | American |
| l' | ami(e) (m/f) | friend |
| s' | amuser | to enjoy oneself |
| l' | an (m) | year |
| l' | ananas (m) | pineapple |
| | ancien(ne) | old, antique |
| | anglais(e) | English |
| l' | Angleterre (f) | England |
| l' | année (f) | year |
| l' | anniversaire (m) | birthday, anniversary |
| l' | annonce (f) | advertisement |
| l' | antibiotique (m) | antibiotic |
| les | Antilles (f) | West Indies |
| l' | antiquaire (m/f) | antique dealer |
| | août | August |
| | appeler | to call |
| s' | appeler | to be called |
| bon | appétit | enjoy your meal |
| | apporter | to bring |
| | apprendre | to learn |
| | après | after |
| l' | argent (m) | money, silver |
| | arrêter | to stop |
| | arriver | to arrive, to come |
| l' | arrondissement (m) | district [in big city] |
| l' | ascenseur (m) | lift, elevator |
| l' | aspirine (f) | aspirin |
| s' | asseoir | to sit down |
| | assez | enough, fairly |
| l' | assiette (f) | plate |
| | assister | to attend |

| | | |
|---|---|---|
| | assorti(e) | matching |
| l' | atout (m) | asset |
| | attendre | to wait (for) |
| | attraper | to catch |
| | aujourd'hui | today |
| | aussi | also, too |
| | aussi … que | as … as |
| l' | automne (m) | autumn, fall |
| | autre | other |
| | autre chose | anything else |
| | autrement | otherwise |
| | avant | before |
| | avec | with |
| l' | avion (m) | aeroplane |
| l' | avocat (m) | avocado |
| | avoir | to have |
| | avoir besoin de | to need |
| | avoir de la chance | to be lucky |
| | avoir chaud | to be hot |
| | avoir envie de | to feel like, to want |
| | avoir faim | to be hungry |
| | avoir froid | to be cold |
| | avoir l'air | to look [happy, etc.] |
| | avoir le moral | to be in good spirits |
| | avoir lieu | to take place |
| | avoir peur (de) | to be afraid (of) |
| | avoir soif | to be thirsty |
| | avril | April |

## B

| | | |
|---|---|---|
| la | bague | ring |
| la | banane | banana |
| la | banque | bank |
| le | basilic | basil |
| le | basket | basketball |
| le | bateau | boat |
| la | batterie | battery |
| | bavard(e) | talkative |
| le | beau-père | father-in-law, stepfather |
| | beau/belle | beautiful, fine |
| | beaucoup | a lot, (very) much, many |
| | belge | Belgian |
| | belle | see beau |
| la | belle-mère | mother-in-law, stepmother |
| la | bicyclette | bicycle |
| | bien | well |
| | bien sûr | of course, sure |
| | bientôt | soon |
| à | bientôt | see you soon |
| | bienvenue | welcome |
| la | bière | beer, ale |
| le | billet | ticket |

237

|     | blanc(he) | white |
|-----|-----------|-------|
|     | bleu(e) | blue |
|     | boire | to drink |
| la | boîte | box |
| la | boîte de nuit | night club |
| le | bol | bowl |
|     | bon(ne) | good |
|     | bonjour | hello, good morning/afternoon |
|     | bonsoir | hello, good evening |
| la | bouche | mouth |
| la | boucle d'oreille | earring |
| le | bracelet | bracelet |
| le | bras | arm |
|     | bravo! | congratulations! |
|     | briller | to shine |
|     | britannique | British |
| le | brouillard | fog |
| le | bruit | noise |
| la | brume | mist |
|     | bruyant(e) | noisy |
| le | bureau | study, office |
| le | bureau de poste | post office |
| le | bus | bus |

**C**

|     | c'est | it's |
|-----|-------|------|
|     | c'est ça | that's right |
|     | ça | it |
|     | ça fait | that comes to, that'll be |
|     | ça va | fine, it's OK |
|     | ça va? | how are you? |
| le | cadeau | present |
| le | café | café, coffee |
|     | calme | quiet |
| la | campagne | countryside |
| le | camping | campsite, campground |
|     | canadien(ne) | Canadian |
| la | cantine | canteen, cafeteria |
| le | car | coach, bus |
|     | carré(e) | square |
| la | carte | card |
| le | cas | case |
| (se) | casser | to break |
| la | cassette | cassette |
| la | cathédrale | cathedral |
|     | ce | this, that |
|     | célèbre | famous |
|     | celui-ci | this one |
|     | cent | hundred |
| le | centime (d'euro) | cent |
| le | centre culturel | arts centre |
|     | cependant | however |
| le | cerf-volant | kite |
|     | cet | this, that |
| la | chaîne | channel [TV] |
| la | chambre | bedroom, hotel room |

| le | champignon | mushroom |
|-----|-----------|----------|
| la | chance | luck |
| la | chanson | song |
|     | chanter | to sing |
| le/la | chanteur/chanteuse | singer |
| le | chapeau | hat |
| le | château | castle |
|     | chaud(e) | hot |
| la | chaussette | sock |
| la | chaussure | shoe |
| la | chemise | shirt |
|     | chercher | to look for |
| le | cheval | horse |
| les | cheveux (m) | hair |
|     | chez | at/to [someone's place] |
|     | chinois(e) | Chinese |
| le | chocolat | chocolate |
|     | choisir | to choose |
| le | chômage | unemployment |
| la | chose | thing |
| le | ciel | sky |
|     | cinq | five |
| la | classe | class |
| la | clé | key |
| le | client | customer |
| le | climat | climate |
| le | cœur | heart |
| le | collant | tights, panty hose |
|     | collectionner | to collect |
| le/la | collègue | colleague |
|     | combien? | how much? how many? |
| la | comédie | comedy |
| le/la | comédien(ne) | actor, actress |
|     | commencer | to start |
|     | comment? | how? |
|     | complet/complète | full (up) |
|     | comprendre | to understand |
| le | comprimé | tablet, pill |
|     | concerner | to regard |
| le | concours | competition |
|     | conduire | to drive |
|     | confidentiel(le) | confidential |
|     | confortable | comfortable |
|     | connaître | to know |
|     | content(e) | happy |
|     | continuer | to continue |
|     | contre | against |
|     | convenir | to suit |
| les | coordonnées (f) | details |
| le | copain | (boy)friend |
| la | copine | (girl)friend |
| la | côte | coast |
| à | côté (de) | next (to) |
| le | coton | cotton |
| se | coucher | to go to bed |
| la | couleur | colour |
| le | coup | blow |
|     | couper | to cut |
| le | courrier | letter, mail |
| le | cours | lesson |

| | | |
|---|---|---|
| le | couteau | knife |
| | coûter | to cost |
| la | crème | cream |
| la | crevette | prawn, shrimp |
| le | cristal | crystal |
| | croire | to believe |
| la | cuiller | spoon |
| la | cuisine | kitchen |
| la | cuisinière | cooker, stove |
| | curieux/curieuse | curious, nosy |

## D

| | | |
|---|---|---|
| | dangereux/dangereuse | dangerous |
| | dans | in, into |
| | de | from, of |
| | de … à | from … until |
| le | débat | debate |
| | décembre | December |
| | découvrir | to discover |
| le | défaut | fault |
| | déjà | already |
| | délicieux/délicieuse | delicious |
| | demain | tomorrow |
| | demander | to ask |
| | demi | half |
| la | dent | tooth |
| | dépanner | to repair |
| | dépassé(e) | overtaken |
| | depuis | for, since |
| | descendre | to go down, to get off |
| | détester | to hate |
| | deux | two |
| | deuxième | second |
| | devoir | to have to |
| | difficile | difficult |
| le | dimanche | Sunday |
| | dîner | to eat dinner |
| le | dîner | dinner |
| | dire | to say |
| | discuter | to discuss |
| se | disputer | to argue |
| le | distributeur de billets | cash dispenser, ATM |
| | divorcer | to get divorced |
| | dix | ten |
| le | documentaire | documentary |
| le | doigt | finger |
| | dommage! | shame! pity! |
| | donner | to give |
| | dormir | to sleep |
| le | dos | back |
| le | dossier | file |
| la | douche | shower |
| la | douzaine | dozen |
| tout droit | | straight on, straight ahead |
| à | droite | on the right |
| | drôle | funny |
| | du … au | from … to |

## E

| | | |
|---|---|---|
| l' | eau (f) | water |
| les | échecs (m) | chess |
| l' | école (f) | school |
| | écossais(e) | Scottish |
| l' | Écosse (f) | Scotland |
| | écouter | to listen (to) |
| | écrire | to write |
| s' | écrire | to be spelt |
| | effectué(e) | done, undertaken |
| l' | église (f) | church |
| l' | électricité (f) | electricity |
| | elle | she, it |
| | elles | they |
| | emmener | to take |
| | en | in, into, to, made of |
| | en face (de) | opposite |
| | encore | yet, again |
| | encourager | to encourage |
| | énervant(e) | annoying |
| | énerver | to annoy |
| l' | enfant (m/f) | child |
| s' | ennuyer | to be bored |
| | ensemble | together |
| | entendre | to hear |
| | entre | between |
| | entrer | to go in |
| | envoyer | to send |
| l' | épicerie (f) | supermarket [on campsite] |
| l' | équipe (f) | team |
| l' | équitation (f) | horseriding, horseback riding |
| l' | escalier (m) | stairs |
| l' | Espagne (f) | Spain |
| | espagnol(e) | Spanish |
| | espérer | to hope |
| l' | essence (f) | petrol, gas(oline) |
| | et | and |
| l' | étage (m) | floor |
| les | États-Unis (m) | United States |
| l' | été (m) | summer |
| l' | étoile (f) | star |
| à l' | étranger | abroad |
| | étranger/étrangère | foreign |
| | être | to be |
| | être en panne | to have broken down |
| l' | étudiant(e) (m/f) | student |
| l' | euro (m) | euro |
| | eux | them, themselves |
| | exactement | exactly |
| | exclus(e) | excluded |
| | excuser | to excuse, to forgive |
| | exister | to exist |
| s' | expliquer | to be explained |
| l' | exposition (f) | exhibition |

## F

| | | |
|---|---|---|
| | facile | easy |
| | facilement | easily |
| | faible | light |
| la | faim | hunger |
| | faire | to do, to make, to be, to cost |
| | faire la vaisselle | to do the washing up, to do the dishes |
| | faire mal | to hurt |
| au | fait | by the way |
| | fatigué(e) | tired |
| il | faut | it is necessary to, you must |
| | faux/fausse | false |
| la | femme | woman, wife |
| le | feu | fire, (traffic) light |
| | février | February |
| | fier/fière | proud |
| la | fièvre | fever, temperature |
| la | fille | daughter |
| le | film | film, movie |
| le | fils | son |
| | finir | to finish, to end |
| le | fleuve | river |
| la | fois | time |
| la | forme | form, shape |
| le | foulard | scarf |
| le | four | oven |
| la | fourchette | fork |
| la | fraise | strawberry |
| la | framboise | raspberry |
| | français(e) | French |
| la | France | France |
| le | frein | brake |
| le | frère | brother |
| | froid(e) | cold |
| le | fromage | cheese |
| le | fruit | fruit |
| | fumer | to smoke |

## G

| | | |
|---|---|---|
| | gallois(e) | Welsh |
| le | gant | glove |
| | garder | to keep, to look after |
| la | gare (SNCF) | (French train) station |
| le | gâteau | gâteau, cake |
| | gâter | to spoil |
| à | gauche | on the left |
| le | genou | knee |
| les | gens | people |
| | gentil/gentille | kind, nice |
| | gentiment | kindly |
| la | glace | ice cream |
| la | gorge | throat |
| | grand(e) | big, large, tall |
| la | grand-mère | grandmother |
| le | grand-père | grandfather |

| | | |
|---|---|---|
| la | Grande-Bretagne | Great Britain |
| les | grands-parents (m) | grandparents |
| | gratuit(e) | free |
| la | grippe | flu |
| | gris(e) | grey |
| | gros/grosse | fat, big |
| la | guitare | guitar |

## H

| | | |
|---|---|---|
| s' | habiller | to get dressed |
| | habiter | to live |
| le | haricot | bean |
| le | haricot vert | green bean |
| l' | heure (f) | hour, time, o'clock |
| | heureusement | fortunately |
| | heureux/heureuse | happy |
| | hier | yesterday |
| l' | histoire (f) | story |
| l' | hiver (m) | winter |
| l' | homme (m) | man |
| l' | hôpital (m) | hospital |
| l' | horaire (m) | timetable |
| l' | hôtel (m) | hotel |
| l' | huile (f) | oil |
| | huit | eight |
| l' | humeur (f) | mood |

## I

| | | |
|---|---|---|
| | ici | here |
| l' | idée (f) | idea |
| | il | he, it |
| | il y a | there is, there are, … ago |
| l' | illustrateur (m) | illustrator |
| | ils | they |
| | immédiatement | immediately |
| l' | imperméable (m) | raincoat |
| l' | informaticien(ne) | computer engineer |
| s' | inquiéter | to worry |
| | inspirer | to inspire |
| | intéressant(e) | interesting |
| l' | interview (f) | interview |
| l' | invité(e) | guest |
| | irlandais(e) | Irish |
| l' | Irlande (f) | Ireland |
| l' | Italie (f) | Italy |
| | italien(ne) | Italian |

## J

| | | |
|---|---|---|
| | j'/je | I |
| (ne … ) | jamais | never |
| la | jambe | leg |
| le | jambon | ham |
| | janvier | January |
| | japonais(e) | Japanese |
| le | jardin | garden |
| le | jardin public | park |
| | jaune | yellow |
| le | jean | jeans |
| le | jeudi | Thursday |
| | jeune | young |

| | | |
|---|---|---|
| | **joli(e)** | pretty |
| | **jouer** | to play |
| le | **jour** | day |
| la | **journée** | day |
| | **juillet** | July |
| | **juin** | June |
| la | **jupe** | skirt |
| le | **jus (de fruit)** | (fruit) juice |
| | **jusqu'à** | as far as, until |

**L**

| | | |
|---|---|---|
| | **la** | the |
| | **là** | there |
| | **là-bas** | over there |
| le | **lac** | lake |
| la | **laine** | wool |
| la | **langue** | language, tongue |
| le | **lavabo** | wash basin, sink |
| le | **lave-linge** | washing machine |
| le | | the |
| le | **légume** | vegetable |
| | **lent(e)** | slow |
| | **lentement** | slowly |
| | **les** | the |
| la | **lettre** | letter |
| | **leur** | their |
| se | **lever** | to get up |
| | **libre** | free, available |
| la | **limonade** | lemonade |
| | **lire** | to read |
| le | **lit** | bed |
| le | **litre** | litre |
| la | **livre** | pound |
| le | **livre** | book |
| | **long/longue** | long |
| | **longtemps** | a long time |
| | **louer** | to rent |
| | **lui** | him(self), her |
| le | **lundi** | Monday |

**M**

| | | |
|---|---|---|
| | **madame** | Mrs, Ms, Madam |
| | **mademoiselle** | Miss |
| le | **magasin** | shop, store |
| le | **magazine** | magazine |
| | **magnifique** | magnificent |
| | **mai** | May |
| la | **main** | hand |
| | **maintenant** | now |
| | **mais** | but |
| la | **maison** | house |
| | **mal** | bad, badly |
| | **avoir mal au cœur** | to feel sick |
| | **malade** | sick, ill |
| | **malgré** | in spite of |
| | **malheureux/malheureuse** | unhappy |
| la | **maman** | Mum, Mom |
| | **manger** | to eat |
| le | **manteau** | winter coat |
| le | **marché** | market |
| la | **marche à pied** | walking |

| | | |
|---|---|---|
| | **marcher** | to work, to walk |
| le | **mardi** | Tuesday |
| le | **mari** | husband |
| | **marié(e)** | married |
| se | **marier** | to get married |
| | **marocain(e)** | Moroccan |
| | **marron** | brown |
| | **mars** | March |
| le | **match de foot** | football match, soccer game |
| | **mauvais(e)** | bad |
| le | **médecin** | doctor |
| le | **médicament** | medicine |
| | **meilleur(e)** | better |
| le/la | **meilleur(e)** | the best |
| le | **mélange** | mixture |
| | **même** | same |
| la | **menthe** | mint |
| la | **mer** | sea |
| | **merci** | thank you |
| le | **mercredi** | Wednesday |
| la | **mère** | mother |
| le | **message** | message |
| | **Messieurs Dames** | *greeting to a man and a woman* |
| le | **métier** | job |
| le | **métro** | underground, subway |
| | **mettre** | to put, to take |
| | **midi** | midday |
| | **mieux** | better |
| | **mignon(ne)** | sweet, cute |
| | **mille** | thousand |
| | **mince** | slim |
| | **minuit** | midnight |
| | **moderne** | modern |
| | **moi** | me, myself |
| | **moins** | less, under |
| le/la | **moins** | the least |
| le | **moment** | moment |
| | **mon, ma, mes** | my |
| le | **monde** | world, people |
| tout le | **monde** | everybody |
| | **mondial(e)** | world |
| | **monsieur** | Mr, Sir |
| le | **monsieur** | man |
| | **monter** | to go up, to get on |
| | **mort(e)** | dead |
| la | **moto** | motorbike |
| les | **mots croisés** (*m*) | crossword |
| | **mourir** | to die |

**N**

| | | |
|---|---|---|
| | **naître** | to be born |
| la | **natation** | swimming |
| la | **nationalité** | nationality |
| | **nature** | plain |
| | **naturel(le)** | natural, normal |
| | **né(e)** | born |
| | **ne ... pas** | not |
| | **ne ... plus** | not any more, no ... left |

| | | |
|---|---|---|
| la | neige | snow |
| | neiger | to snow |
| | neuf | nine |
| le | nez | nose |
| | noir(e) | black |
| le | nom | name |
| le | nombre | number |
| | nombreux/nombreuses | numerous |
| | normal(e) | normal |
| | normalement | normally |
| | noter | to write down |
| | notre, nos | our |
| | nous | we, us |
| les | nouvelles (f) | news |
| | novembre | November |
| le | nuage | cloud |
| la | nuit | night |
| le | numéro | number |
| le | numéro d'immatriculation | car registration number |

## O

| | | |
|---|---|---|
| l' | objet (m) | item, object |
| | obligé(e) | necessary |
| | occupé(e) | engaged, busy |
| s' | occuper de | to look after |
| | octobre | October |
| l' | œil (m) | eye |
| l' | œuf (m) | egg |
| l' | oignon (m) | onion |
| | on | we |
| l' | ordinateur (m) | computer |
| l' | ordonnance (f) | prescription |
| l' | oreille (f) | ear |
| | où? | where? |
| | oublier | to forget |
| | ouvert(e) | open |

## P

| | | |
|---|---|---|
| le | pain | bread |
| la | panne | breakdown |
| le | pantalon | trousers, pants |
| le | papa | Dad |
| | parce que | because |
| | pardon | excuse me |
| le | pare-brise | windscreen, windshield |
| les | parents | parents |
| | parfait(e) | perfect |
| le | parfum | flavour, perfume |
| | parler | to speak |
| la | part | helping, portion |
| | partager | to share |
| | partir | to go away, to leave |
| le | passage | route |
| | passer | to spend, to put through |
| se | passer | to happen, to go |
| | passionnant(e) | fascinating |
| | patienter | to be patient, to hold |

| | | |
|---|---|---|
| le/la | patron(ne) | boss |
| | pauvre | poor |
| | payer | to pay |
| le | pays | country |
| le | pays de Galles | Wales |
| les | Pays-Bas | Netherlands |
| la | pêche | peach |
| | peindre | to paint |
| le | peintre | painter |
| la | peinture | painting |
| le | père | father |
| la | personne | person |
| | petit(e) | small, short |
| le | petit déjeuner | breakfast |
| le | petit pois | pea |
| les | petits-enfants (m) | grandchildren |
| un | peu (de/d') | a little |
| | peut-être | maybe |
| le/la | pharmacien(ne) | chemist, pharmacist |
| le | pied | foot |
| | pire | worse |
| la | piscine | swimming pool |
| la | place | square, space |
| la | plage | beach |
| | plaisanter | to joke |
| | plat(e) | flat |
| à | plat | flat |
| le | plat | dish |
| le | plâtre | plaster |
| | plein(e) | full |
| | pleuvoir | to rain |
| | plier | to bend |
| la | pluie | rain |
| | plus | more |
| en | plus | on top of that |
| le/la | plus | the most |
| ne ... | plus | not any more, no ... left |
| le | pneu | tyre |
| la | pointure | shoe size |
| la | poire | pear |
| le | poireau | leek |
| le | poivron | capsicum, pepper |
| | poli(e) | polite |
| | poliment | politely |
| la | pomme | apple |
| la | pomme de terre | potato |
| le | pont | bridge |
| le | porc | pork |
| le | port | harbour |
| | portugais(e) | Portuguese |
| | poser une question | to ask a question |
| | possible | possible |
| le | poste | extension |
| le | poulet | chicken |
| | pour | for |
| le | pourboire | tip |
| je | pourrais | I could |
| | pouvoir | to be able to |
| | pratique | convenient |
| | préféré(e) | favourite |

| | | |
|---|---|---|
| | **préférer** | to prefer |
| | **premier/première** | first |
| | **prendre** | to have, to take |
| | **préparer** | to prepare |
| | **près de** | near |
| | **prescrire** | to prescribe |
| le | **printemps** | spring |
| le | **prix** | prize, cost |
| | **prochain(e)** | next |
| le | **projet** | plan, project |
| se | **promener** | to walk |
| | **proposer** | to offer |
| | **propre** | clean |
| la | **pub(licité)** | publicity |
| | **publicitaire** | advertising |
| le | **pull** | sweater |
| le | **pyjama** | pyjamas |

## Q

| | | |
|---|---|---|
| | **qu'est-ce que ... ?** | what ... ? |
| | **quand** | when |
| | **quarante** | forty |
| | **quatre** | four |
| | **que** | than, which, that |
| | **quel(le)** | what, which |
| | **quelquefois** | sometimes |
| | **quelques** | a few |
| | **qui** | who, which, that |
| | **quitter** | to leave |
| ne | **quittez pas** | hold the line, hold on |

## R

| | | |
|---|---|---|
| | **raconter** | to tell |
| | **rafraîchissant(e)** | refreshing |
| | **rapide** | fast, quick |
| | **rapidement** | rapidly |
| le/la | **réceptionniste** (*m/f*) | receptionist |
| la | **recette** | revenue, recipe |
| | **recevoir** | to receive |
| | **recommander** | to recommend |
| le | **réfrigérateur** | refrigerator |
| | **regarder** | to look at, to watch |
| | **regretter** | to be sorry |
| la | **remise des prix** | award ceremony |
| | **rencontrer** | to meet |
| le | **rendez-vous** | appointment |
| | **rendez-vous** | let's meet |
| se | **rendre** | to go to |
| le | **renseignement** | information |
| | **rentrer** | to come back |
| le | **repas** | meal |
| | **répéter** | to repeat |
| | **répondre** | to answer, to reply |
| se | **reposer** | to rest |
| la | **réservation** | reservation |
| | **réserver** | to book, to reserve |
| | **rester** | to stay |
| de | **retour** | back |

| | | |
|---|---|---|
| le | **retour** | return journey, roundtrip |
| se | **retrouver** | to meet |
| la | **réunion** | meeting |
| se | **réveiller** | to wake up |
| au | **revoir** | goodbye |
| les | **rhumatismes** (*m*) | rheumatism |
| le | **rhume** | cold |
| | **ridicule** | ridiculous |
| la | **robe** | dress |
| le | **roi** | king |
| | **rond(e)** | round |
| | **rouge** | red |
| la | **rue** | street |

## S

| | | |
|---|---|---|
| | **s'il te/vous plaît** | please |
| la | **saison** | season |
| la | **salade** | salad |
| la | **salle de bains** | bathroom |
| la | **salle de concert** | concert hall |
| | **salut** | hi, hello, goodbye |
| le | **samedi** | Saturday |
| le | **sandwich** | sandwich |
| le | **saumon** | salmon |
| le | **saut** | jump |
| | **sauter** | to jump |
| | **savoir** | to know |
| | **second(e)** | second |
| le/la | **secrétaire** (*m/f*) | secretary |
| le | **séjour** | stay; living room |
| le | **sel** | salt |
| la | **semaine** | week |
| | **sentir** | to smell, to feel |
| | **sept** | seven |
| | **septembre** | September |
| la | **série** | series |
| le/la | **serveur/se** | waiter, waitress |
| | **seul(e)** | alone |
| | **seulement** | only |
| | **si** | if |
| | **six** | six |
| le | **ski** | skiing |
| la | **sœur** | sister |
| la | **soie** | silk |
| la | **soif** | thirst |
| le | **soir** | evening |
| le | **soleil** | sun |
| | **son, sa, ses** | his, her, its |
| | **sortir** | to go out |
| | **souffler** | to blow |
| | **souffrir** | to suffer |
| | **souhaiter** | to wish |
| la | **soupe** | soup |
| | **souvent** | often |
| le/la | **stagiaire** | trainee |
| le | **style** | style |
| la | **Suède** | Sweden |
| | **suisse** | Swiss |
| la | **Suisse** | Switzerland |
| | **super** | great |

| | | |
|---|---|---|
| | sur | on, about |
| | sûr(e) | sure |
| | sympa | nice, friendly |

**T**

| | | |
|---|---|---|
| le | tabac | tobacco |
| la | table | table |
| le | tableau | painting |
| la | taille | size |
| | tant pis | never mind |
| la | tante | aunt |
| | tard | late |
| le | tarif | rates |
| la | tarte | tart |
| la | télé(vision) | TV, television |
| | téléphoner | to ring, to call |
| le | temps | time, weather |
| la | tente | tent |
| la | terrine | pâté |
| la | tête | head |
| le | thé | tea |
| le | timbre | stamp |
| la | tisane | herbal tea |
| | toi | you |
| les | toilettes (f) | toilet |
| la | tomate | tomato |
| | tomber | to fall |
| | ton, ta, tes | your |
| | tôt | early |
| | toujours | always |
| | tourner | to turn |
| le | tournesol | sunflower |
| | tout(e) | all |
| | tout de suite | right away |
| | tout seul | on his own |
| le | train | train |
| le | trajet | journey, trip |
| | tranquille | quiet |
| | transmettre | to pass on to |
| | travailler | to work |
| | trente | thirty |
| | très | very |
| | triste | sad |
| | tristement | sadly |
| | trois | three |
| | troisième | third |
| | trouver | to find |
| | tu | you |
| le | tube | tube |
| | tunisien(ne) | Tunisian |
| | tutoyer | to say **tu** |

**U**

| | | |
|---|---|---|
| | un(e) | a, one |
| l' | usine (f) | factory |

**V**

| | | |
|---|---|---|
| les | vacances (f) | holiday, vacation |
| la | vanille | vanilla |
| | varié(e) | varied |
| | végétarien(ne) | vegetarian |

| | | |
|---|---|---|
| le | vélo | bike |
| le/la | vendeur/se | sales assistant, salesman/woman |
| | vendre | to sell |
| le | vendredi | Friday |
| | venir | to come |
| le | vent | wind |
| le | ventre | belly |
| le | verre | glass |
| | vers | towards, around |
| | vert(e) | green |
| la | veste | jacket |
| le | vêtement | item of clothing |
| je | veux bien | I'd like to |
| la | viande | meat |
| la | vidéo | video |
| la | vie | life |
| | vieille | *see* **vieux** |
| | vieux/vieille | old |
| la | ville | town, city |
| le | vin | wine |
| | violet(te) | purple |
| la | visite | visit |
| | voici | here's |
| | voilà | here it is, here you are |
| | voir | to see |
| la | voiture | car |
| le | vol | flight |
| | votre, vos | your |
| | vouloir | to want |
| | vous | you |
| le | voyage | journey, trip |
| | voyager | to travel |
| | vrai | true |
| | vraiment | really |

**W**

| | | |
|---|---|---|
| les | WC | toilet |

**Y**

| | | |
|---|---|---|
| le | yaourt | yoghurt |
| les | yeux | eyes |

**Z**

| | | |
|---|---|---|
| | zut! | bother! damn! |

# Glossary of grammatical terms

**Adjective:** A word used to give information about a noun.

un pantalon **noir** black trousers
votre jardin est **beau** your garden is beautiful

**Adverb:** A word used to give information about a verb, an adjective, or another adverb. In French, most adverbs end in **-ment**.

marcher **lentement** to walk slowly
**très** honnêtement very honestly
**assez** grand quite big

**Agree:** To match another word in number (singular or plural), gender (masculine or feminine), or grammatical person (I, you, etc.).

**Article:** In English 'the' is the definite article and 'a' and 'an' are the indefinite articles. See *Definite article, Indefinite article*.

**Auxiliary verbs:** The verbs **avoir** and **être** when they are used to form some verb tenses such as the *passé composé* in French.

elle **a** choisi she has chosen/she chose

**Comparative:** The form of an adjective or adverb used to express higher or lower degree. See also *Superlative*.

Louise est **moins fatiguée** que sa sœur. Louise is less tired than her sister.
Pierre marche **plus vite** que son frère. Pierre walks more quickly than his brother.

**Conditional:** A verb form used to express wishes or preferences, or to make polite requests or suggestions. It is also used to expres what might happen if something else occurred.

Je **voudrais** parler au directeur. I would like to speak to the director.
On **pourrait** aller au théâtre. We could go to the theatre

**Definite article:** In English, the definite article is 'the'. In French, the definite articles are **le, la, l', les**.

**Direct object:** The noun, pronoun, or phrase directly affected by the action of the verb.

Je **les** adore. I love them.
Il apprend **le français**. He's learning French.

**Disjunctive pronoun:** The form of a pronoun used in certain situations, such as after prepositions or for emphasis.

Nous allons **chez elle**. We're going to her house.
**Moi**, je n'aime pas la viande. I don't like meat.

**Ending:** A letter or letters added to the stem of the verb to show the tense, subject, and number; also to nouns and adjectives, to show the number and gender.

je parl**e**, vous parl**ez**
les grand**s** arbre**s**

**Feminine:** One of the two genders in French. See *Gender*.

**Future tense:** The form of a verb used to express what will happen in the future.

Demain il **prendra** l'avion pour Londres. He will fly to London tomorrow.

**Gender:** In French, all nouns have a gender, either masculine or feminine, although a very few can have both. Gender is reflected in the form of the definite or indefinite article used (**le/la**; **un/une**). Gender also affects the form of accompanying words such as adjectives, possessive forms, etc.

masculine: **le bureau, un grand arbre, son livre**
feminine: **la voiture, une grande maison, sa mère**

**Imperative:** The form of a verb that is used to give orders or instructions, or to suggest that someone does something.

**Téléphone-moi/Téléphonez-moi**. Give me a call.
**Allons**-y! Let's go!

**Imperfect tense:** The form of a verb used to express a continuous or habitual action in the past.

Annie **lisait** le journal quand Marc est arrivé.
Annie was reading the newspaper when Marc arrived.
Quand j'**étais** petite, je **jouais** du piano.
When I was little, I used to play the piano.

**Indefinite article:** In English, the indefinite articles are 'a' and 'an'. In French they are **un**, **une**, and the plural form **des**, which has no English equivalent.

J'ai **un** problème. I've got a problem.
J'ai **des** problèmes. I've got problems.

**Indirect object:** The noun, pronoun, or phrase indirectly affected by the action of the verb.

Qu'est-ce que tu **lui** as dit? What did you say to him?
Elle a écrit à **son père**. She wrote to her father.

**Infinitive:** The basic form of a verb which does not indicate a particular tense or number or person. The verb form given in a dictionary.

**parler** to speak    **vouloir** to want
**être** to be        **attendre** to wait
**finir** to finish

**Intonation:** The pattern of sounds made in a sentence as the speaker's voice rises and falls.

**Irregular verb:** A verb that does not follow one of the set patterns and has its own individual forms. Many common verbs such as **avoir** ('to have'), **être** ('to be'), and **aller** ('to go') are irregular.

**Masculine:** One of the two genders in French. See *Gender*.

**Noun:** A word that identifies a person, thing, place, or concept.

**frère** brother
**livre** book
**M. Dupont** M. Dupont
**jardin** garden
**chat** cat
**sagesse** wisdom

**Number:** Indicating whether a noun or pronoun is singular or plural. Number is one of the factors determining the form of accompanying words such as adjectives and possessive forms.

singular: **un homme** a man
         **une femme** a woman
plural:   **deux hommes** two men
         **deux femmes** two women
         **quelques grands arbres** a few large trees

**Object:** The noun, pronoun, or phrase affected by the action of the verb. See *Direct object, Indirect object*.

**Past participle:** The form of a verb used either on its own as an adjective or in combination with the auxiliary verbs **avoir** or **être** in tenses such as the *passé composé*.

**marié** married    **été** been
**voulu** wanted    **parlé** spoken
**divorcé** divorced **fini** finished

**Passé composé:** The form of a verb used to relate completed actions in the past.

Elle **a fini**. She has finished.
Il **est venu** à la maison. He came to the house.
Hier, il **a téléphoné** à tous ses amis. Yesterday he telephoned all his friends.

**Person:** A category used to distinguish between the 'I'/'we' (first person), 'you' (second person), and 'he'/'she'/'it'/'they' (third person) forms of the verb. The person is reflected in the verb and/or in the pronoun accompanying it.

**Je parle.** (first person singular)
**Elle prend.** (third person singular)
**Vous travaillez.** (second person plural)

**Plural:** Denoting more than one. See *Number*.

**Possessive forms:** Adjectives and pronouns used to show belonging.

Il m'a donné **son** livre. He gave me his book.
Il m'a donné **le sien.** He gave me his.

**Preposition:** A word (e.g. **à**, **pour**, **avec**, **de**, etc.) or phrase (e.g. **en face de**, **à côté de**, **jusqu'à**, etc.) used before a noun or pronoun to relate it to another part of the sentence.

Je serai là **à** six heures. I'll be there at six o'clock.
Vos livres sont **sur** la table. Your books are on the table.
Il est **à côté de** la chaise. It's next to the chair.

**Present tense:** The form of a verb used to express something happening or in existence now, or as a habitual occurrence.

Paul **a** mal au dos. Paul has backache.
Nous nous **parlons** tous les jours. We speak to each other every day.

**Pronoun:** A word used to stand for a noun. Pronouns may refer to things or concepts ('it', 'them'), or people ('she', 'him'), and may be indefinite ('someone', 'something').

Ton frère? **Il** est là-bas. Your brother? He's over there.
**Elle** pense que **tu** as raison. She thinks you are right.
**Je** voudrais **celui-ci.** I'd like this one.

**Reflexive verb:** A verb whose object refers to the same person as its subject. The verb form contains an object pronoun, to indicate this reflexive action.

Ma mère **se lève** à sept heures. My mother gets [herself] up at seven.

**Regular verb:** A verb that follows a common set pattern.

**Singular:** Denoting only one. See *Number*.

**Stem:** The part of a verb to which endings showing tense, number, and person are added.

**par**ler    je **par**le, tu **par**les, nous **par**lons

**Subject:** The noun, pronoun, or phrase that performs the action indicated by the verb.

**Ma mère** était malade. My mother was ill.
**Elle** a quinze ans. She's 15.
**La petite fille** a chanté. The little girl sang.

**Superlative:** The form of an adjective or adverb used to express the highest or lowest degree. See also *Comparative*.

les avions **les plus rapides** the fastest planes
C'est Pierre qui chante **le mieux.** Pierre sings (the) best.

**Syllable:** A unit of pronunciation which forms either the whole or part of a word.

**part** (one syllable) **par/ti** (two syllables) **par/ti/ra** (three syllables)

**Tense:** The form of a verb which indicates when the action takes place, i.e. in the past, present, or future.

**Verb:** A word or phrase used to express what is being done or what is happening. It can also be used to express a state.

Elle **jardine.** She is gardening.
Il **est parti.** He has gone.
Le train **partait.** The train was setting off.
Il **fera** froid. It will be cold.

**Word order:** The grammatically appropriate way in which words go together in a sentence.

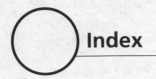

# Index

*In addition to the Language Building pages listed below, see also the relevant section of the Grammar Summary.*

adjectives 53, 63
  demonstrative 77
  interrogative 33
  possessive 65
adverbs 113, 139
articles
  definite 5
  indefinite 5
comparatives 157, 159
colours 77
days 33
**depuis** + present tense 139
gender 5
**il y a** 17, 185
imperative 19, 127
months 51
negatives 35, 93, 127
numbers 7, 21, 33, 49
plurals 17
prepositions
  à 19, 109, 183
  **de** 19, 65, 79,
  **en** 183
pronouns
  demonstrative 77
  direct object 81
  disjunctive 91, 155
  indirect object 93
  position of 187
  possessive 159
  **en** 79, 109
  **y** 109

**que/qui** 173
question forms 35, 95
superlatives 157, 159
time 31, 111
titles 3
**tu** 31
verbs
  future 197, 201
  imperfect 141
  followed by the infinitive 127, 169, 171, 185
  irregular verbs 21, 49, 77, 81, 91, 93, 111, 123
  *passé composé* 125, 127, 137
  regular **-er** 31, **-ir** 35, **-re** 51
  reflexive 67
**vous** 31